THE END

Fantastic Four

Story & Pencils: **Alan Davis**
Inks: **Mark Farmer**
Colors: **John Kalisz**
Letters: **Dave Lanphear**

Assistant Editors: **Molly Lazer & Aubrey Sitterson**
Editor: **Tom Brevoort**

Collection Editor: **Jennifer Grünwald**
Assistant Editors: **Cory Levine & John Denning**
Associate Editor: **Mark D. Beazley**
Senior Editor, Special Projects: **Jeff Youngquist**
Senior Vice President of Sales: **David Gabriel**
Production: **Jerry Kalinowski**
Book Designer: **Dave Barry**
Vice President of Creative: **Tom Marvelli**

Editor in Chief: **Joe Quesada**
Publisher: **Dan Buckley**

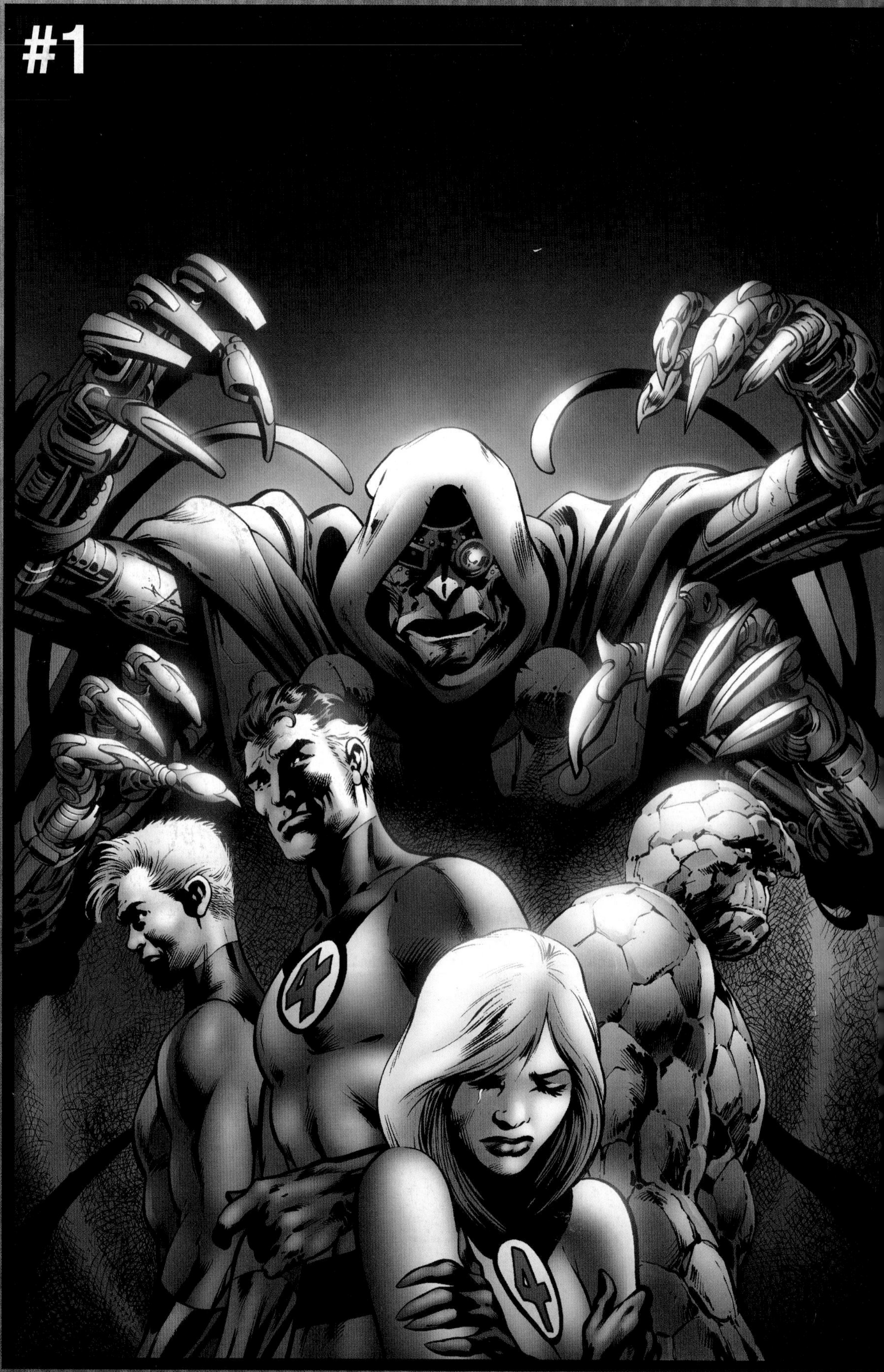
#1

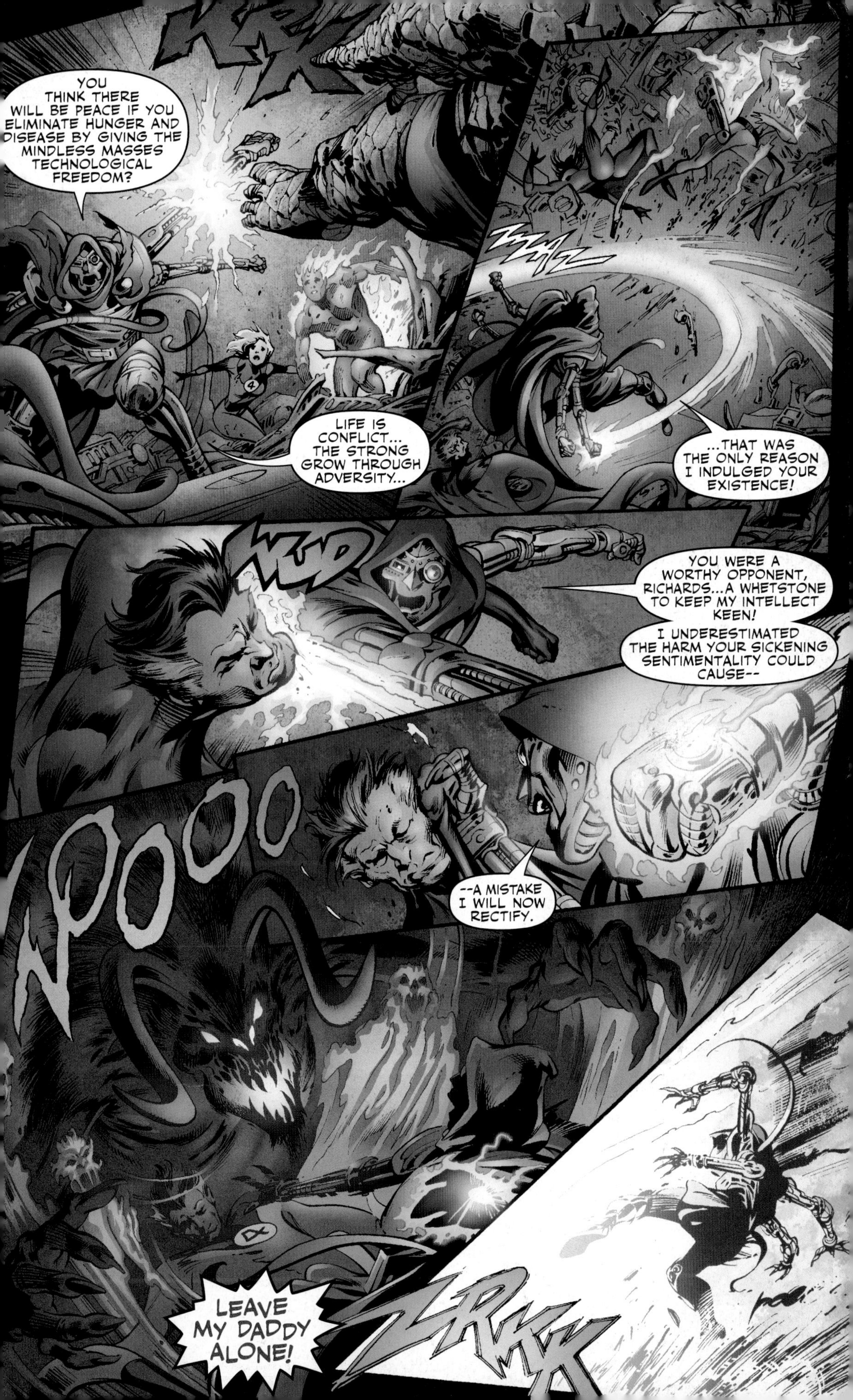
KRAKK
YOU THINK THERE WILL BE PEACE IF YOU ELIMINATE HUNGER AND DISEASE BY GIVING THE MINDLESS MASSES TECHNOLOGICAL FREEDOM?
ZZZAZ
LIFE IS CONFLICT... THE STRONG GROW THROUGH ADVERSITY...
...THAT WAS THE ONLY REASON I INDULGED YOUR EXISTENCE!
WUD
YOU WERE A WORTHY OPPONENT, RICHARDS...A WHETSTONE TO KEEP MY INTELLECT KEEN!
I UNDERESTIMATED THE HARM YOUR SICKENING SENTIMENTALITY COULD CAUSE--
ZOOOOO
--A MISTAKE I WILL NOW RECTIFY.
LEAVE MY DADDY ALONE!

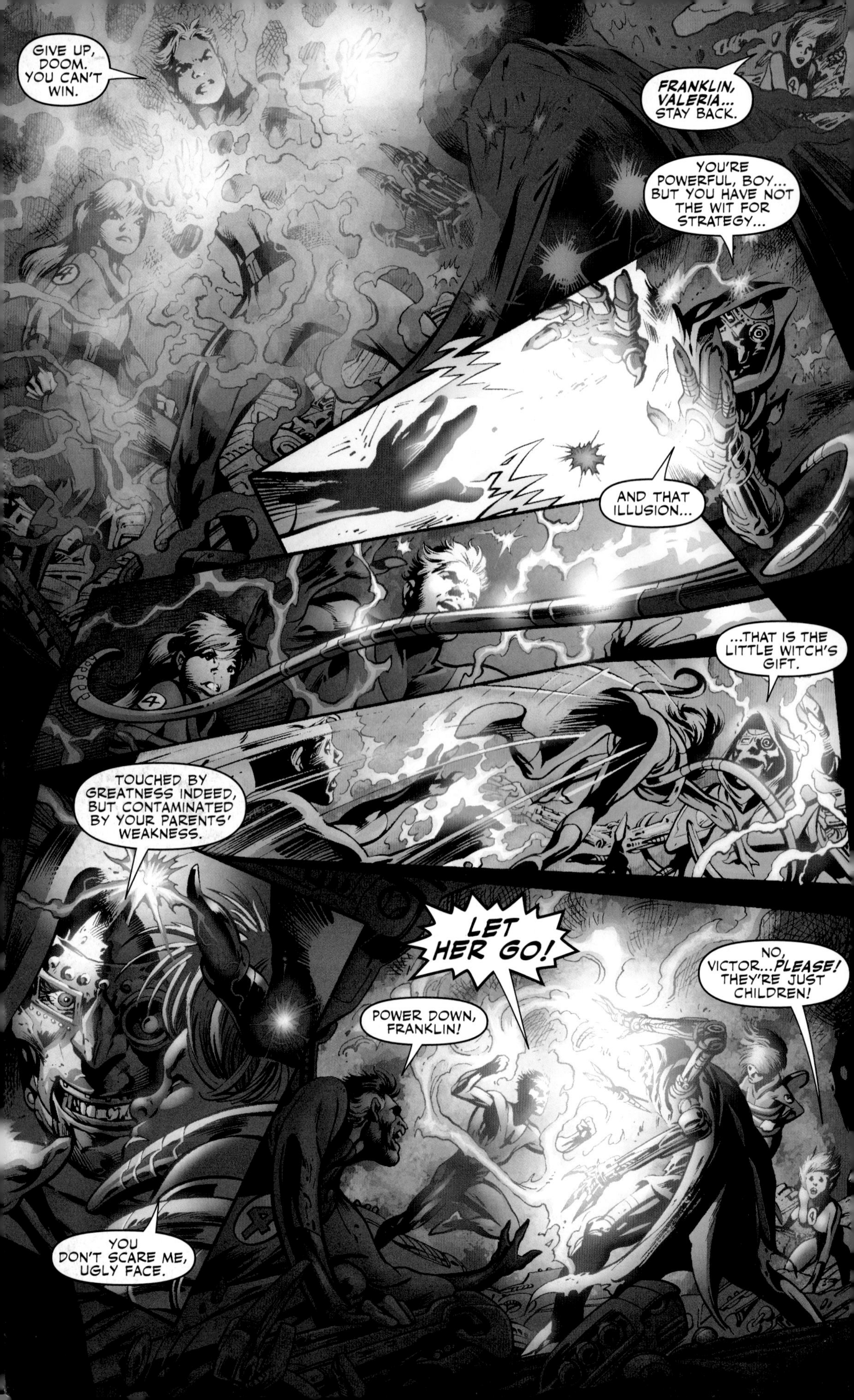
GIVE UP, DOOM. YOU CAN'T WIN.
FRANKLIN, VALERIA... STAY BACK.
YOU'RE POWERFUL, BOY... BUT YOU HAVE NOT THE WIT FOR STRATEGY...
AND THAT ILLUSION...
...THAT IS THE LITTLE WITCH'S GIFT.
TOUCHED BY GREATNESS INDEED, BUT CONTAMINATED BY YOUR PARENTS' WEAKNESS.
LET HER GO!
NO, VICTOR...PLEASE! THEY'RE JUST CHILDREN!
POWER DOWN, FRANKLIN!
YOU DON'T SCARE ME, UGLY FACE.

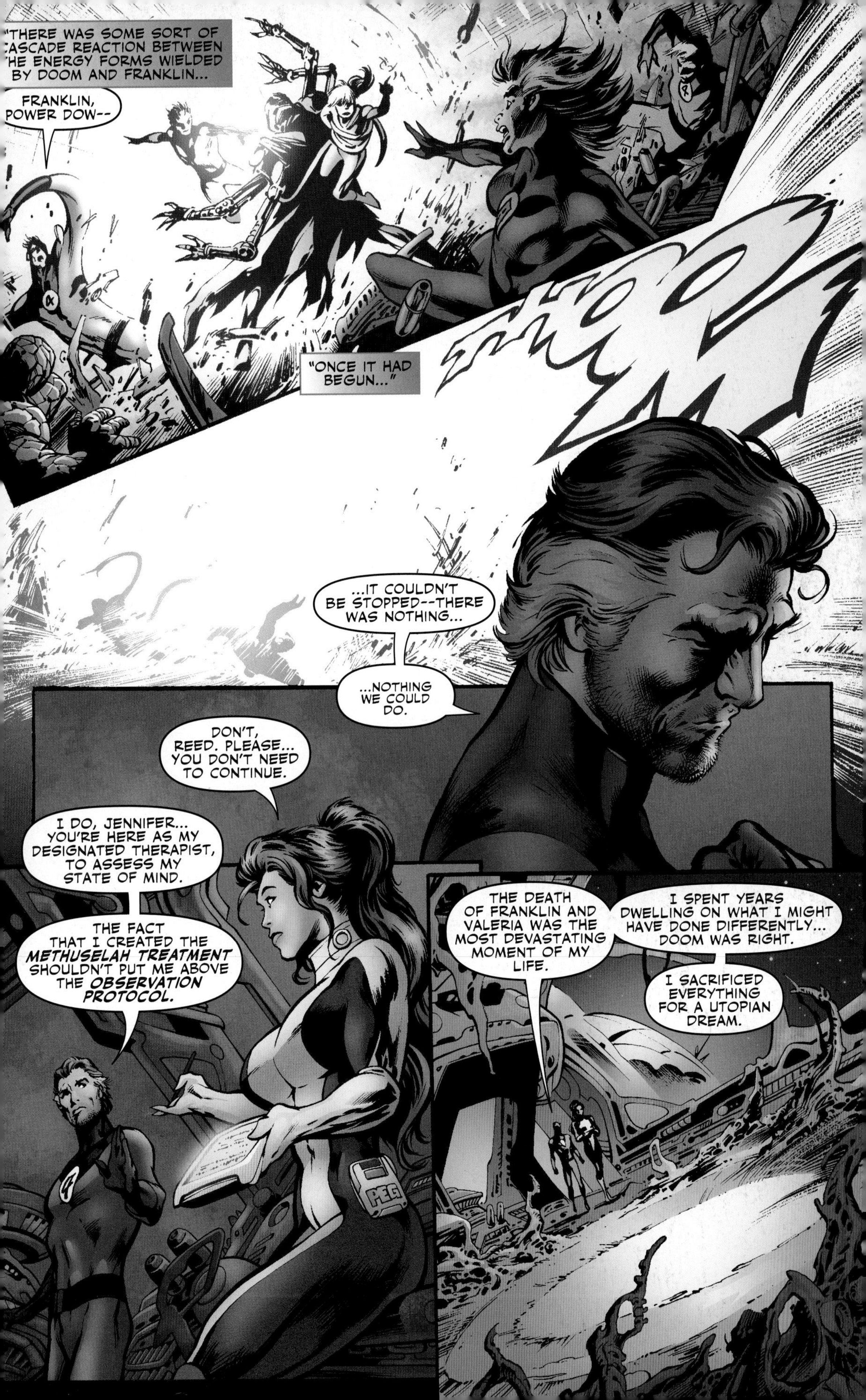
"THERE WAS SOME SORT OF CASCADE REACTION BETWEEN THE ENERGY FORMS WIELDED BY DOOM AND FRANKLIN...
FRANKLIN, POWER DOW--
"ONCE IT HAD BEGUN..."
...IT COULDN'T BE STOPPED--THERE WAS NOTHING...
...NOTHING WE COULD DO.
DON'T, REED. PLEASE... YOU DON'T NEED TO CONTINUE.
I DO, JENNIFER... YOU'RE HERE AS MY DESIGNATED THERAPIST, TO ASSESS MY STATE OF MIND.
THE FACT THAT I CREATED THE *METHUSELAH TREATMENT* SHOULDN'T PUT ME ABOVE THE *OBSERVATION PROTOCOL*.
THE DEATH OF FRANKLIN AND VALERIA WAS THE MOST DEVASTATING MOMENT OF MY LIFE.
I SPENT YEARS DWELLING ON WHAT I MIGHT HAVE DONE DIFFERENTLY... DOOM WAS RIGHT.
I SACRIFICED EVERYTHING FOR A UTOPIAN DREAM.

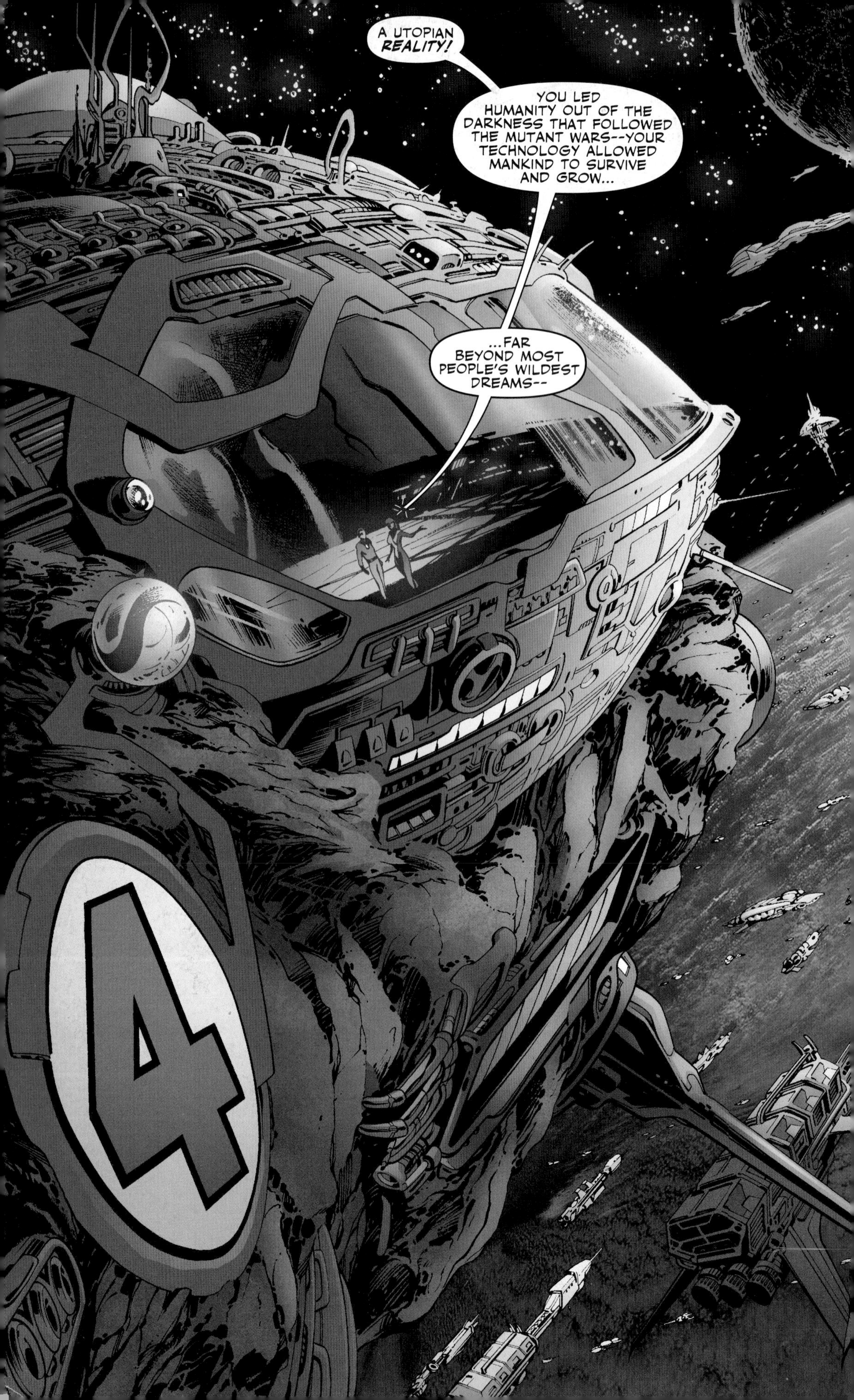
A UTOPIAN *REALITY!*
YOU LED HUMANITY OUT OF THE DARKNESS THAT FOLLOWED THE MUTANT WARS--YOUR TECHNOLOGY ALLOWED MANKIND TO SURVIVE AND GROW...
...FAR BEYOND MOST PEOPLE'S WILDEST DREAMS--

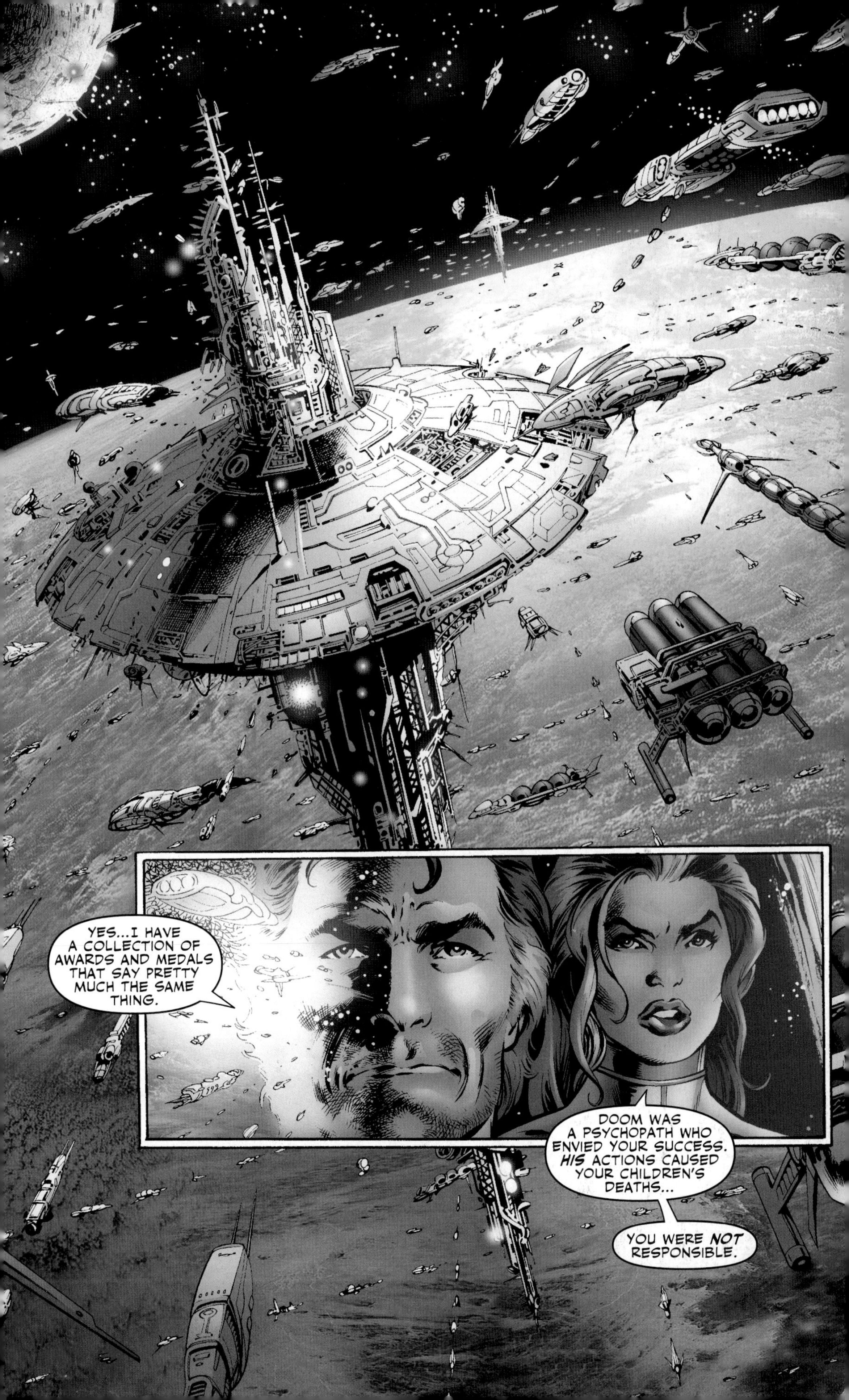
YES...I HAVE A COLLECTION OF AWARDS AND MEDALS THAT SAY PRETTY MUCH THE SAME THING.
DOOM WAS A PSYCHOPATH WHO ENVIED YOUR SUCCESS. HIS ACTIONS CAUSED YOUR CHILDREN'S DEATHS...
YOU WERE NOT RESPONSIBLE.

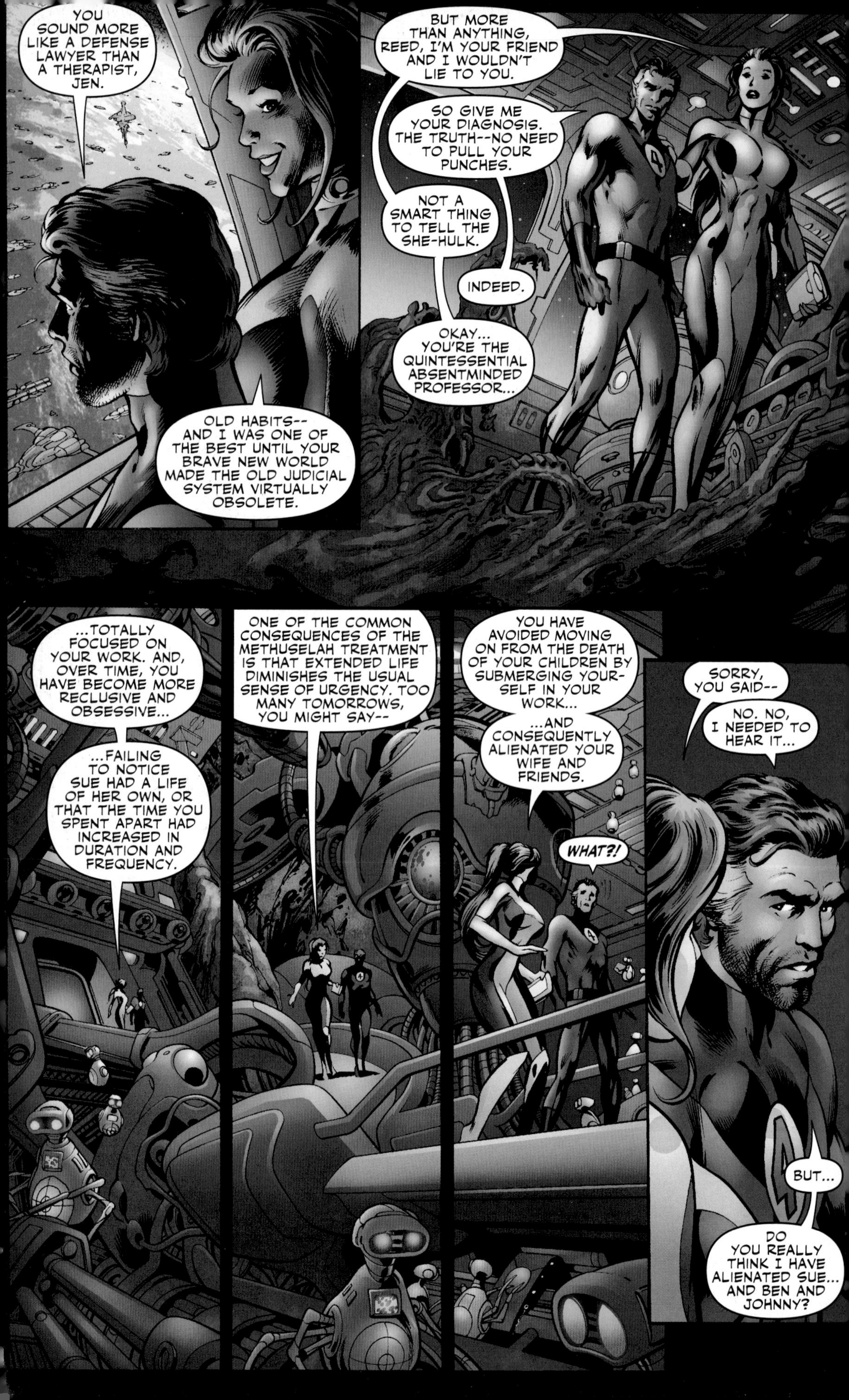
YOU SOUND MORE LIKE A DEFENSE LAWYER THAN A THERAPIST, JEN.
OLD HABITS-- AND I WAS ONE OF THE BEST UNTIL YOUR BRAVE NEW WORLD MADE THE OLD JUDICIAL SYSTEM VIRTUALLY OBSOLETE.
BUT MORE THAN ANYTHING, REED, I'M YOUR FRIEND AND I WOULDN'T LIE TO YOU.
SO GIVE ME YOUR DIAGNOSIS. THE TRUTH--NO NEED TO PULL YOUR PUNCHES.
NOT A SMART THING TO TELL THE SHE-HULK.
INDEED.
OKAY... YOU'RE THE QUINTESSENTIAL ABSENTMINDED PROFESSOR...
...TOTALLY FOCUSED ON YOUR WORK. AND, OVER TIME, YOU HAVE BECOME MORE RECLUSIVE AND OBSESSIVE...
...FAILING TO NOTICE SUE HAD A LIFE OF HER OWN, OR THAT THE TIME YOU SPENT APART HAD INCREASED IN DURATION AND FREQUENCY.
ONE OF THE COMMON CONSEQUENCES OF THE METHUSELAH TREATMENT IS THAT EXTENDED LIFE DIMINISHES THE USUAL SENSE OF URGENCY. TOO MANY TOMORROWS, YOU MIGHT SAY--
YOU HAVE AVOIDED MOVING ON FROM THE DEATH OF YOUR CHILDREN BY SUBMERGING YOUR-SELF IN YOUR WORK...
...AND CONSEQUENTLY ALIENATED YOUR WIFE AND FRIENDS.
WHAT?!
SORRY, YOU SAID--
NO. NO, I NEEDED TO HEAR IT...
BUT...
DO YOU REALLY THINK I HAVE ALIENATED SUE... AND BEN AND JOHNNY?

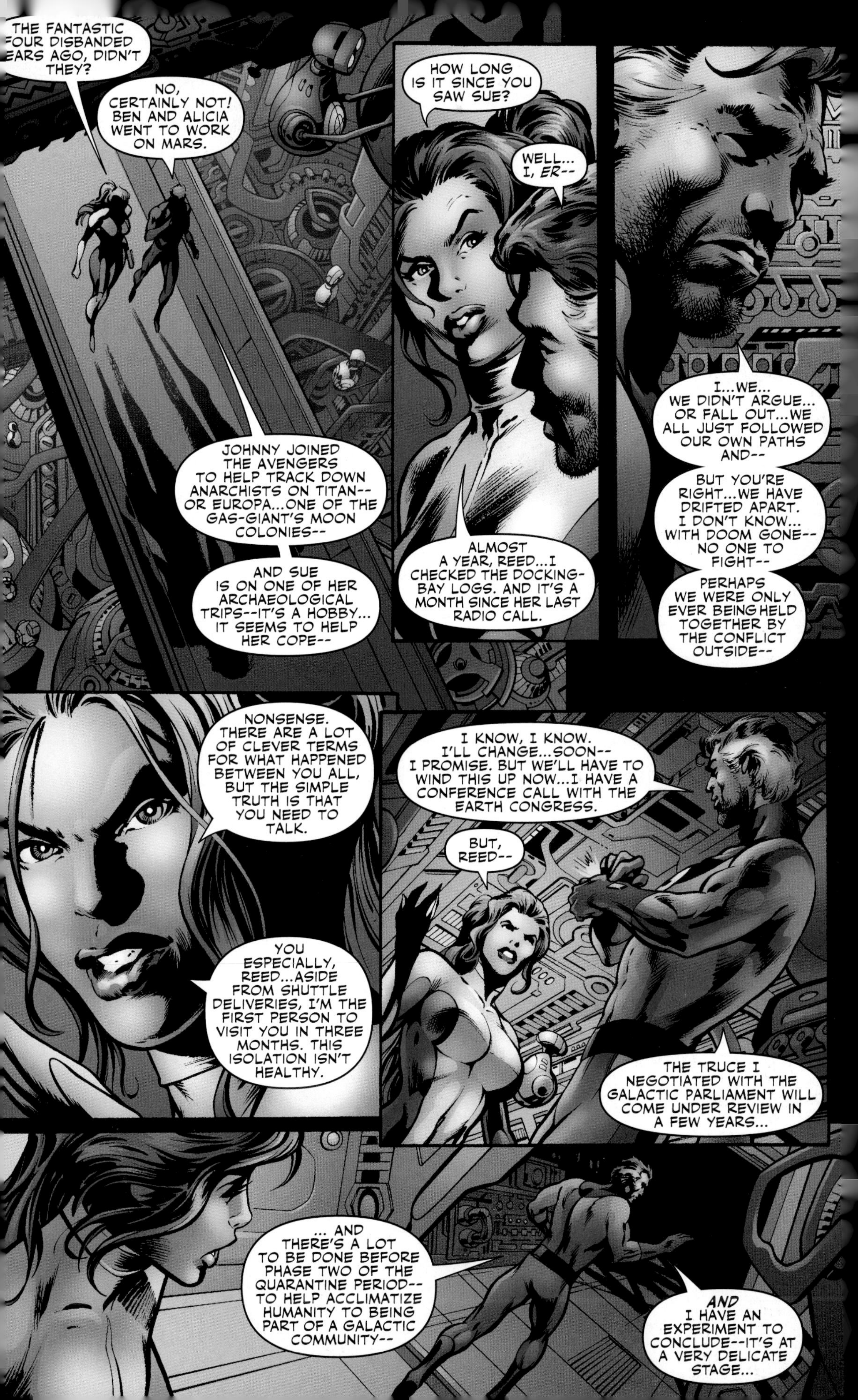
THE FANTASTIC FOUR DISBANDED EARS AGO, DIDN'T THEY?
NO, CERTAINLY NOT! BEN AND ALICIA WENT TO WORK ON MARS.
JOHNNY JOINED THE AVENGERS TO HELP TRACK DOWN ANARCHISTS ON TITAN-- OR EUROPA...ONE OF THE GAS-GIANT'S MOON COLONIES--
AND SUE IS ON ONE OF HER ARCHAEOLOGICAL TRIPS--IT'S A HOBBY... IT SEEMS TO HELP HER COPE--
HOW LONG IS IT SINCE YOU SAW SUE?
WELL... I, ER--
ALMOST A YEAR, REED...I CHECKED THE DOCKING-BAY LOGS. AND IT'S A MONTH SINCE HER LAST RADIO CALL.
I...WE... WE DIDN'T ARGUE... OR FALL OUT...WE ALL JUST FOLLOWED OUR OWN PATHS AND--
BUT YOU'RE RIGHT...WE HAVE DRIFTED APART. I DON'T KNOW... WITH DOOM GONE-- NO ONE TO FIGHT--
PERHAPS WE WERE ONLY EVER BEING HELD TOGETHER BY THE CONFLICT OUTSIDE--
NONSENSE. THERE ARE A LOT OF CLEVER TERMS FOR WHAT HAPPENED BETWEEN YOU ALL, BUT THE SIMPLE TRUTH IS THAT YOU NEED TO TALK.
YOU ESPECIALLY, REED...ASIDE FROM SHUTTLE DELIVERIES, I'M THE FIRST PERSON TO VISIT YOU IN THREE MONTHS. THIS ISOLATION ISN'T HEALTHY.
I KNOW, I KNOW. I'LL CHANGE...SOON-- I PROMISE. BUT WE'LL HAVE TO WIND THIS UP NOW...I HAVE A CONFERENCE CALL WITH THE EARTH CONGRESS.
BUT, REED--
THE TRUCE I NEGOTIATED WITH THE GALACTIC PARLIAMENT WILL COME UNDER REVIEW IN A FEW YEARS...
... AND THERE'S A LOT TO BE DONE BEFORE PHASE TWO OF THE QUARANTINE PERIOD-- TO HELP ACCLIMATIZE HUMANITY TO BEING PART OF A GALACTIC COMMUNITY--
AND I HAVE AN EXPERIMENT TO CONCLUDE--IT'S AT A VERY DELICATE STAGE...

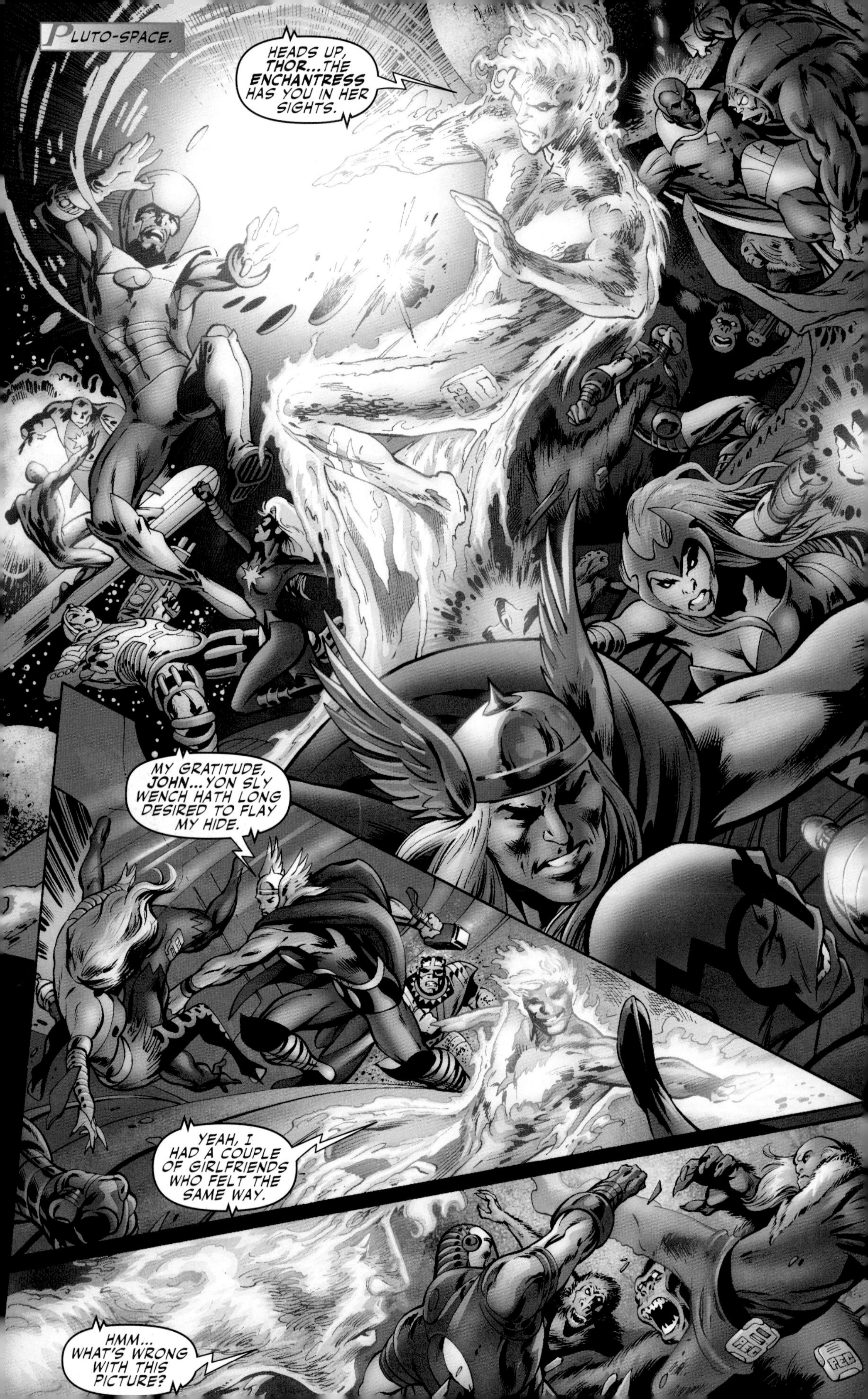
PLUTO-SPACE.
HEADS UP, THOR...THE ENCHANTRESS HAS YOU IN HER SIGHTS.
MY GRATITUDE, JOHN...YON SLY WENCH HATH LONG DESIRED TO FLAY MY HIDE.
YEAH, I HAD A COUPLE OF GIRLFRIENDS WHO FELT THE SAME WAY.
HMM... WHAT'S WRONG WITH THIS PICTURE?

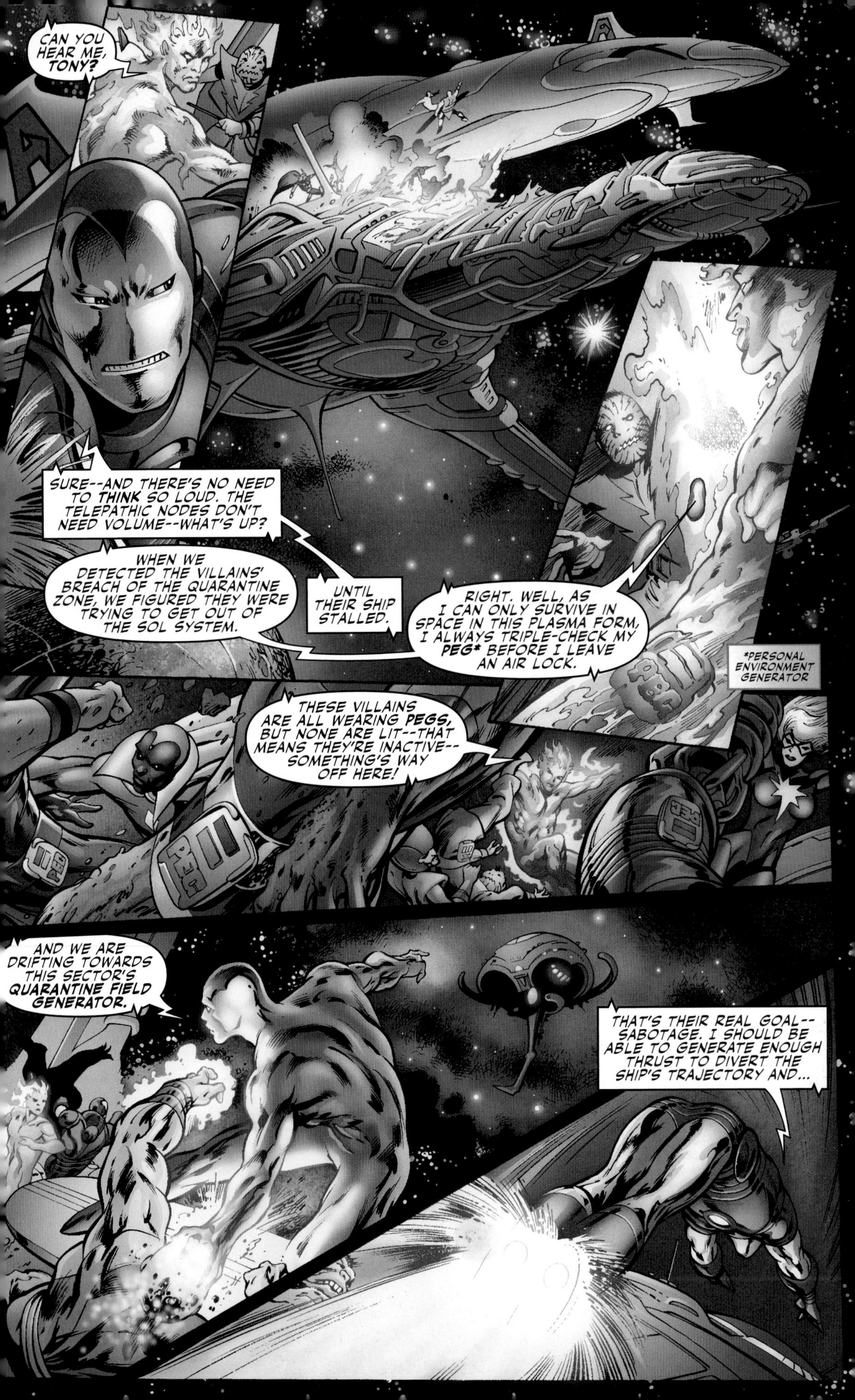
CAN YOU HEAR ME, TONY?
SURE--AND THERE'S NO NEED TO THINK SO LOUD. THE TELEPATHIC NODES DON'T NEED VOLUME--WHAT'S UP?
WHEN WE DETECTED THE VILLAINS' BREACH OF THE QUARANTINE ZONE, WE FIGURED THEY WERE TRYING TO GET OUT OF THE SOL SYSTEM.
UNTIL THEIR SHIP STALLED.
RIGHT. WELL, AS I CAN ONLY SURVIVE IN SPACE IN THIS PLASMA FORM, I ALWAYS TRIPLE-CHECK MY PEG* BEFORE I LEAVE AN AIR LOCK.
*PERSONAL ENVIRONMENT GENERATOR
THESE VILLAINS ARE ALL WEARING PEGS, BUT NONE ARE LIT--THAT MEANS THEY'RE INACTIVE--SOMETHING'S WAY OFF HERE!
AND WE ARE DRIFTING TOWARDS THIS SECTOR'S QUARANTINE FIELD GENERATOR.
THAT'S THEIR REAL GOAL--SABOTAGE. I SHOULD BE ABLE TO GENERATE ENOUGH THRUST TO DIVERT THE SHIP'S TRAJECTORY AND...

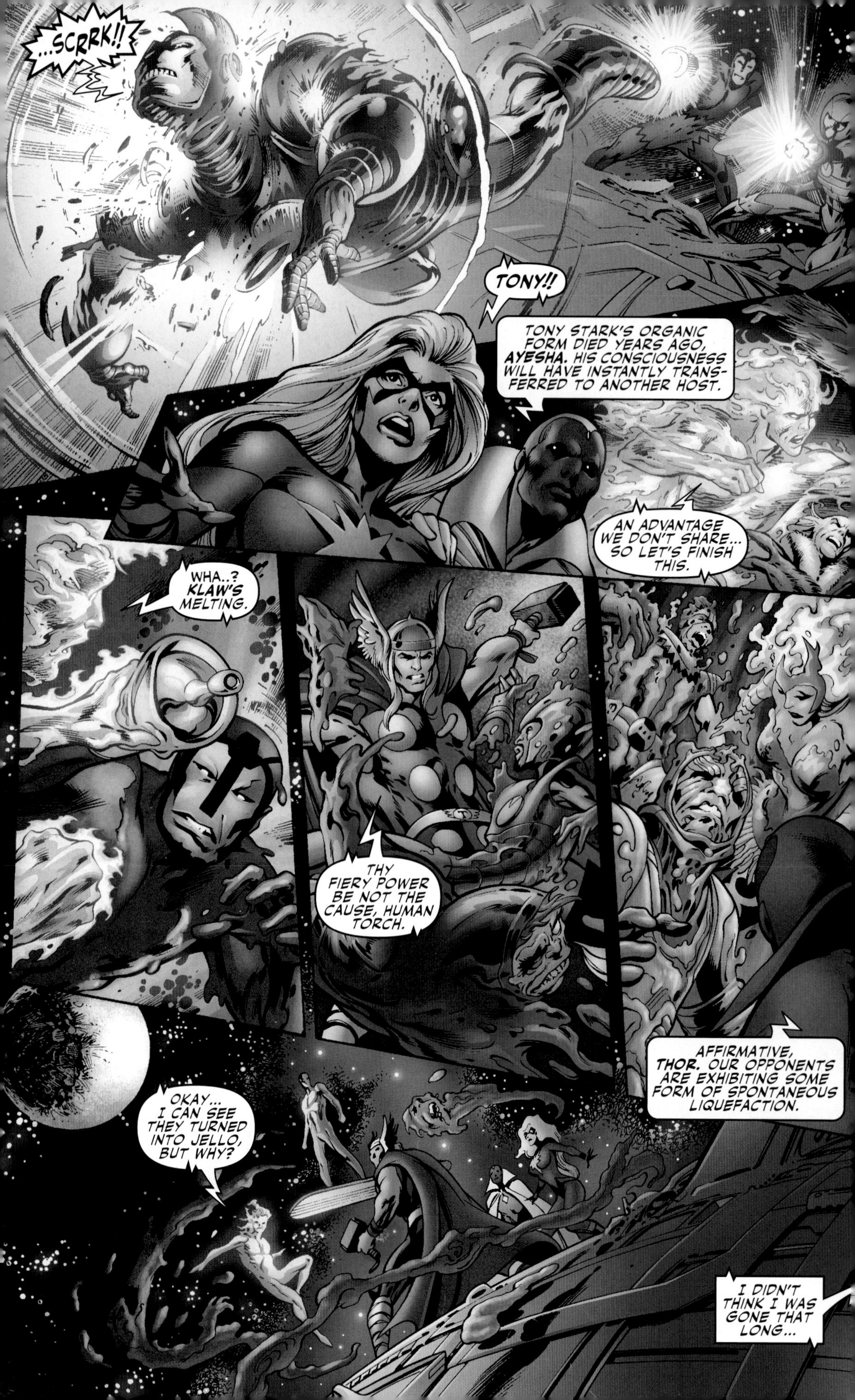
...SCRRK!!
TONY!!
TONY STARK'S ORGANIC FORM DIED YEARS AGO, AYESHA. HIS CONSCIOUSNESS WILL HAVE INSTANTLY TRANSFERRED TO ANOTHER HOST.
AN ADVANTAGE WE DON'T SHARE... SO LET'S FINISH THIS.
WHA..? KLAW'S MELTING.
THY FIERY POWER BE NOT THE CAUSE, HUMAN TORCH.
AFFIRMATIVE, THOR. OUR OPPONENTS ARE EXHIBITING SOME FORM OF SPONTANEOUS LIQUEFACTION.
OKAY... I CAN SEE THEY TURNED INTO JELLO, BUT WHY?
I DIDN'T THINK I WAS GONE THAT LONG...

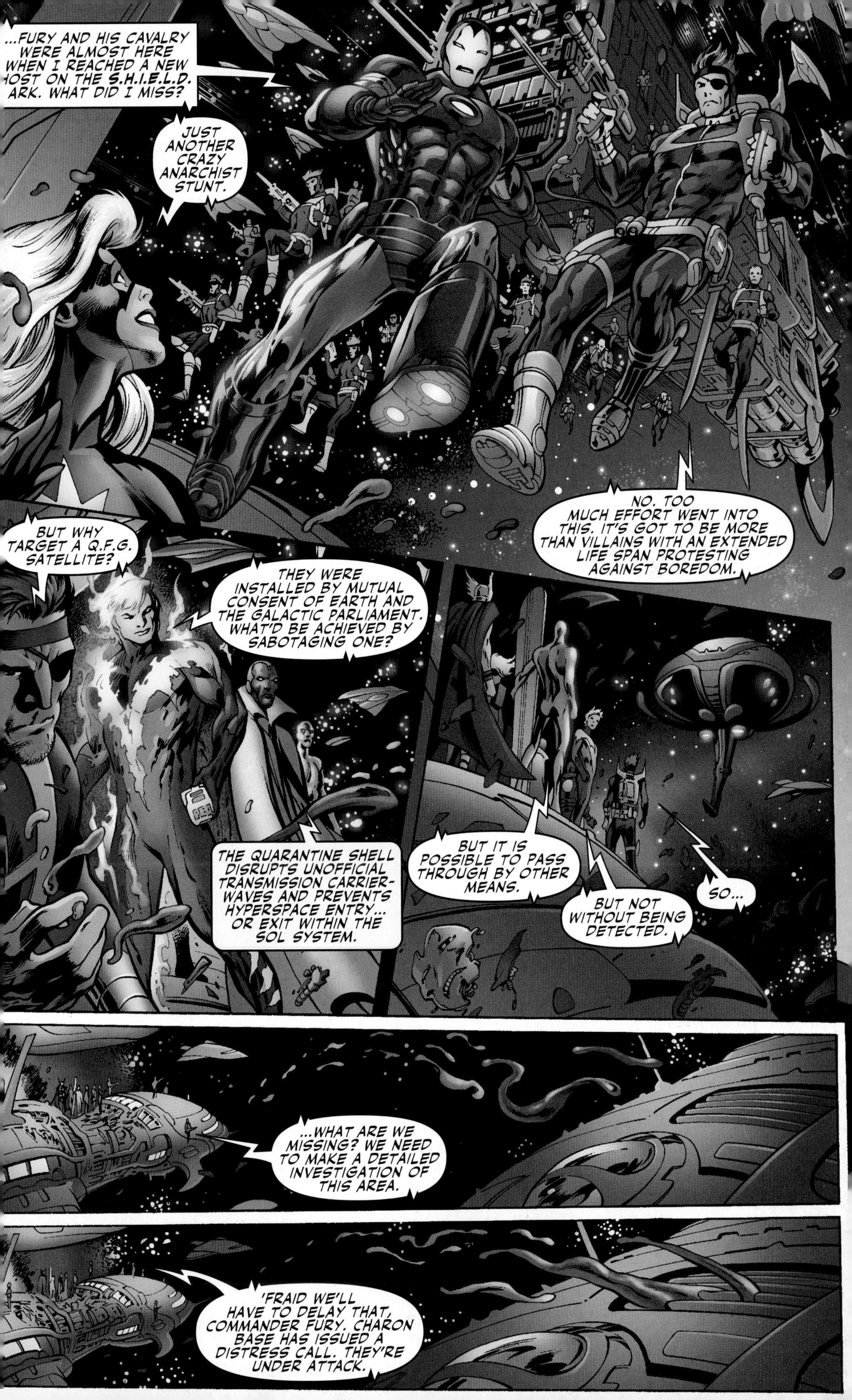
...FURY AND HIS CAVALRY WERE ALMOST HERE WHEN I REACHED A NEW HOST ON THE S.H.I.E.L.D. ARK. WHAT DID I MISS?
JUST ANOTHER CRAZY ANARCHIST STUNT.
NO. TOO MUCH EFFORT WENT INTO THIS. IT'S GOT TO BE MORE THAN VILLAINS WITH AN EXTENDED LIFE SPAN PROTESTING AGAINST BOREDOM.
BUT WHY TARGET A Q.F.G. SATELLITE?
THEY WERE INSTALLED BY MUTUAL CONSENT OF EARTH AND THE GALACTIC PARLIAMENT. WHAT'D BE ACHIEVED BY SABOTAGING ONE?
THE QUARANTINE SHELL DISRUPTS UNOFFICIAL TRANSMISSION CARRIER-WAVES AND PREVENTS HYPERSPACE ENTRY... OR EXIT WITHIN THE SOL SYSTEM.
BUT IT IS POSSIBLE TO PASS THROUGH BY OTHER MEANS.
BUT NOT WITHOUT BEING DETECTED.
SO...
...WHAT ARE WE MISSING? WE NEED TO MAKE A DETAILED INVESTIGATION OF THIS AREA.
'FRAID WE'LL HAVE TO DELAY THAT, COMMANDER FURY. CHARON BASE HAS ISSUED A DISTRESS CALL. THEY'RE UNDER ATTACK.

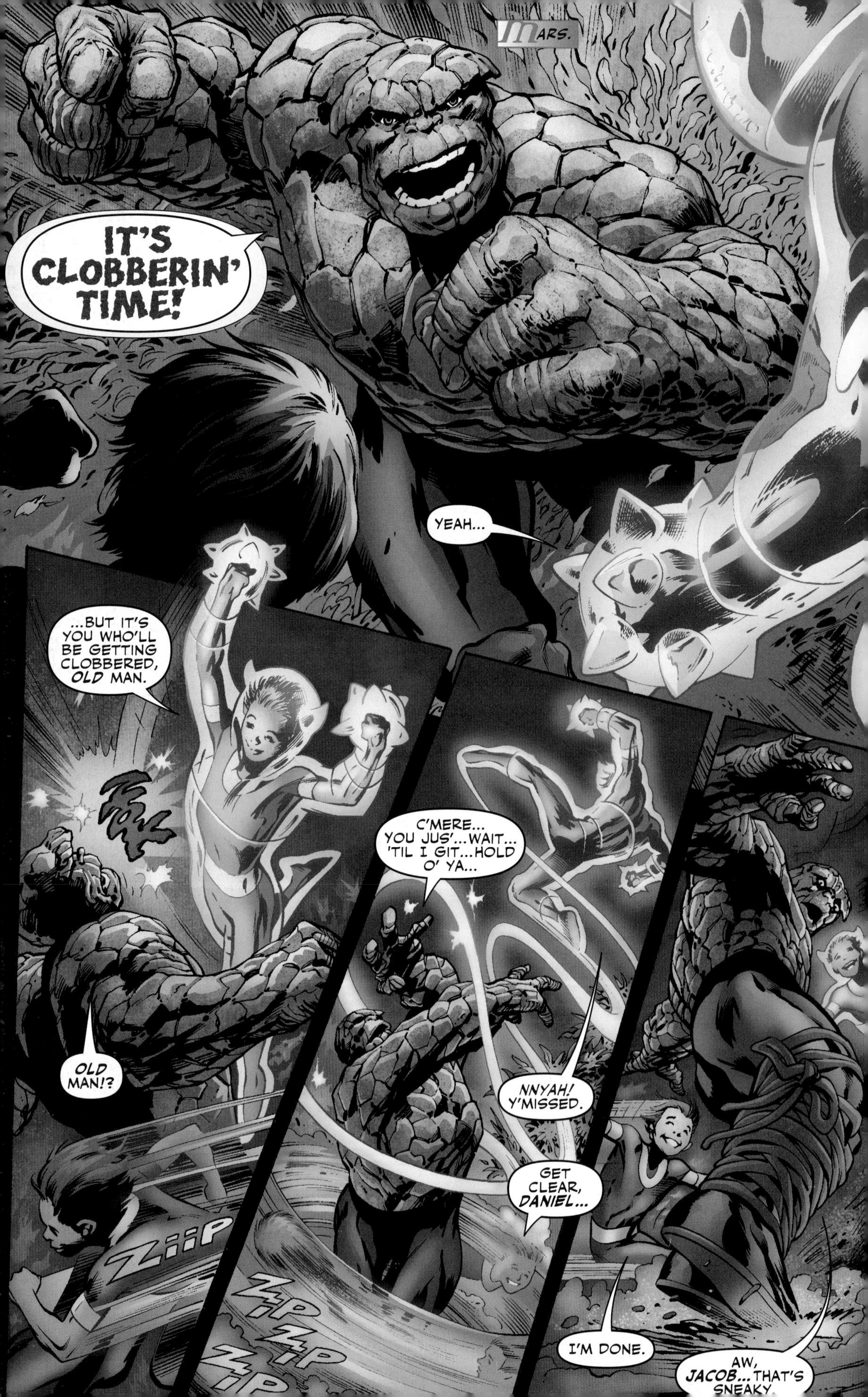
MARS.
IT'S CLOBBERIN' TIME!
YEAH...
...BUT IT'S YOU WHO'LL BE GETTING CLOBBERED, OLD MAN.
OLD MAN!?
ZIIP
C'MERE... YOU JUS'...WAIT... 'TIL I GIT...HOLD O' YA...
NNYAH! Y'MISSED.
GET CLEAR, DANIEL...
ZIP ZIP ZIP
I'M DONE.
AW, JACOB... THAT'S SNEAKY.

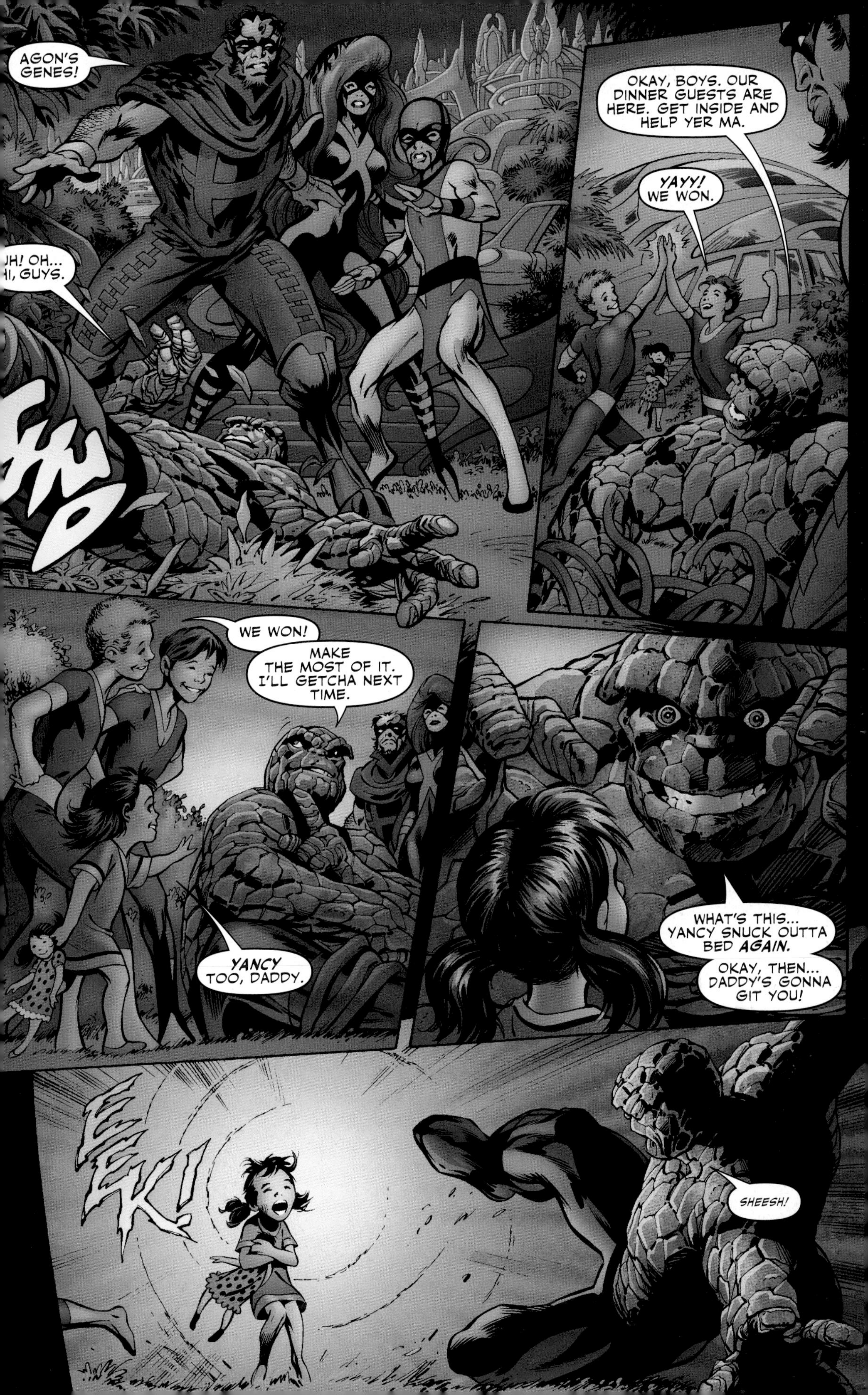
AGON'S GENES!
UH! OH... HI, GUYS.
OKAY, BOYS. OUR DINNER GUESTS ARE HERE. GET INSIDE AND HELP YER MA.
YAYY! WE WON.
WE WON!
MAKE THE MOST OF IT. I'LL GETCHA NEXT TIME.
YANCY TOO, DADDY.
WHAT'S THIS... YANCY SNUCK OUTTA BED AGAIN.
OKAY, THEN... DADDY'S GONNA GIT YOU!
EEEK!
SHEESH!

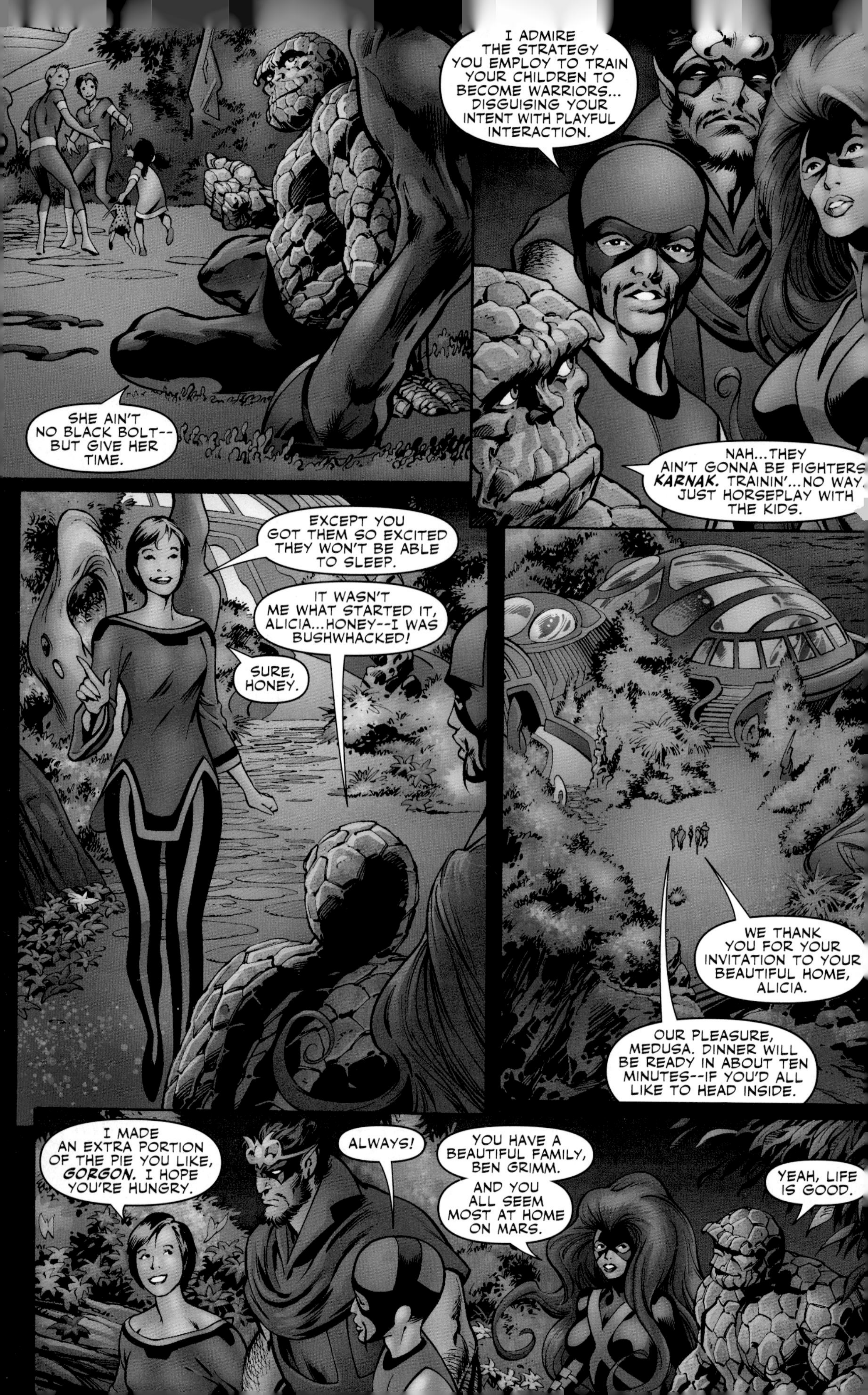
SHE AIN'T NO BLACK BOLT-- BUT GIVE HER TIME.
I ADMIRE THE STRATEGY YOU EMPLOY TO TRAIN YOUR CHILDREN TO BECOME WARRIORS... DISGUISING YOUR INTENT WITH PLAYFUL INTERACTION.
NAH...THEY AIN'T GONNA BE FIGHTERS KARNAK. TRAININ'...NO WAY. JUST HORSEPLAY WITH THE KIDS.
EXCEPT YOU GOT THEM SO EXCITED THEY WON'T BE ABLE TO SLEEP.
IT WASN'T ME WHAT STARTED IT, ALICIA...HONEY--I WAS BUSHWHACKED!
SURE, HONEY.
WE THANK YOU FOR YOUR INVITATION TO YOUR BEAUTIFUL HOME, ALICIA.
OUR PLEASURE, MEDUSA. DINNER WILL BE READY IN ABOUT TEN MINUTES--IF YOU'D ALL LIKE TO HEAD INSIDE.
I MADE AN EXTRA PORTION OF THE PIE YOU LIKE, GORGON. I HOPE YOU'RE HUNGRY.
ALWAYS!
YOU HAVE A BEAUTIFUL FAMILY, BEN GRIMM.
AND YOU ALL SEEM MOST AT HOME ON MARS.
YEAH, LIFE IS GOOD.

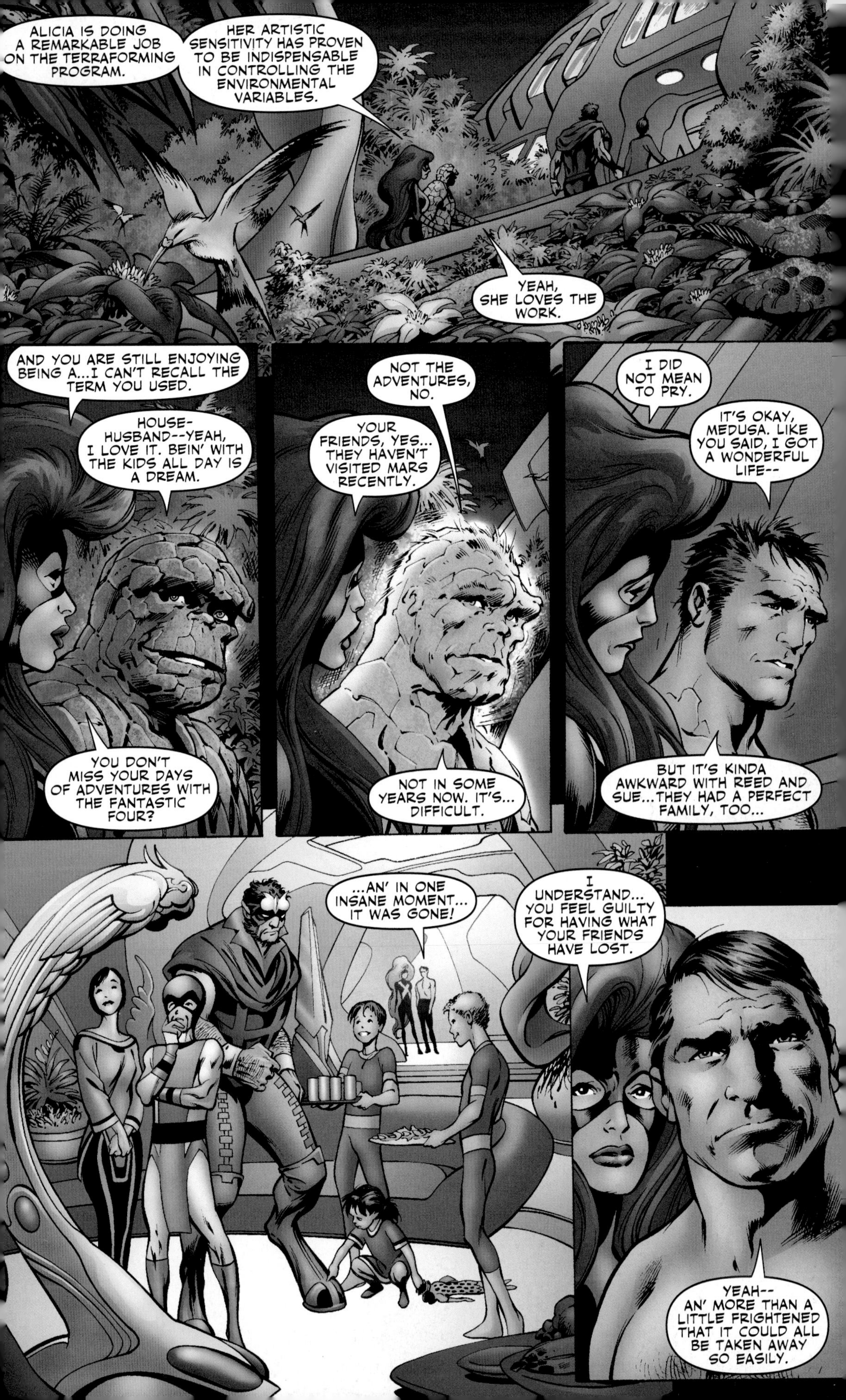
ALICIA IS DOING A REMARKABLE JOB ON THE TERRAFORMING PROGRAM.
HER ARTISTIC SENSITIVITY HAS PROVEN TO BE INDISPENSABLE IN CONTROLLING THE ENVIRONMENTAL VARIABLES.
YEAH, SHE LOVES THE WORK.
AND YOU ARE STILL ENJOYING BEING A...I CAN'T RECALL THE TERM YOU USED.
HOUSE-HUSBAND--YEAH, I LOVE IT. BEIN' WITH THE KIDS ALL DAY IS A DREAM.
YOU DON'T MISS YOUR DAYS OF ADVENTURES WITH THE FANTASTIC FOUR?
NOT THE ADVENTURES, NO.
YOUR FRIENDS, YES... THEY HAVEN'T VISITED MARS RECENTLY.
NOT IN SOME YEARS NOW. IT'S... DIFFICULT.
I DID NOT MEAN TO PRY.
IT'S OKAY, MEDUSA. LIKE YOU SAID, I GOT A WONDERFUL LIFE--
BUT IT'S KINDA AWKWARD WITH REED AND SUE...THEY HAD A PERFECT FAMILY, TOO...
...AN' IN ONE INSANE MOMENT... IT WAS GONE!
I UNDERSTAND... YOU FEEL GUILTY FOR HAVING WHAT YOUR FRIENDS HAVE LOST.
YEAH-- AN' MORE THAN A LITTLE FRIGHTENED THAT IT COULD ALL BE TAKEN AWAY SO EASILY.

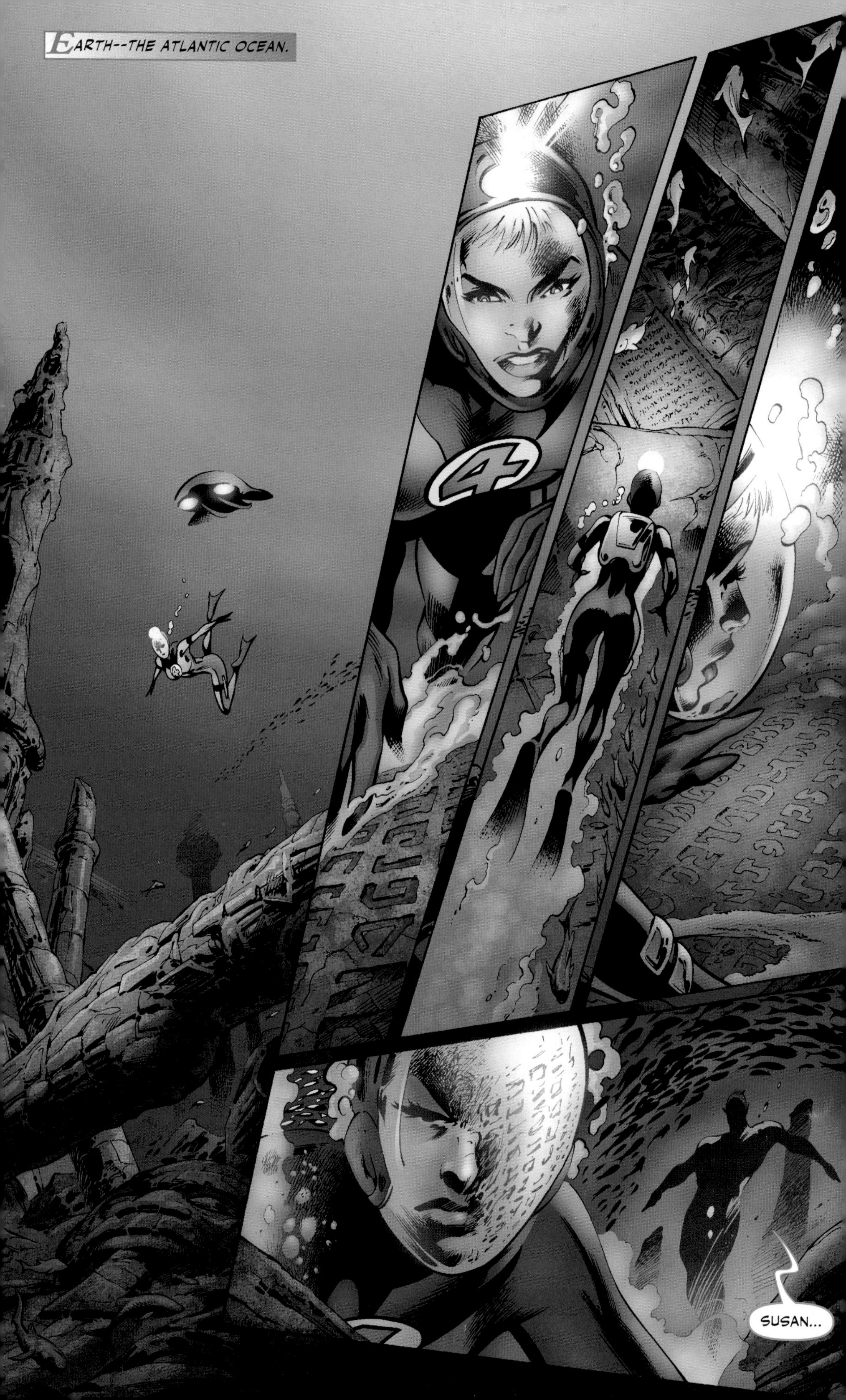
EARTH--THE ATLANTIC OCEAN.
SUSAN...

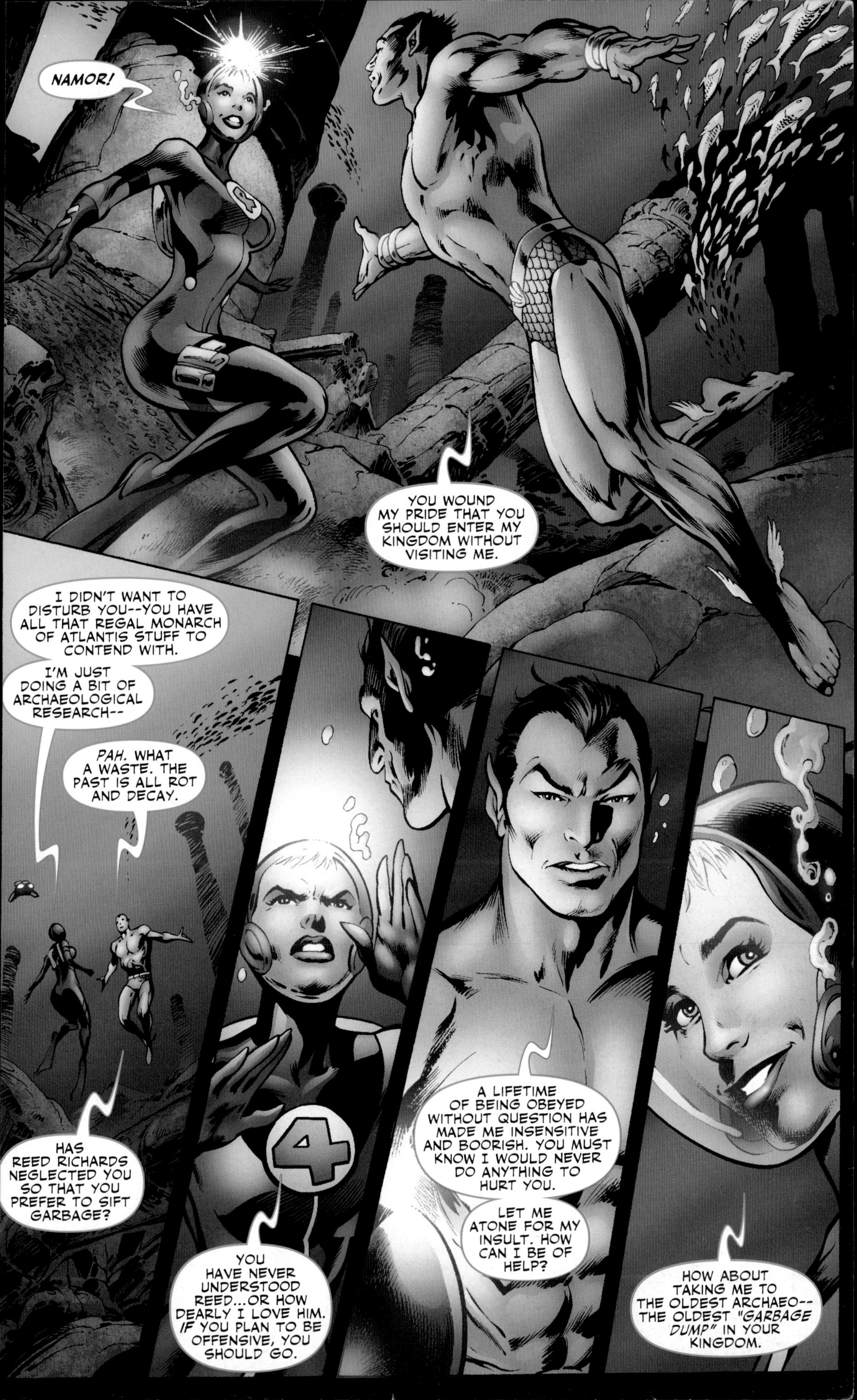
NAMOR!
YOU WOUND MY PRIDE THAT YOU SHOULD ENTER MY KINGDOM WITHOUT VISITING ME.
I DIDN'T WANT TO DISTURB YOU--YOU HAVE ALL THAT REGAL MONARCH OF ATLANTIS STUFF TO CONTEND WITH.
I'M JUST DOING A BIT OF ARCHAEOLOGICAL RESEARCH--
PAH. WHAT A WASTE. THE PAST IS ALL ROT AND DECAY.
HAS REED RICHARDS NEGLECTED YOU SO THAT YOU PREFER TO SIFT GARBAGE?
YOU HAVE NEVER UNDERSTOOD REED...OR HOW DEARLY I LOVE HIM. IF YOU PLAN TO BE OFFENSIVE, YOU SHOULD GO.
A LIFETIME OF BEING OBEYED WITHOUT QUESTION HAS MADE ME INSENSITIVE AND BOORISH. YOU MUST KNOW I WOULD NEVER DO ANYTHING TO HURT YOU.
LET ME ATONE FOR MY INSULT. HOW CAN I BE OF HELP?
HOW ABOUT TAKING ME TO THE OLDEST ARCHAEO-- THE OLDEST "GARBAGE DUMP" IN YOUR KINGDOM.

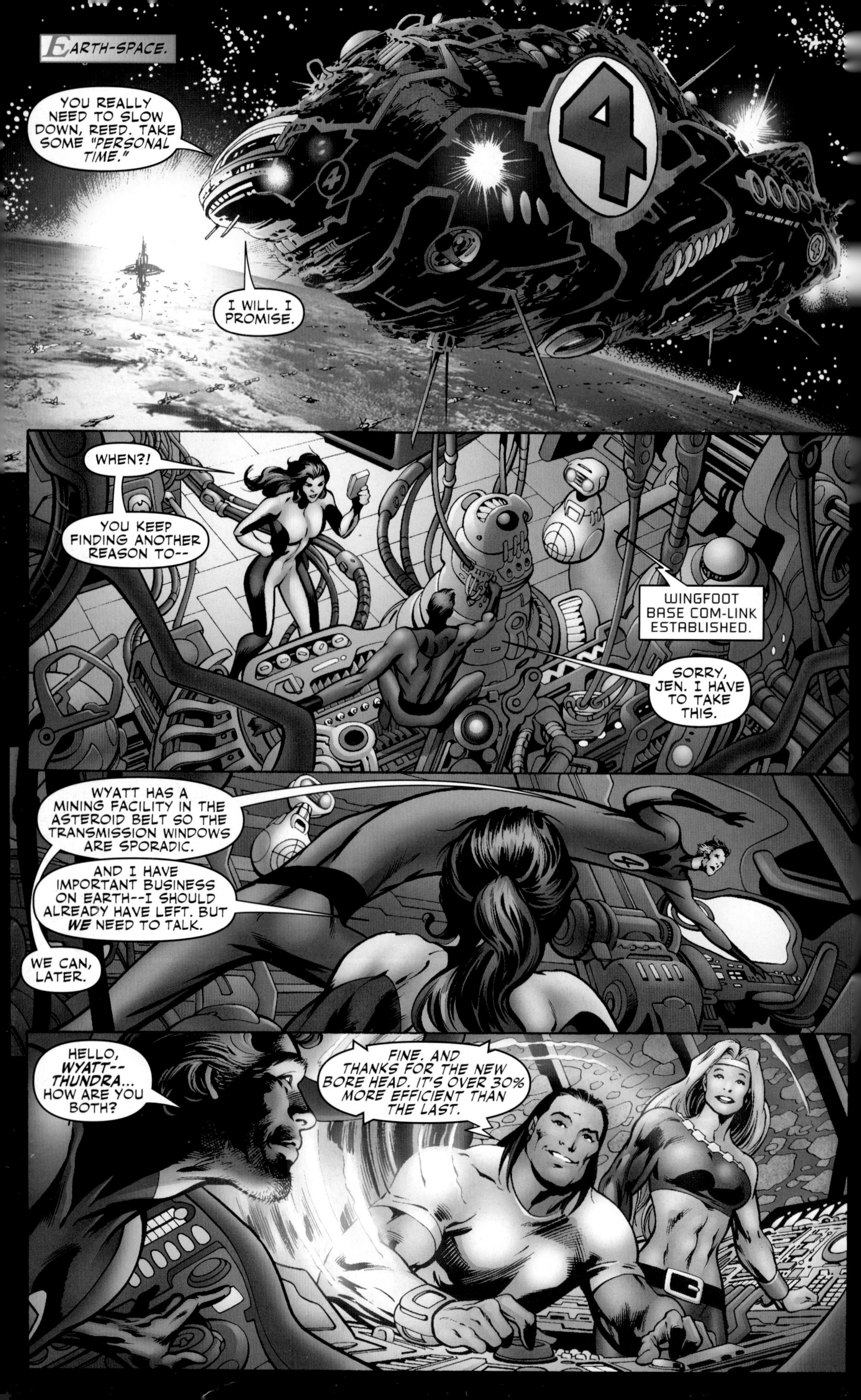
EARTH-SPACE.
YOU REALLY NEED TO SLOW DOWN, REED. TAKE SOME "PERSONAL TIME."
I WILL. I PROMISE.
WHEN?!
YOU KEEP FINDING ANOTHER REASON TO--
WINGFOOT BASE COM-LINK ESTABLISHED.
SORRY, JEN. I HAVE TO TAKE THIS.
WYATT HAS A MINING FACILITY IN THE ASTEROID BELT SO THE TRANSMISSION WINDOWS ARE SPORADIC.
AND I HAVE IMPORTANT BUSINESS ON EARTH--I SHOULD ALREADY HAVE LEFT. BUT WE NEED TO TALK.
WE CAN, LATER.
HELLO, WYATT-- THUNDRA... HOW ARE YOU BOTH?
FINE. AND THANKS FOR THE NEW BORE HEAD. IT'S OVER 30% MORE EFFICIENT THAN THE LAST.

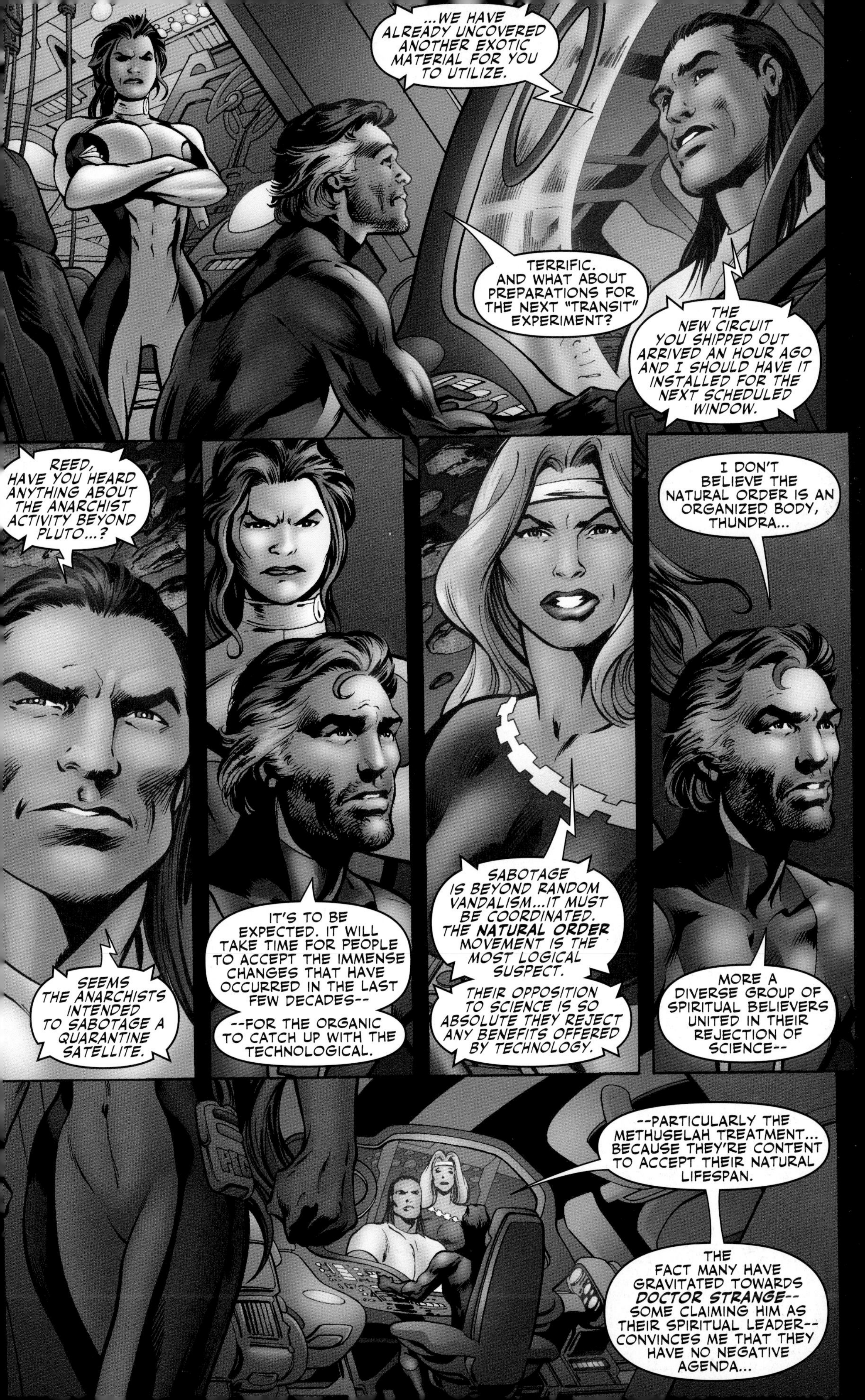
...WE HAVE ALREADY UNCOVERED ANOTHER EXOTIC MATERIAL FOR YOU TO UTILIZE.
TERRIFIC. AND WHAT ABOUT PREPARATIONS FOR THE NEXT "TRANSIT" EXPERIMENT?
THE NEW CIRCUIT YOU SHIPPED OUT ARRIVED AN HOUR AGO AND I SHOULD HAVE IT INSTALLED FOR THE NEXT SCHEDULED WINDOW.
REED, HAVE YOU HEARD ANYTHING ABOUT THE ANARCHIST ACTIVITY BEYOND PLUTO...?
SEEMS THE ANARCHISTS INTENDED TO SABOTAGE A QUARANTINE SATELLITE.
IT'S TO BE EXPECTED. IT WILL TAKE TIME FOR PEOPLE TO ACCEPT THE IMMENSE CHANGES THAT HAVE OCCURRED IN THE LAST FEW DECADES--
--FOR THE ORGANIC TO CATCH UP WITH THE TECHNOLOGICAL.
SABOTAGE IS BEYOND RANDOM VANDALISM...IT MUST BE COORDINATED. THE **NATURAL ORDER** MOVEMENT IS THE MOST LOGICAL SUSPECT.
THEIR OPPOSITION TO SCIENCE IS SO ABSOLUTE THEY REJECT ANY BENEFITS OFFERED BY TECHNOLOGY.
I DON'T BELIEVE THE NATURAL ORDER IS AN ORGANIZED BODY, THUNDRA...
MORE A DIVERSE GROUP OF SPIRITUAL BELIEVERS UNITED IN THEIR REJECTION OF SCIENCE--
--PARTICULARLY THE METHUSELAH TREATMENT... BECAUSE THEY'RE CONTENT TO ACCEPT THEIR NATURAL LIFESPAN.
THE FACT MANY HAVE GRAVITATED TOWARDS ***DOCTOR STRANGE***-- SOME CLAIMING HIM AS THEIR SPIRITUAL LEADER-- CONVINCES ME THAT THEY HAVE NO NEGATIVE AGENDA...

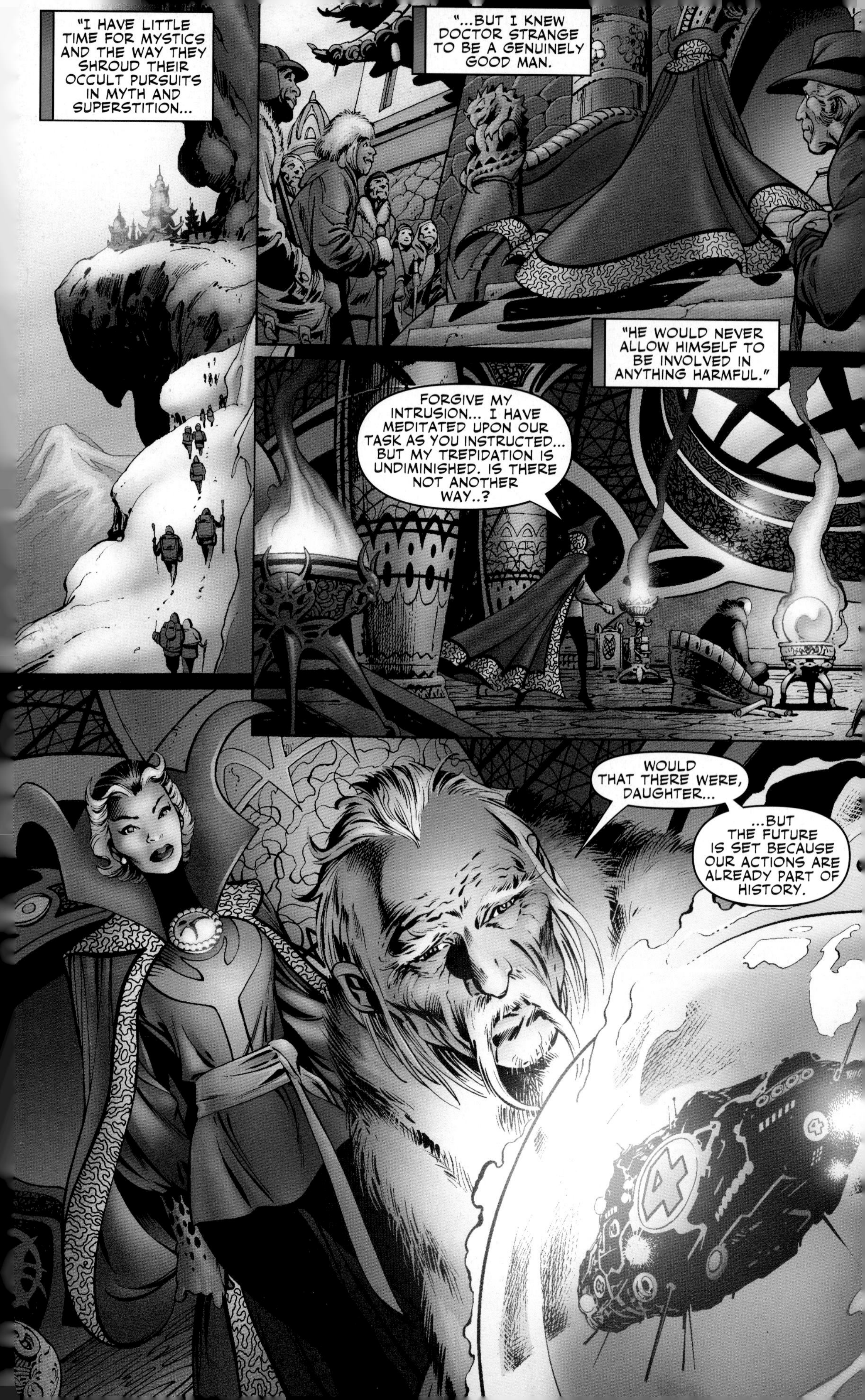
"I HAVE LITTLE TIME FOR MYSTICS AND THE WAY THEY SHROUD THEIR OCCULT PURSUITS IN MYTH AND SUPERSTITION...
"...BUT I KNEW DOCTOR STRANGE TO BE A GENUINELY GOOD MAN.
"HE WOULD NEVER ALLOW HIMSELF TO BE INVOLVED IN ANYTHING HARMFUL."
FORGIVE MY INTRUSION... I HAVE MEDITATED UPON OUR TASK AS YOU INSTRUCTED... BUT MY TREPIDATION IS UNDIMINISHED. IS THERE NOT ANOTHER WAY..?
WOULD THAT THERE WERE, DAUGHTER...
...BUT THE FUTURE IS SET BECAUSE OUR ACTIONS ARE ALREADY PART OF HISTORY.

THE END

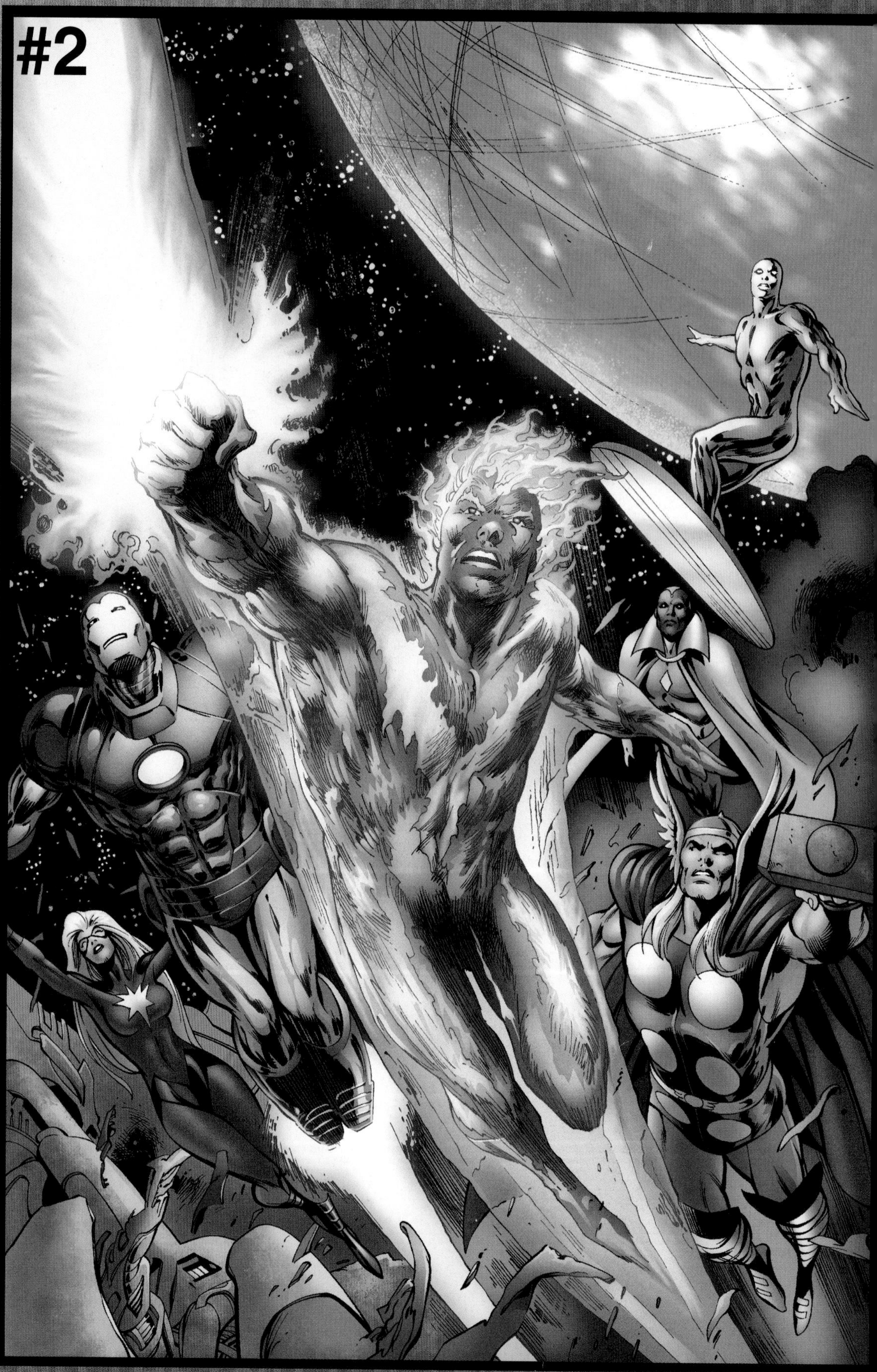
#2

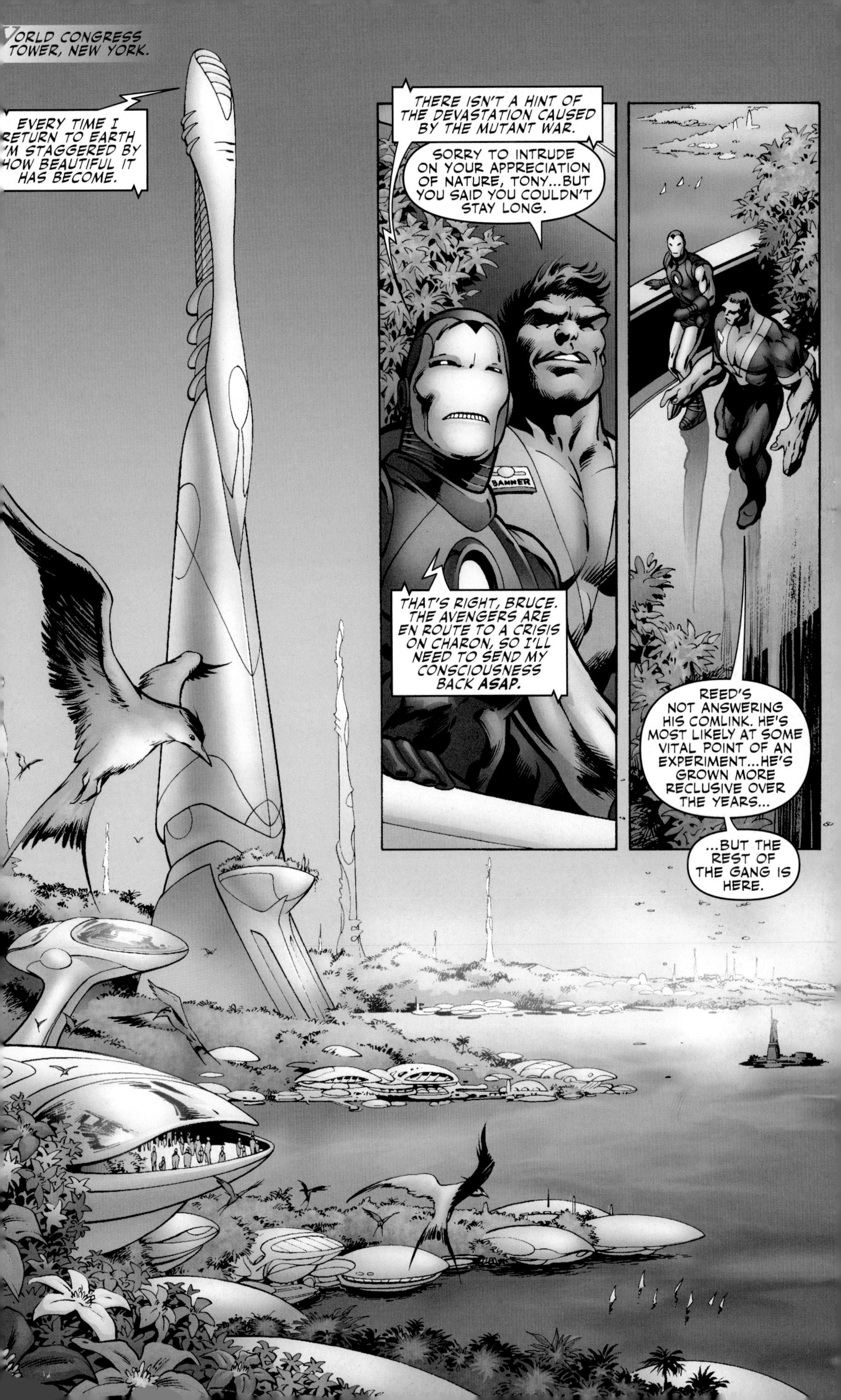
ORLD CONGRESS TOWER, NEW YORK.
EVERY TIME I RETURN TO EARTH 'M STAGGERED BY HOW BEAUTIFUL IT HAS BECOME.
THERE ISN'T A HINT OF THE DEVASTATION CAUSED BY THE MUTANT WAR.
SORRY TO INTRUDE ON YOUR APPRECIATION OF NATURE, TONY...BUT YOU SAID YOU COULDN'T STAY LONG.
BANNER
THAT'S RIGHT, BRUCE. THE AVENGERS ARE EN ROUTE TO A CRISIS ON CHARON, SO I'LL NEED TO SEND MY CONSCIOUSNESS BACK ASAP.
REED'S NOT ANSWERING HIS COMLINK. HE'S MOST LIKELY AT SOME VITAL POINT OF AN EXPERIMENT...HE'S GROWN MORE RECLUSIVE OVER THE YEARS...
...BUT THE REST OF THE GANG IS HERE.

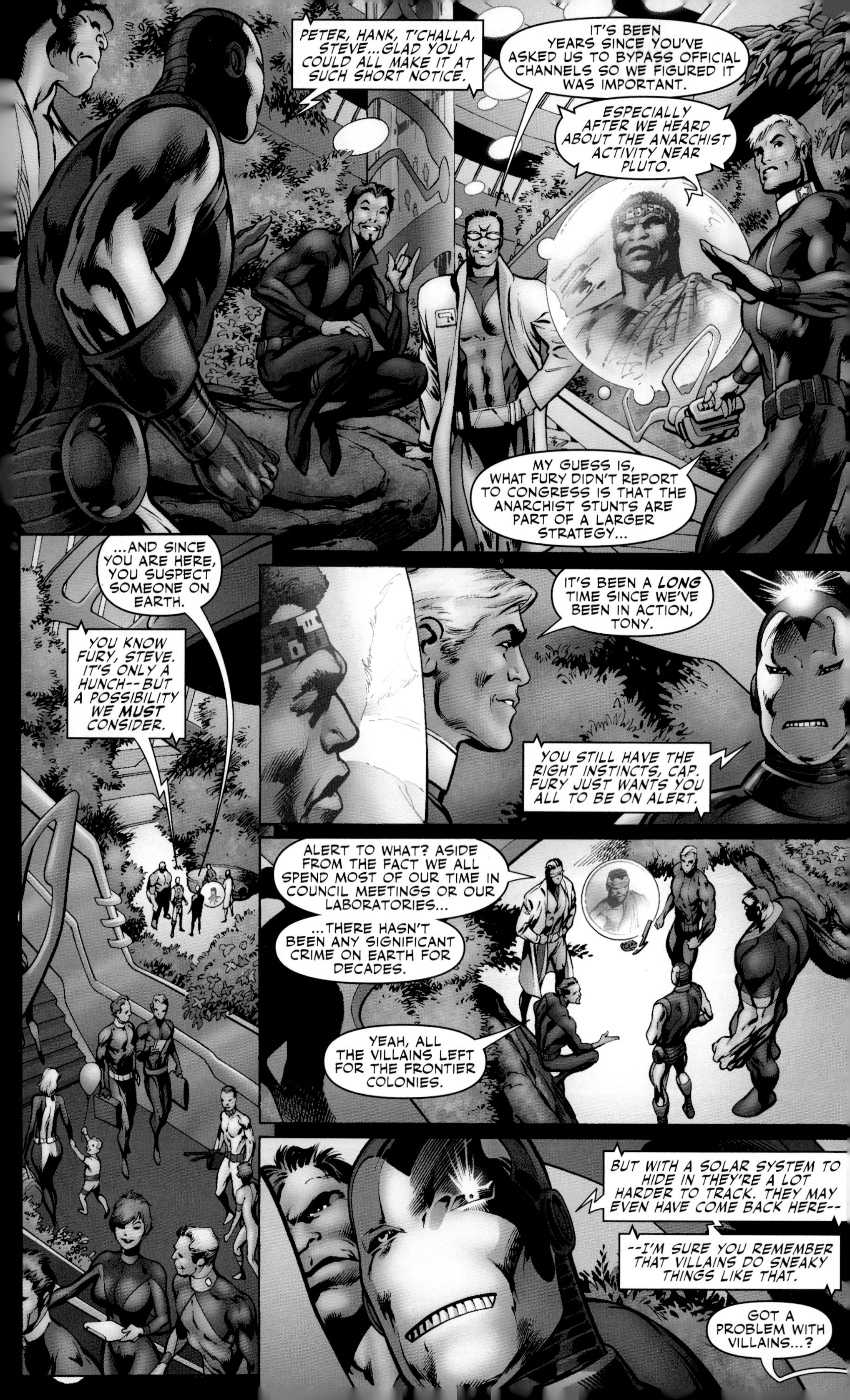
PETER, HANK, T'CHALLA, STEVE...GLAD YOU COULD ALL MAKE IT AT SUCH SHORT NOTICE.
IT'S BEEN YEARS SINCE YOU'VE ASKED US TO BYPASS OFFICIAL CHANNELS SO WE FIGURED IT WAS IMPORTANT.
ESPECIALLY AFTER WE HEARD ABOUT THE ANARCHIST ACTIVITY NEAR PLUTO.
MY GUESS IS, WHAT FURY DIDN'T REPORT TO CONGRESS IS THAT THE ANARCHIST STUNTS ARE PART OF A LARGER STRATEGY...
...AND SINCE YOU ARE HERE, YOU SUSPECT SOMEONE ON EARTH.
YOU KNOW FURY, STEVE. IT'S ONLY A HUNCH--BUT A POSSIBILITY WE MUST CONSIDER.
IT'S BEEN A LONG TIME SINCE WE'VE BEEN IN ACTION, TONY.
YOU STILL HAVE THE RIGHT INSTINCTS, CAP. FURY JUST WANTS YOU ALL TO BE ON ALERT.
ALERT TO WHAT? ASIDE FROM THE FACT WE ALL SPEND MOST OF OUR TIME IN COUNCIL MEETINGS OR OUR LABORATORIES...
...THERE HASN'T BEEN ANY SIGNIFICANT CRIME ON EARTH FOR DECADES.
YEAH, ALL THE VILLAINS LEFT FOR THE FRONTIER COLONIES.
BUT WITH A SOLAR SYSTEM TO HIDE IN THEY'RE A LOT HARDER TO TRACK. THEY MAY EVEN HAVE COME BACK HERE--
--I'M SURE YOU REMEMBER THAT VILLAINS DO SNEAKY THINGS LIKE THAT.
GOT A PROBLEM WITH VILLAINS...?

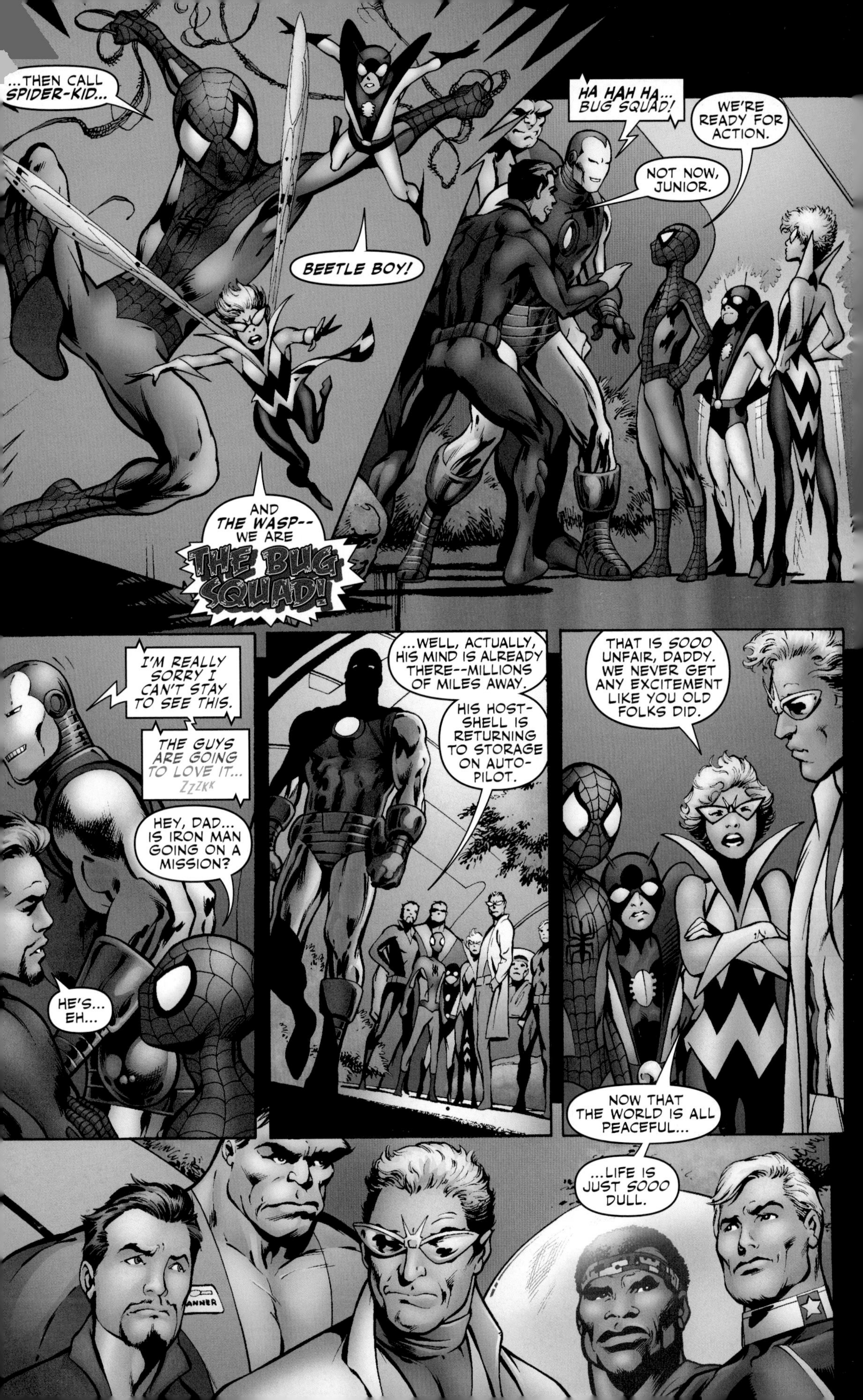
...THEN CALL SPIDER-KID...
BEETLE BOY!
AND THE WASP-- WE ARE
THE BUG SQUAD!
HA HAH HA... BUG SQUAD!
WE'RE READY FOR ACTION.
NOT NOW, JUNIOR.
I'M REALLY SORRY I CAN'T STAY TO SEE THIS.
THE GUYS ARE GOING TO LOVE IT... ZZZKK
HEY, DAD... IS IRON MAN GOING ON A MISSION?
HE'S... EH...
...WELL, ACTUALLY, HIS MIND IS ALREADY THERE--MILLIONS OF MILES AWAY.
HIS HOST-SHELL IS RETURNING TO STORAGE ON AUTO-PILOT.
THAT IS SOOO UNFAIR, DADDY. WE NEVER GET ANY EXCITEMENT LIKE YOU OLD FOLKS DID.
NOW THAT THE WORLD IS ALL PEACEFUL...
...LIFE IS JUST SOOO DULL.

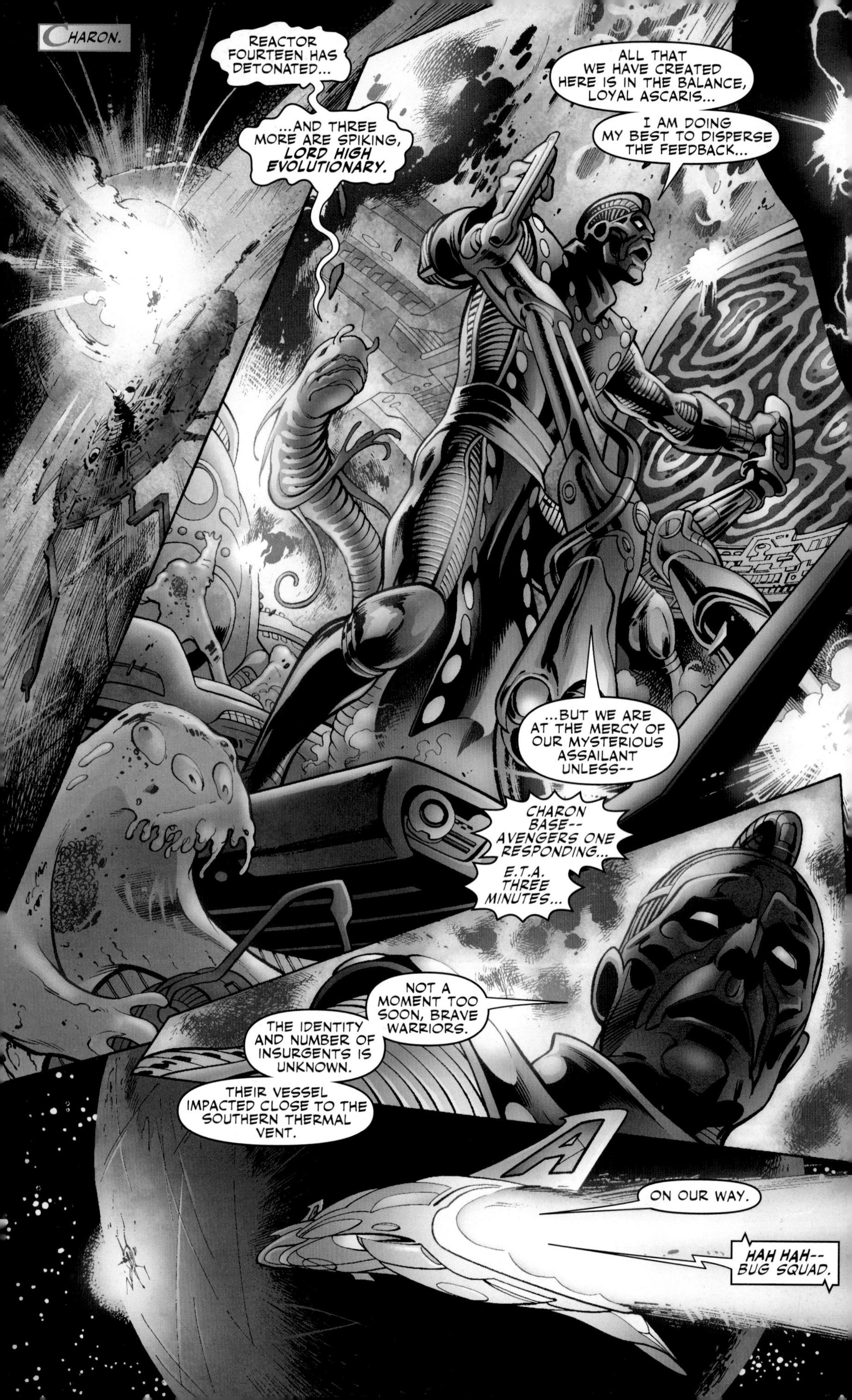
CHARON.
REACTOR FOURTEEN HAS DETONATED...
...AND THREE MORE ARE SPIKING, LORD HIGH EVOLUTIONARY.
ALL THAT WE HAVE CREATED HERE IS IN THE BALANCE, LOYAL ASCARIS...
I AM DOING MY BEST TO DISPERSE THE FEEDBACK...
...BUT WE ARE AT THE MERCY OF OUR MYSTERIOUS ASSAILANT UNLESS--
CHARON BASE-- AVENGERS ONE RESPONDING...
E.T.A. THREE MINUTES...
NOT A MOMENT TOO SOON, BRAVE WARRIORS.
THE IDENTITY AND NUMBER OF INSURGENTS IS UNKNOWN.
THEIR VESSEL IMPACTED CLOSE TO THE SOUTHERN THERMAL VENT.
ON OUR WAY.
HAH HAH-- BUG SQUAD.

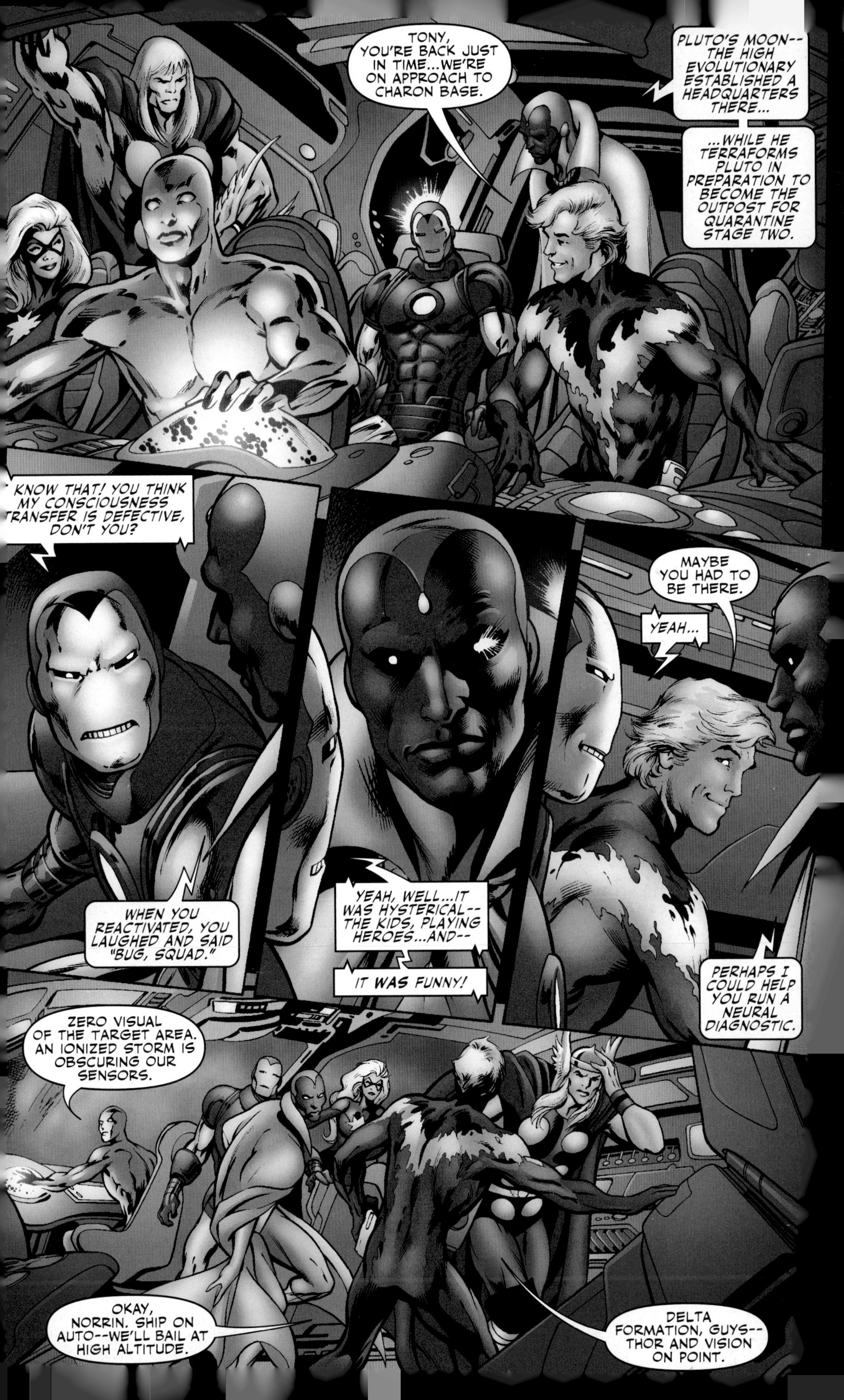
TONY, YOU'RE BACK JUST IN TIME...WE'RE ON APPROACH TO CHARON BASE.
PLUTO'S MOON--THE HIGH EVOLUTIONARY ESTABLISHED A HEADQUARTERS THERE...
...WHILE HE TERRAFORMS PLUTO IN PREPARATION TO BECOME THE OUTPOST FOR QUARANTINE STAGE TWO.
I KNOW THAT! YOU THINK MY CONSCIOUSNESS TRANSFER IS DEFECTIVE, DON'T YOU?
WHEN YOU REACTIVATED, YOU LAUGHED AND SAID "BUG, SQUAD."
YEAH, WELL...IT WAS HYSTERICAL--THE KIDS, PLAYING HEROES...AND--
IT WAS FUNNY!
MAYBE YOU HAD TO BE THERE.
YEAH...
PERHAPS I COULD HELP YOU RUN A NEURAL DIAGNOSTIC.
ZERO VISUAL OF THE TARGET AREA. AN IONIZED STORM IS OBSCURING OUR SENSORS.
OKAY, NORRIN. SHIP ON AUTO--WE'LL BAIL AT HIGH ALTITUDE.
DELTA FORMATION, GUYS--THOR AND VISION ON POINT.

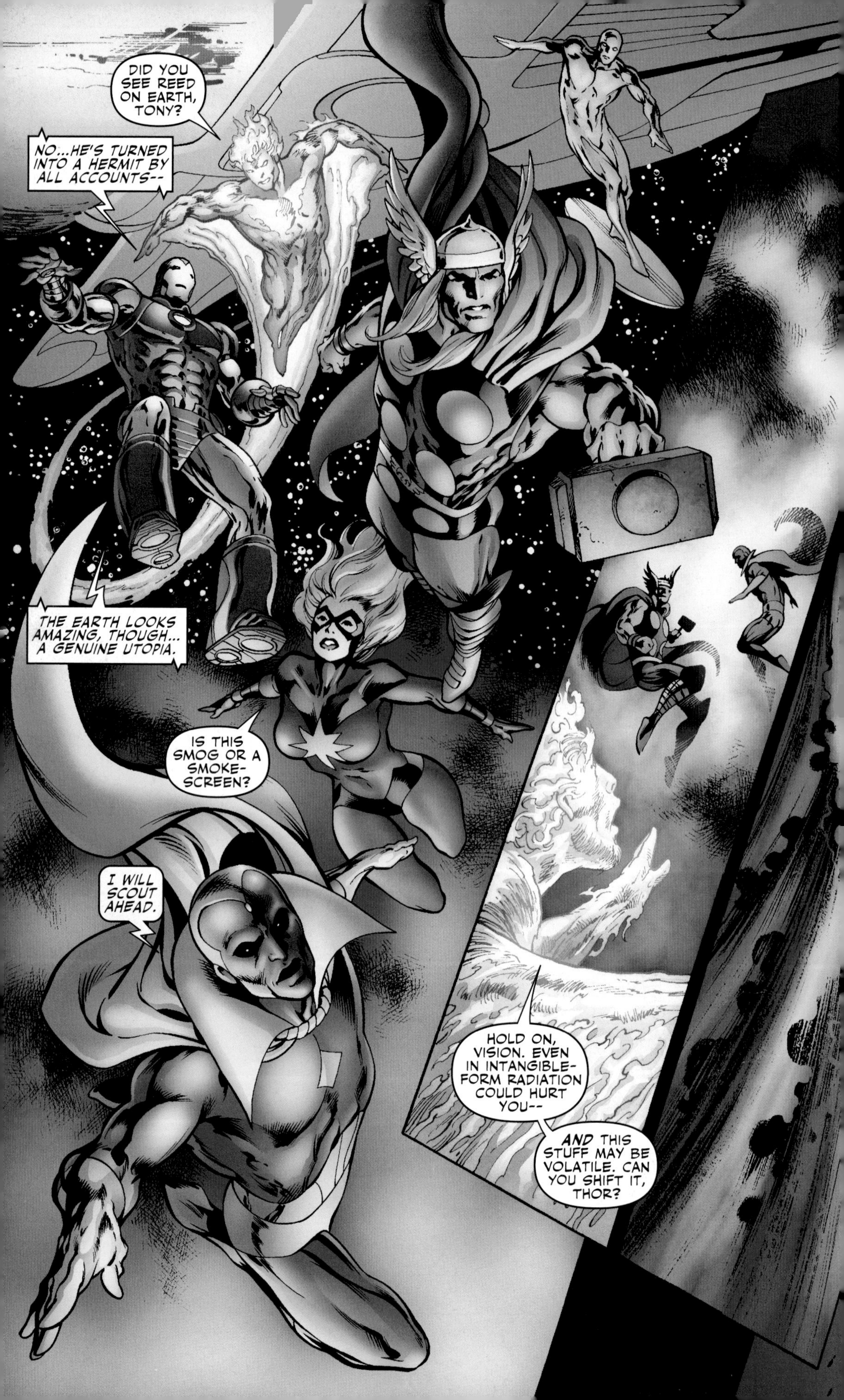
DID YOU SEE REED ON EARTH, TONY?
NO...HE'S TURNED INTO A HERMIT BY ALL ACCOUNTS--
THE EARTH LOOKS AMAZING, THOUGH... A GENUINE UTOPIA.
IS THIS SMOG OR A SMOKE-SCREEN?
I WILL SCOUT AHEAD.
HOLD ON, VISION. EVEN IN INTANGIBLE-FORM RADIATION COULD HURT YOU--
AND THIS STUFF MAY BE VOLATILE. CAN YOU SHIFT IT, THOR?

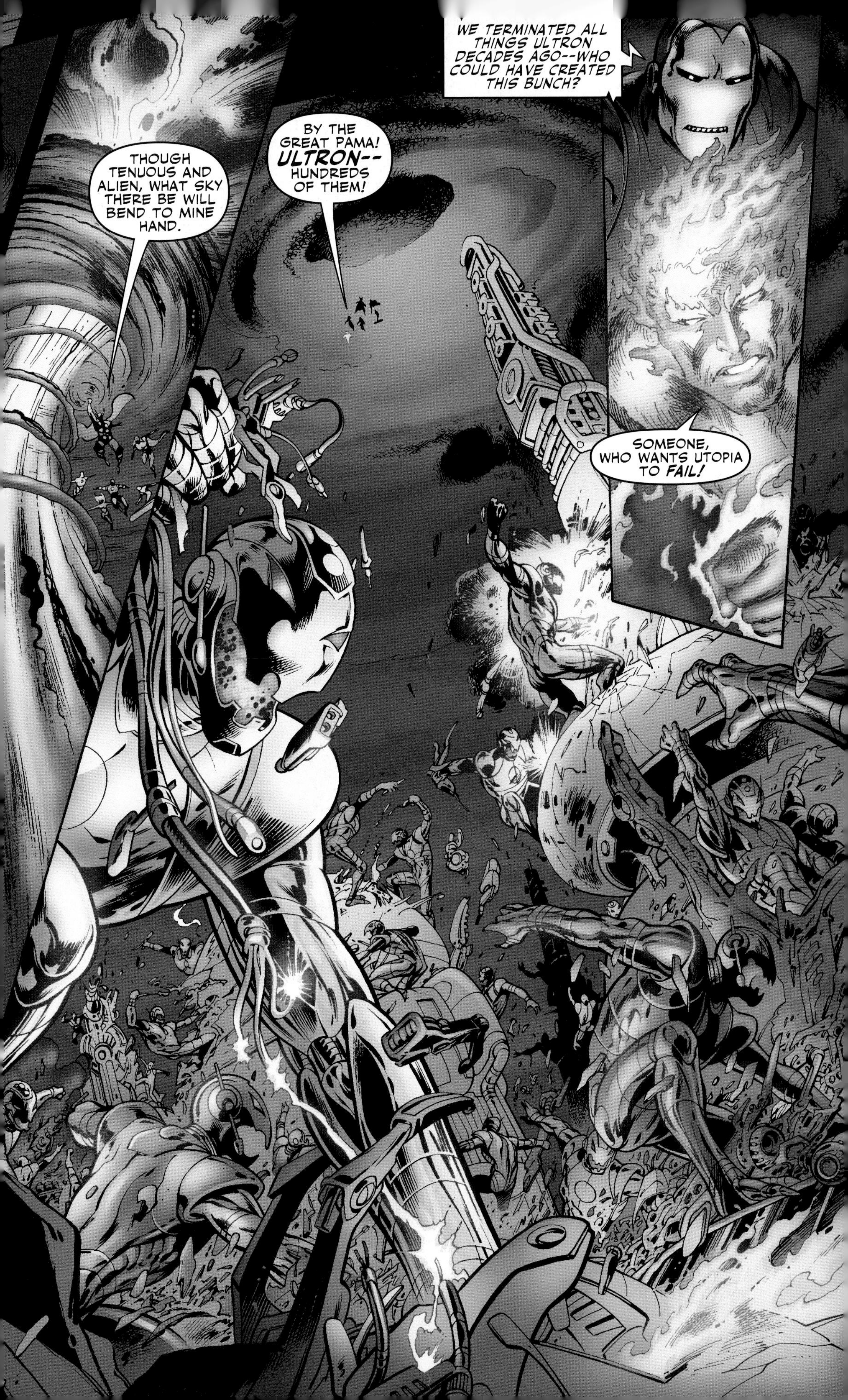
THOUGH TENUOUS AND ALIEN, WHAT SKY THERE BE WILL BEND TO MINE HAND.
BY THE GREAT PAMA! ULTRON-- HUNDREDS OF THEM!
WE TERMINATED ALL THINGS ULTRON DECADES AGO--WHO COULD HAVE CREATED THIS BUNCH?
SOMEONE, WHO WANTS UTOPIA TO FAIL!

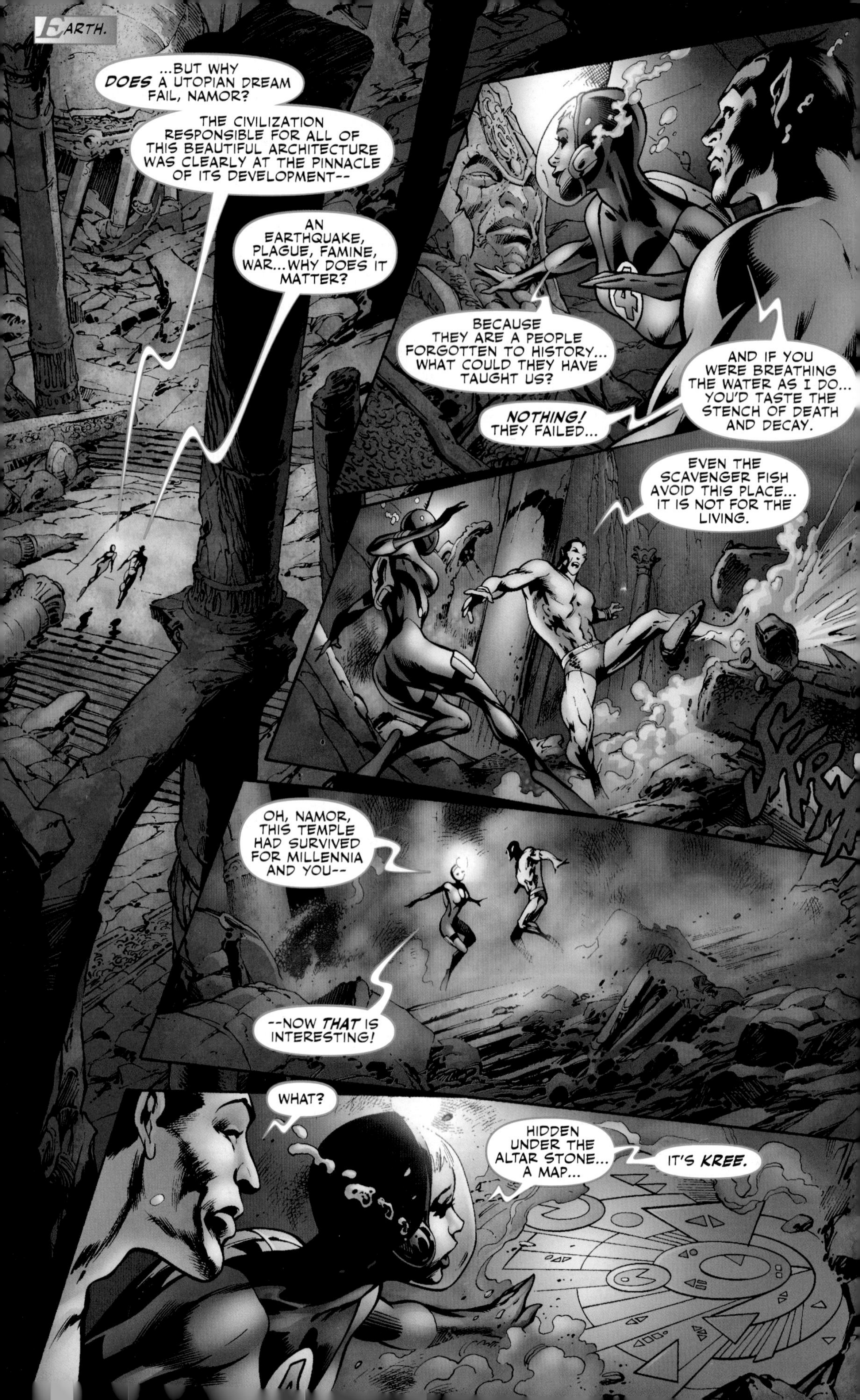
EARTH.
...BUT WHY DOES A UTOPIAN DREAM FAIL, NAMOR?
THE CIVILIZATION RESPONSIBLE FOR ALL OF THIS BEAUTIFUL ARCHITECTURE WAS CLEARLY AT THE PINNACLE OF ITS DEVELOPMENT--
AN EARTHQUAKE, PLAGUE, FAMINE, WAR...WHY DOES IT MATTER?
BECAUSE THEY ARE A PEOPLE FORGOTTEN TO HISTORY... WHAT COULD THEY HAVE TAUGHT US?
NOTHING! THEY FAILED...
AND IF YOU WERE BREATHING THE WATER AS I DO... YOU'D TASTE THE STENCH OF DEATH AND DECAY.
EVEN THE SCAVENGER FISH AVOID THIS PLACE... IT IS NOT FOR THE LIVING.
SKRAM
OH, NAMOR, THIS TEMPLE HAD SURVIVED FOR MILLENNIA AND YOU--
--NOW THAT IS INTERESTING!
WHAT?
HIDDEN UNDER THE ALTAR STONE... A MAP...
IT'S KREE.

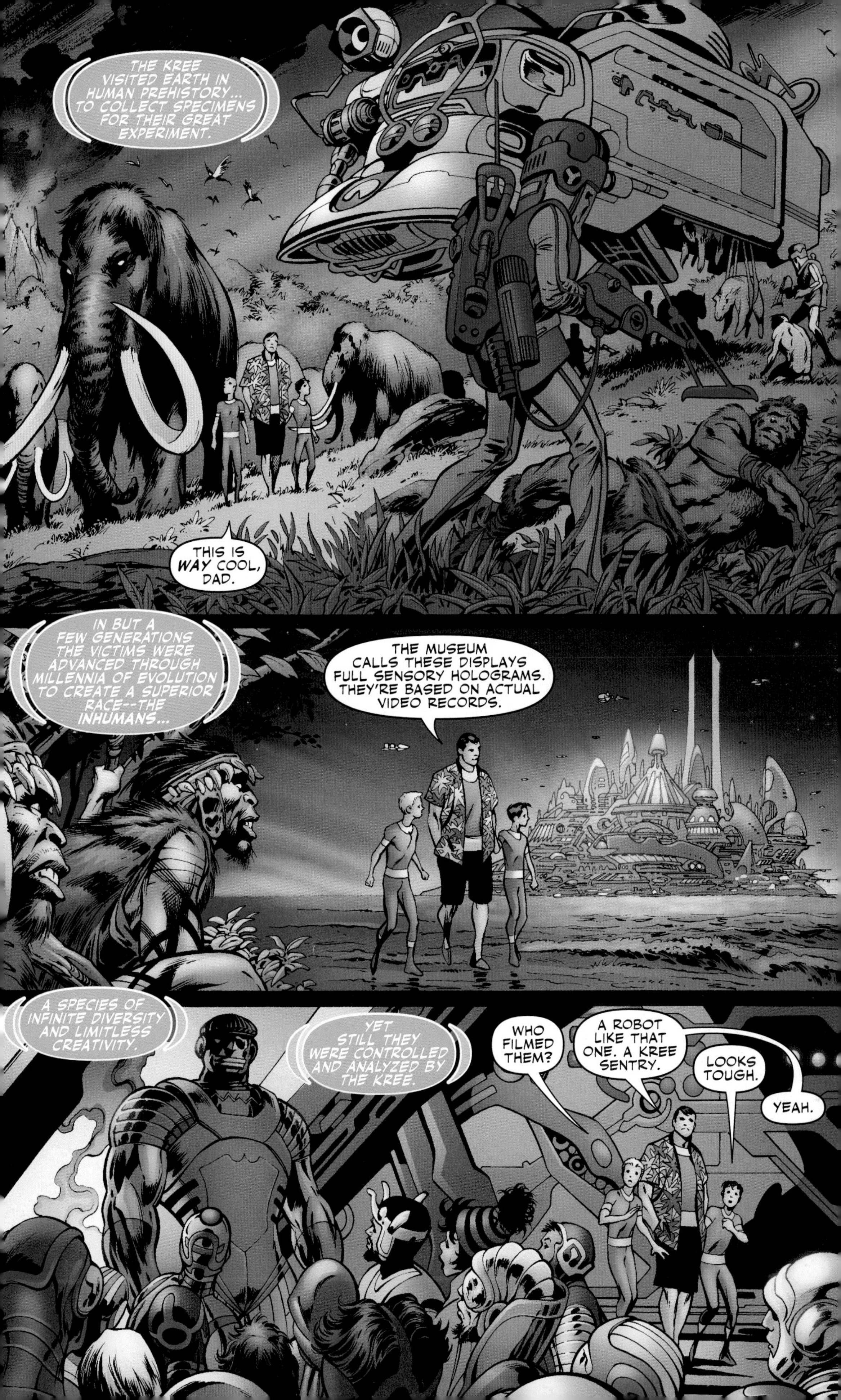
THE KREE VISITED EARTH IN HUMAN PREHISTORY... TO COLLECT SPECIMENS FOR THEIR GREAT EXPERIMENT.
THIS IS WAY COOL, DAD.
IN BUT A FEW GENERATIONS THE VICTIMS WERE ADVANCED THROUGH MILLENNIA OF EVOLUTION TO CREATE A SUPERIOR RACE--THE INHUMANS...
THE MUSEUM CALLS THESE DISPLAYS FULL SENSORY HOLOGRAMS. THEY'RE BASED ON ACTUAL VIDEO RECORDS.
A SPECIES OF INFINITE DIVERSITY AND LIMITLESS CREATIVITY.
YET STILL THEY WERE CONTROLLED AND ANALYZED BY THE KREE.
WHO FILMED THEM?
A ROBOT LIKE THAT ONE. A KREE SENTRY.
LOOKS TOUGH.
YEAH.

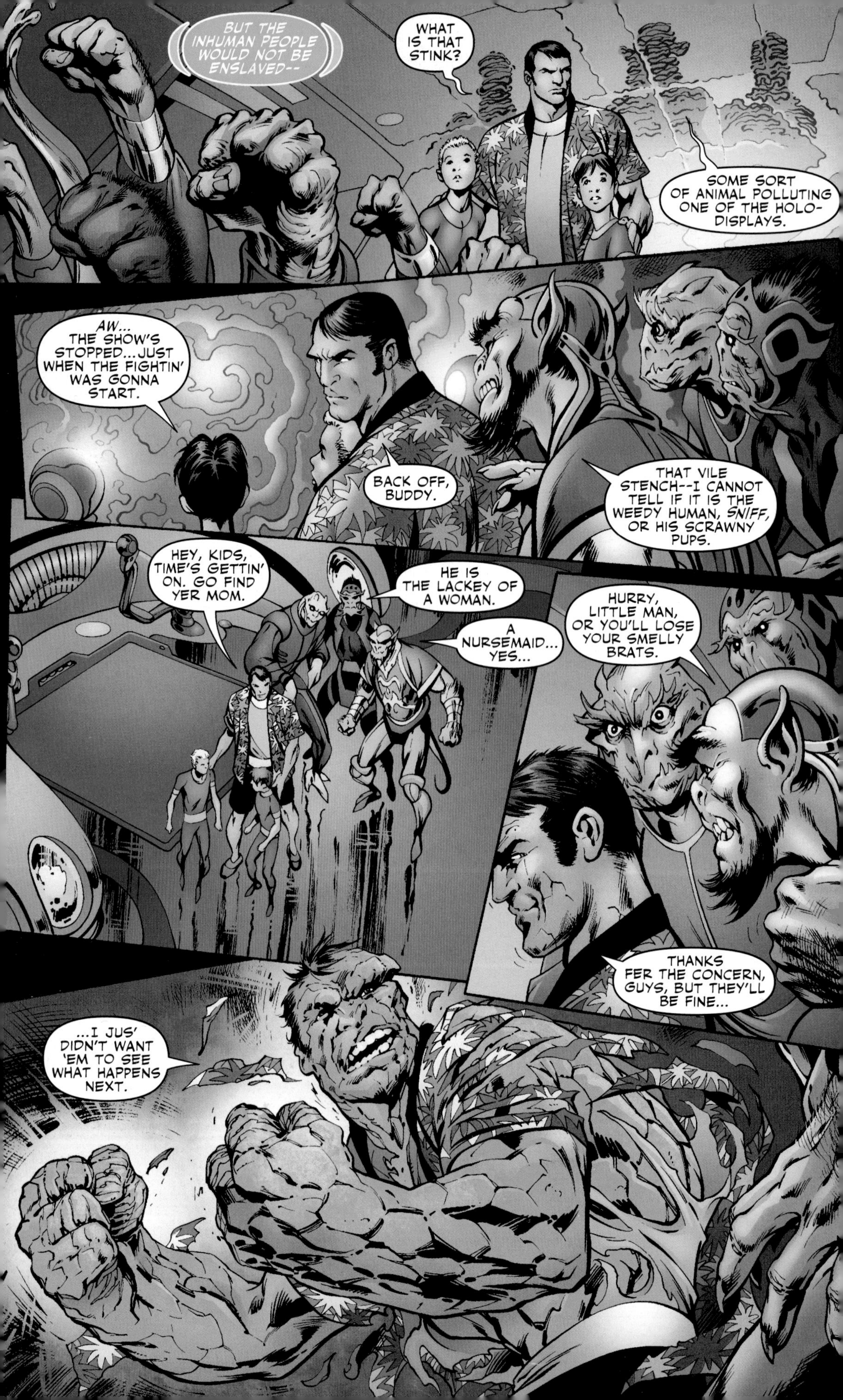
BUT THE INHUMAN PEOPLE WOULD NOT BE ENSLAVED--
WHAT IS THAT STINK?
SOME SORT OF ANIMAL POLLUTING ONE OF THE HOLO-DISPLAYS.
AW... THE SHOW'S STOPPED...JUST WHEN THE FIGHTIN' WAS GONNA START.
BACK OFF, BUDDY.
THAT VILE STENCH--I CANNOT TELL IF IT IS THE WEEDY HUMAN, SNIFF, OR HIS SCRAWNY PUPS.
HEY, KIDS, TIME'S GETTIN' ON. GO FIND YER MOM.
HE IS THE LACKEY OF A WOMAN.
A NURSEMAID... YES...
HURRY, LITTLE MAN, OR YOU'LL LOSE YOUR SMELLY BRATS.
THANKS FER THE CONCERN, GUYS, BUT THEY'LL BE FINE...
...I JUS' DIDN'T WANT 'EM TO SEE WHAT HAPPENS NEXT.

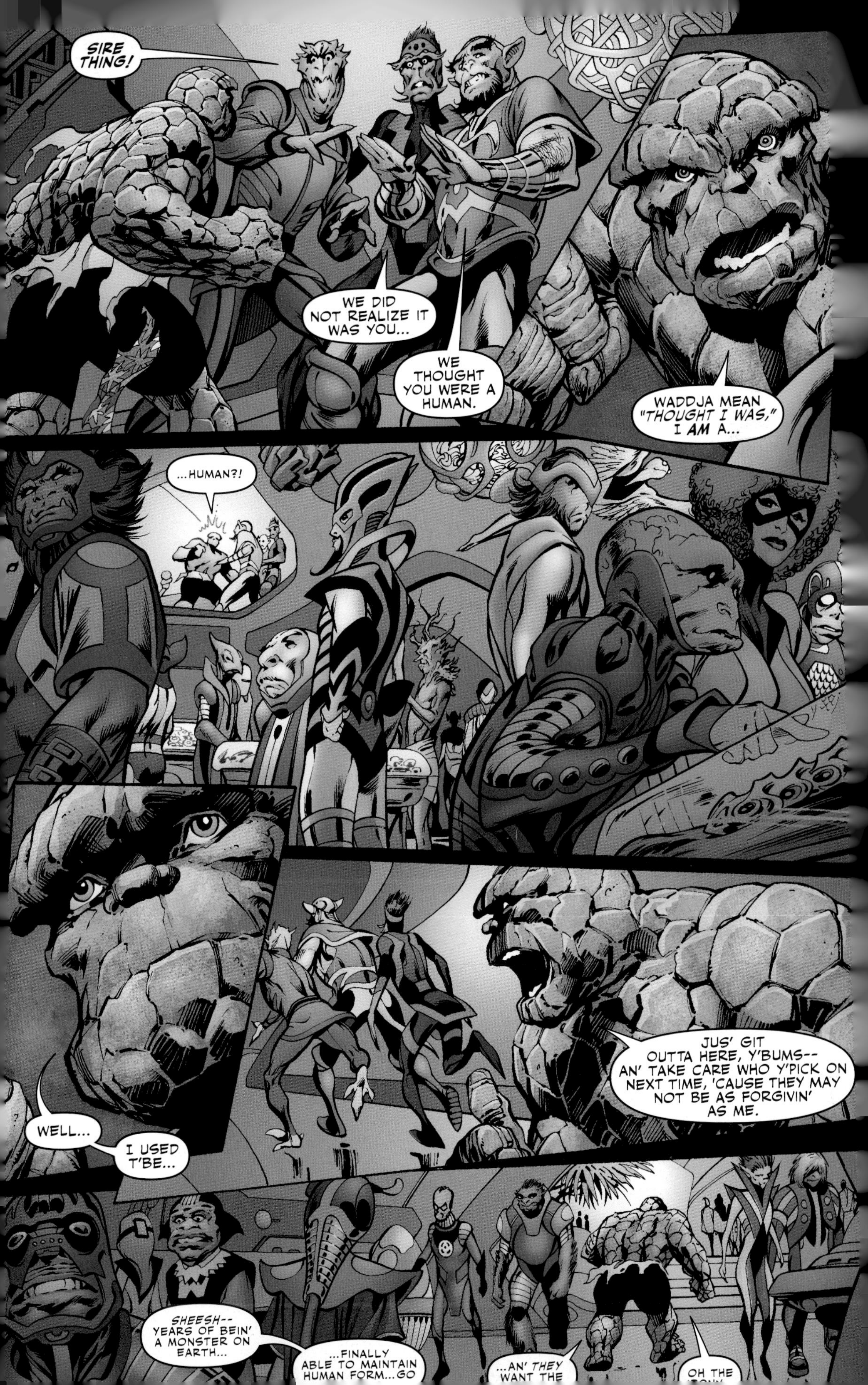
SIRE THING!
WE DID NOT REALIZE IT WAS YOU...
WE THOUGHT YOU WERE A HUMAN.
WADDJA MEAN "THOUGHT I WAS," I AM A...
...HUMAN?!
WELL...
I USED T'BE...
JUS' GIT OUTTA HERE, Y'BUMS-- AN' TAKE CARE WHO Y'PICK ON NEXT TIME, 'CAUSE THEY MAY NOT BE AS FORGIVIN' AS ME.
SHEESH-- YEARS OF BEIN' A MONSTER ON EARTH...
...FINALLY ABLE TO MAINTAIN HUMAN FORM...GO
...AN' THEY WANT THE
OH THE

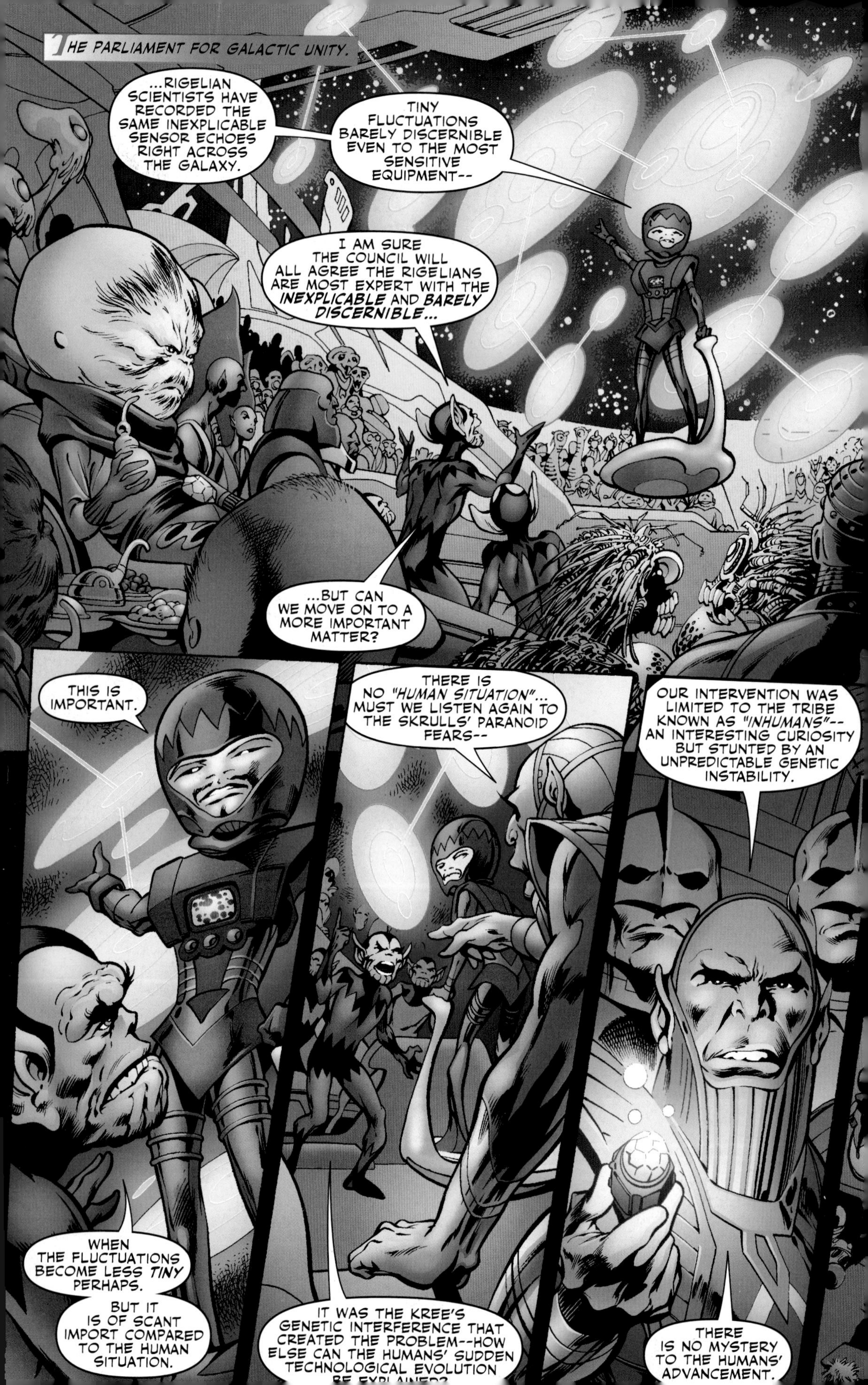
THE PARLIAMENT FOR GALACTIC UNITY.
...RIGELIAN SCIENTISTS HAVE RECORDED THE SAME INEXPLICABLE SENSOR ECHOES RIGHT ACROSS THE GALAXY.
TINY FLUCTUATIONS BARELY DISCERNIBLE EVEN TO THE MOST SENSITIVE EQUIPMENT--
I AM SURE THE COUNCIL WILL ALL AGREE THE RIGELIANS ARE MOST EXPERT WITH THE *INEXPLICABLE* AND *BARELY DISCERNIBLE*...
...BUT CAN WE MOVE ON TO A MORE IMPORTANT MATTER?
THIS IS IMPORTANT.
WHEN THE FLUCTUATIONS BECOME LESS *TINY* PERHAPS.
BUT IT IS OF SCANT IMPORT COMPARED TO THE HUMAN SITUATION.
THERE IS NO *"HUMAN SITUATION"*... MUST WE LISTEN AGAIN TO THE SKRULLS' PARANOID FEARS--
IT WAS THE KREE'S GENETIC INTERFERENCE THAT CREATED THE PROBLEM--HOW ELSE CAN THE HUMANS' SUDDEN TECHNOLOGICAL EVOLUTION
OUR INTERVENTION WAS LIMITED TO THE TRIBE KNOWN AS *"INHUMANS"*-- AN INTERESTING CURIOSITY BUT STUNTED BY AN UNPREDICTABLE GENETIC INSTABILITY.
THERE IS NO MYSTERY TO THE HUMANS' ADVANCEMENT.

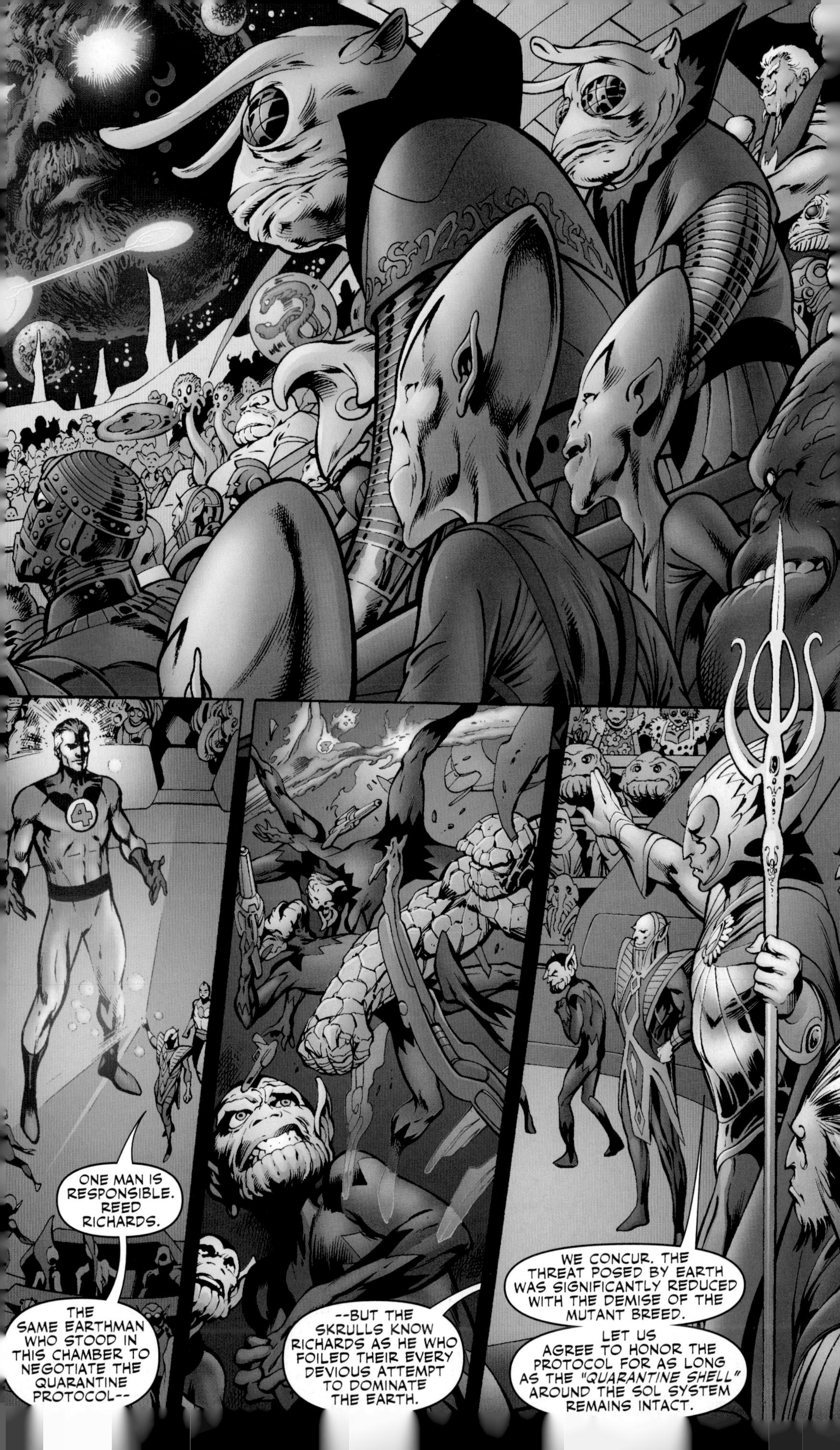
ONE MAN IS RESPONSIBLE. REED RICHARDS.
THE SAME EARTHMAN WHO STOOD IN THIS CHAMBER TO NEGOTIATE THE QUARANTINE PROTOCOL--
--BUT THE SKRULLS KNOW RICHARDS AS HE WHO FOILED THEIR EVERY DEVIOUS ATTEMPT TO DOMINATE THE EARTH.
WE CONCUR. THE THREAT POSED BY EARTH WAS SIGNIFICANTLY REDUCED WITH THE DEMISE OF THE MUTANT BREED.
LET US AGREE TO HONOR THE PROTOCOL FOR AS LONG AS THE "QUARANTINE SHELL" AROUND THE SOL SYSTEM REMAINS INTACT.

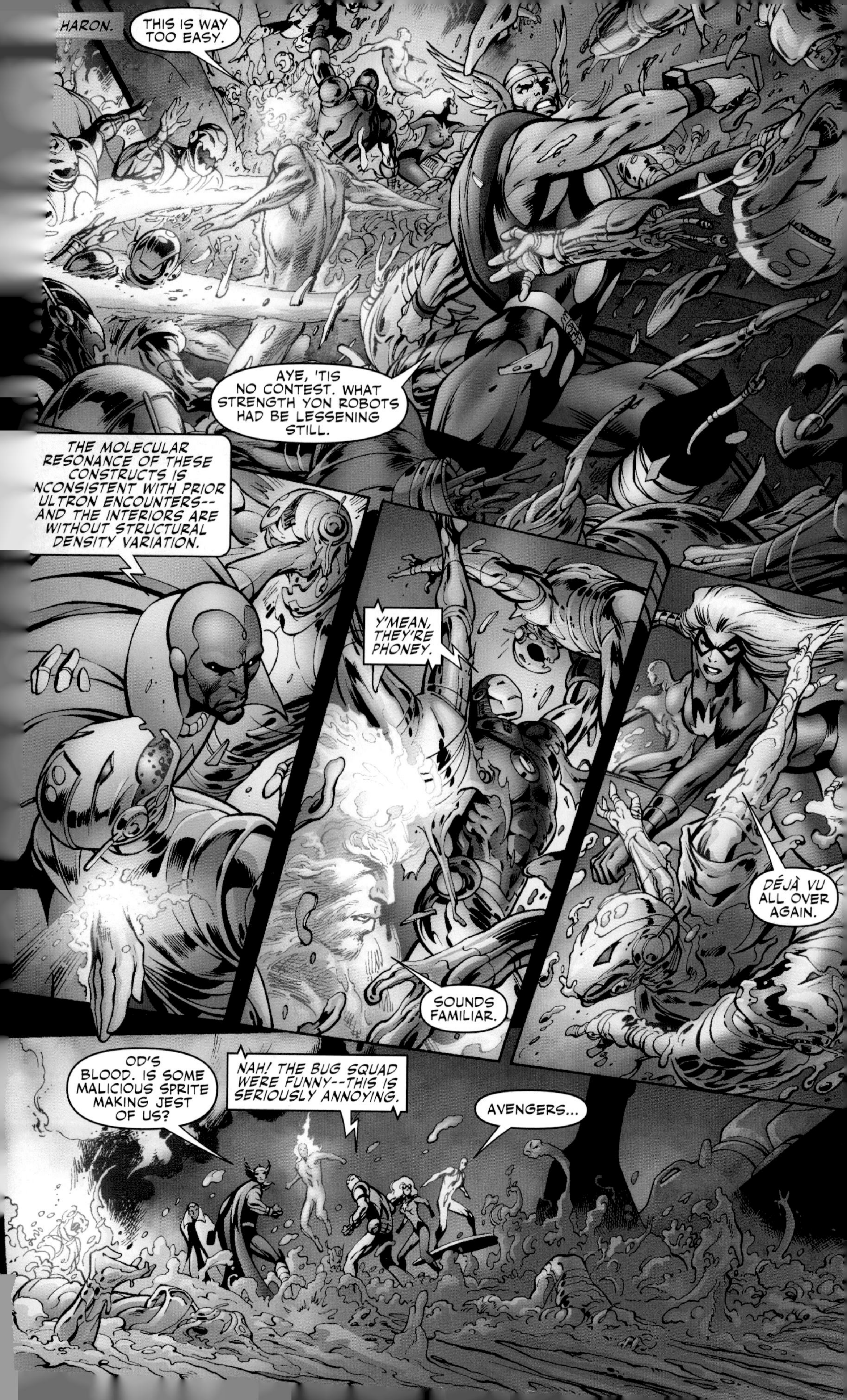
HARON.
THIS IS WAY TOO EASY.
AYE, 'TIS NO CONTEST. WHAT STRENGTH YON ROBOTS HAD BE LESSENING STILL.
THE MOLECULAR RESONANCE OF THESE CONSTRUCTS IS NCONSISTENT WITH PRIOR ULTRON ENCOUNTERS-- AND THE INTERIORS ARE WITHOUT STRUCTURAL DENSITY VARIATION.
Y'MEAN, THEY'RE PHONEY.
SOUNDS FAMILIAR.
DÉJÀ VU ALL OVER AGAIN.
OD'S BLOOD. IS SOME MALICIOUS SPRITE MAKING JEST OF US?
NAH! THE BUG SQUAD WERE FUNNY--THIS IS SERIOUSLY ANNOYING.
AVENGERS...

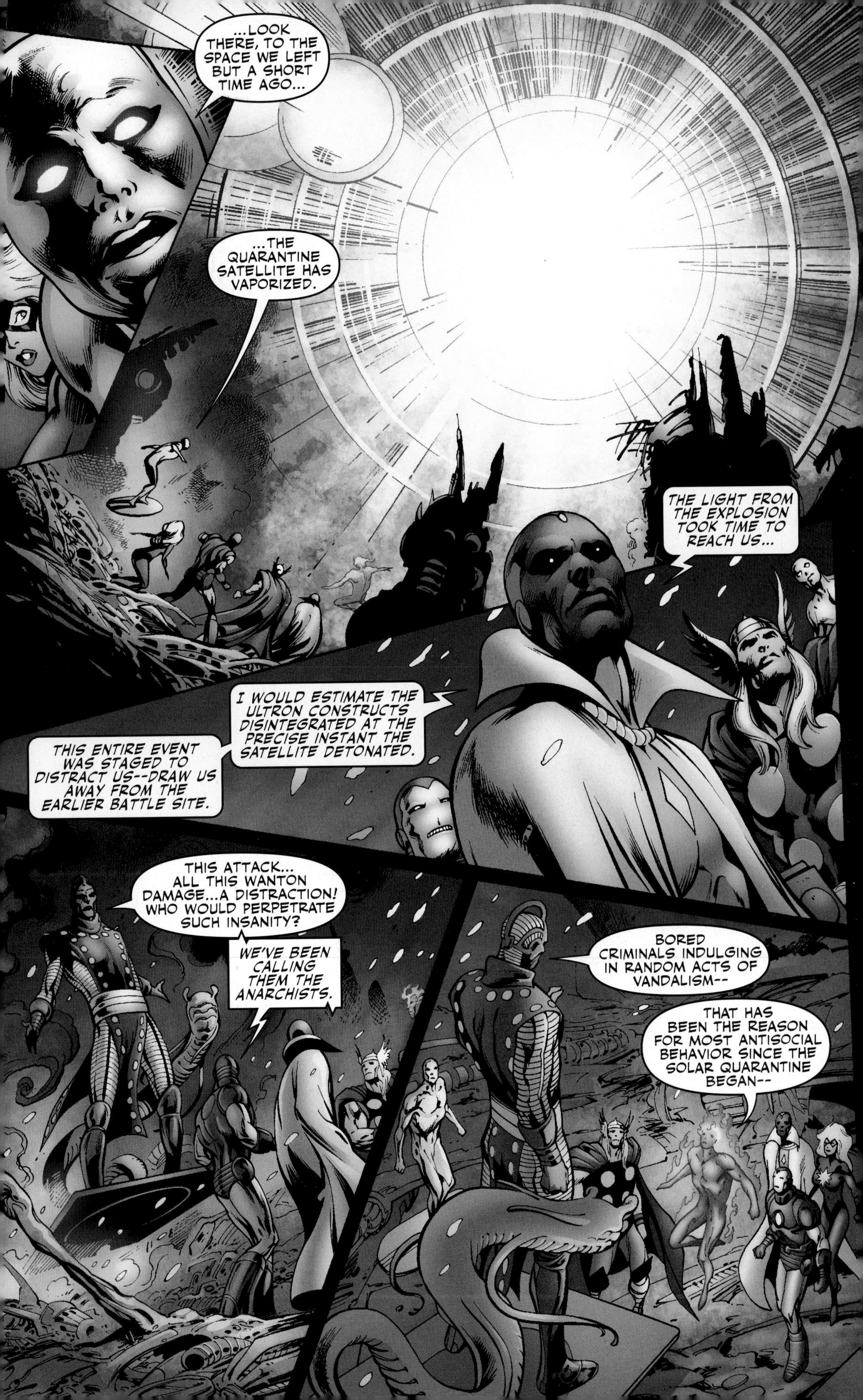
...LOOK THERE, TO THE SPACE WE LEFT BUT A SHORT TIME AGO...
...THE QUARANTINE SATELLITE HAS VAPORIZED.
THE LIGHT FROM THE EXPLOSION TOOK TIME TO REACH US...
I WOULD ESTIMATE THE ULTRON CONSTRUCTS DISINTEGRATED AT THE PRECISE INSTANT THE SATELLITE DETONATED.
THIS ENTIRE EVENT WAS STAGED TO DISTRACT US--DRAW US AWAY FROM THE EARLIER BATTLE SITE.
THIS ATTACK... ALL THIS WANTON DAMAGE...A DISTRACTION! WHO WOULD PERPETRATE SUCH INSANITY?
WE'VE BEEN CALLING THEM THE ANARCHISTS.
BORED CRIMINALS INDULGING IN RANDOM ACTS OF VANDALISM--
THAT HAS BEEN THE REASON FOR MOST ANTISOCIAL BEHAVIOR SINCE THE SOLAR QUARANTINE BEGAN--

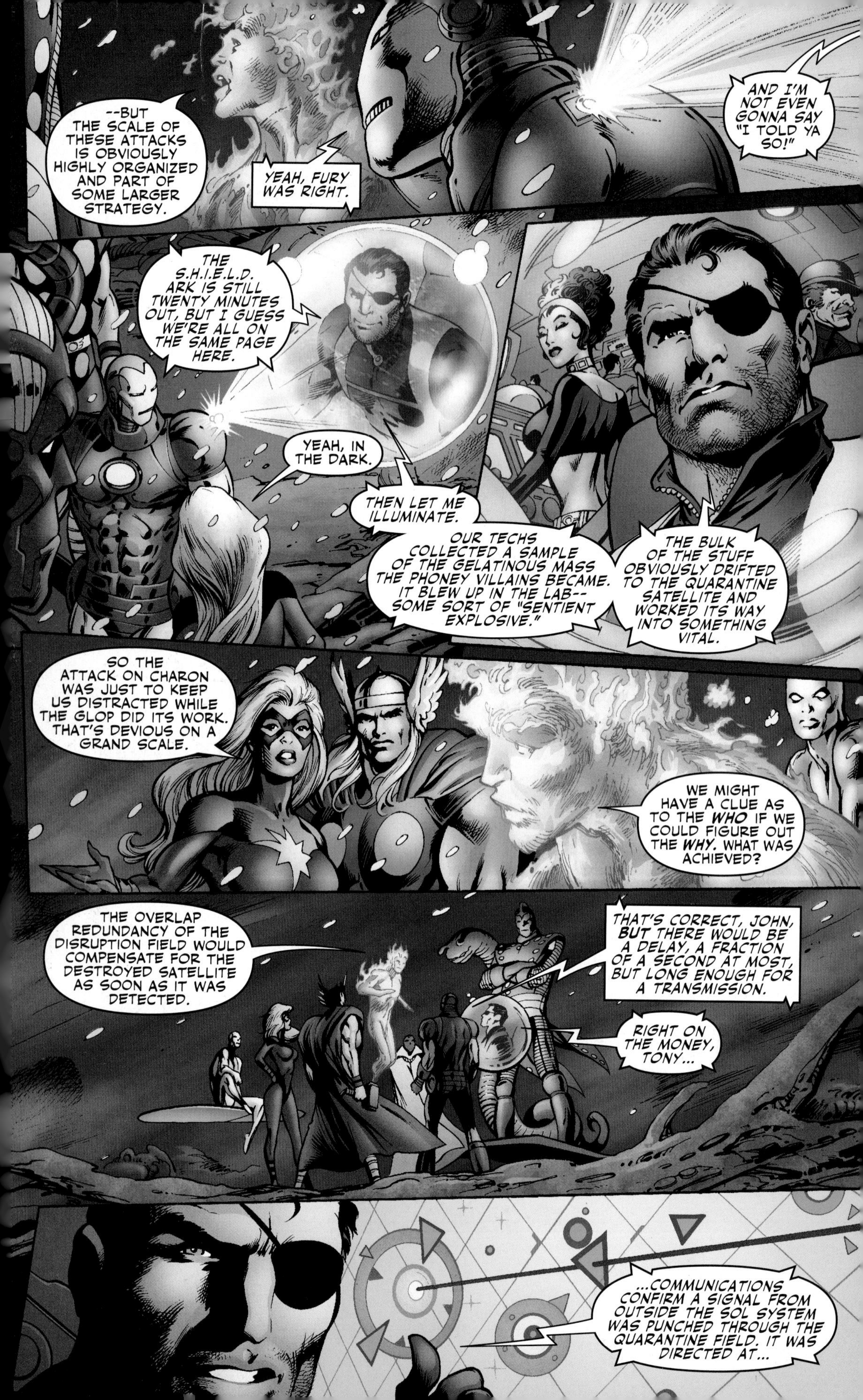
--BUT THE SCALE OF THESE ATTACKS IS OBVIOUSLY HIGHLY ORGANIZED AND PART OF SOME LARGER STRATEGY.
YEAH, FURY WAS RIGHT.
AND I'M NOT EVEN GONNA SAY "I TOLD YA SO!"
THE S.H.I.E.L.D. ARK IS STILL TWENTY MINUTES OUT, BUT I GUESS WE'RE ALL ON THE SAME PAGE HERE.
YEAH, IN THE DARK.
THEN LET ME ILLUMINATE.
OUR TECHS COLLECTED A SAMPLE OF THE GELATINOUS MASS THE PHONEY VILLAINS BECAME. IT BLEW UP IN THE LAB-- SOME SORT OF "SENTIENT EXPLOSIVE."
THE BULK OF THE STUFF OBVIOUSLY DRIFTED TO THE QUARANTINE SATELLITE AND WORKED ITS WAY INTO SOMETHING VITAL.
SO THE ATTACK ON CHARON WAS JUST TO KEEP US DISTRACTED WHILE THE GLOP DID ITS WORK. THAT'S DEVIOUS ON A GRAND SCALE.
WE MIGHT HAVE A CLUE AS TO THE WHO IF WE COULD FIGURE OUT THE WHY. WHAT WAS ACHIEVED?
THE OVERLAP REDUNDANCY OF THE DISRUPTION FIELD WOULD COMPENSATE FOR THE DESTROYED SATELLITE AS SOON AS IT WAS DETECTED.
THAT'S CORRECT, JOHN, BUT THERE WOULD BE A DELAY, A FRACTION OF A SECOND AT MOST, BUT LONG ENOUGH FOR A TRANSMISSION.
RIGHT ON THE MONEY, TONY...
...COMMUNICATIONS CONFIRM A SIGNAL FROM OUTSIDE THE SOL SYSTEM WAS PUNCHED THROUGH THE QUARANTINE FIELD. IT WAS DIRECTED AT...

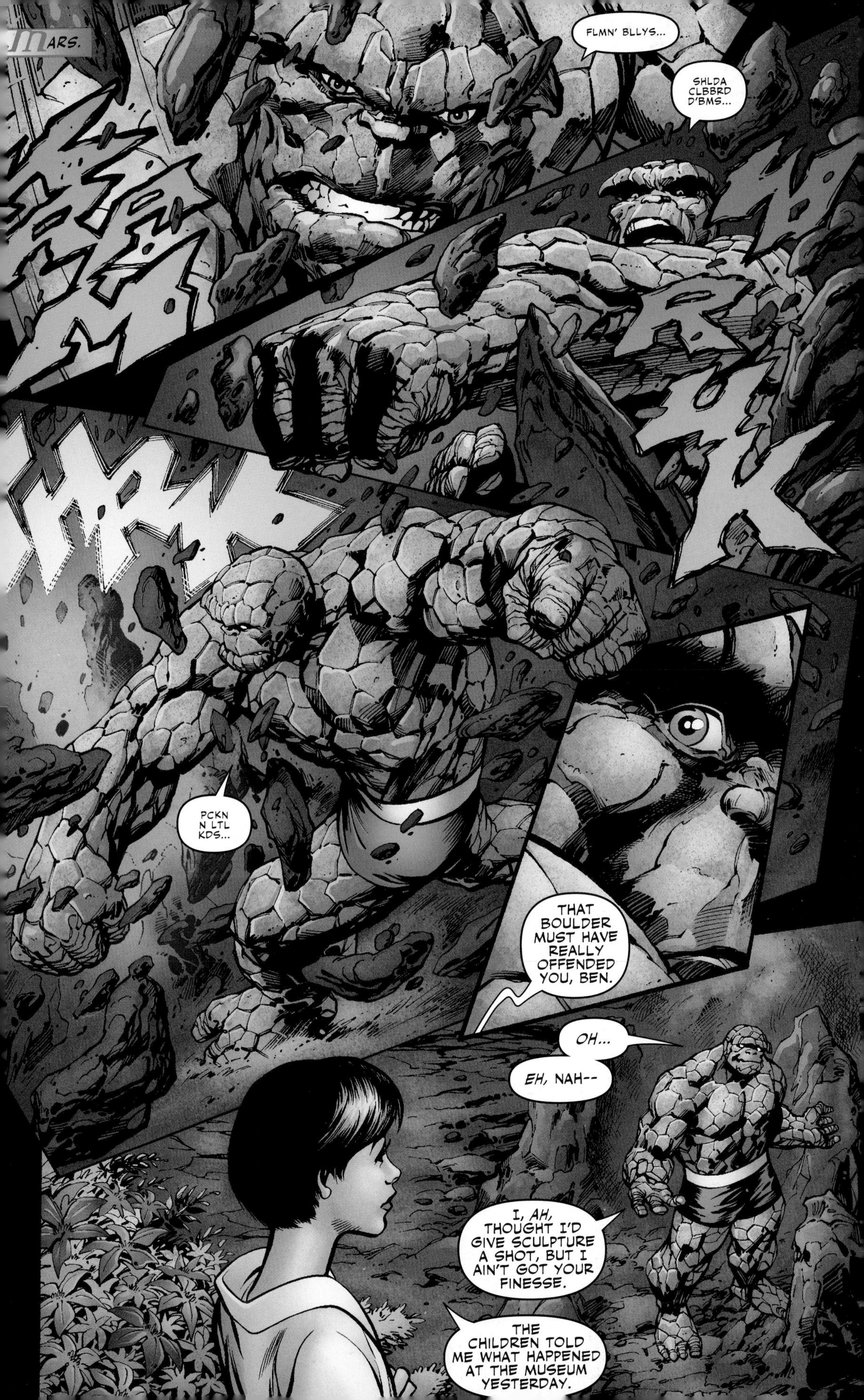
MARS.
FLMN' BLLYS...
SHLDA CLBBRD D'BMS...
PCKN N LTL KDS...
THAT BOULDER MUST HAVE REALLY OFFENDED YOU, BEN.
OH...
EH, NAH--
I, AH, THOUGHT I'D GIVE SCULPTURE A SHOT, BUT I AIN'T GOT YOUR FINESSE.
THE CHILDREN TOLD ME WHAT HAPPENED AT THE MUSEUM YESTERDAY.

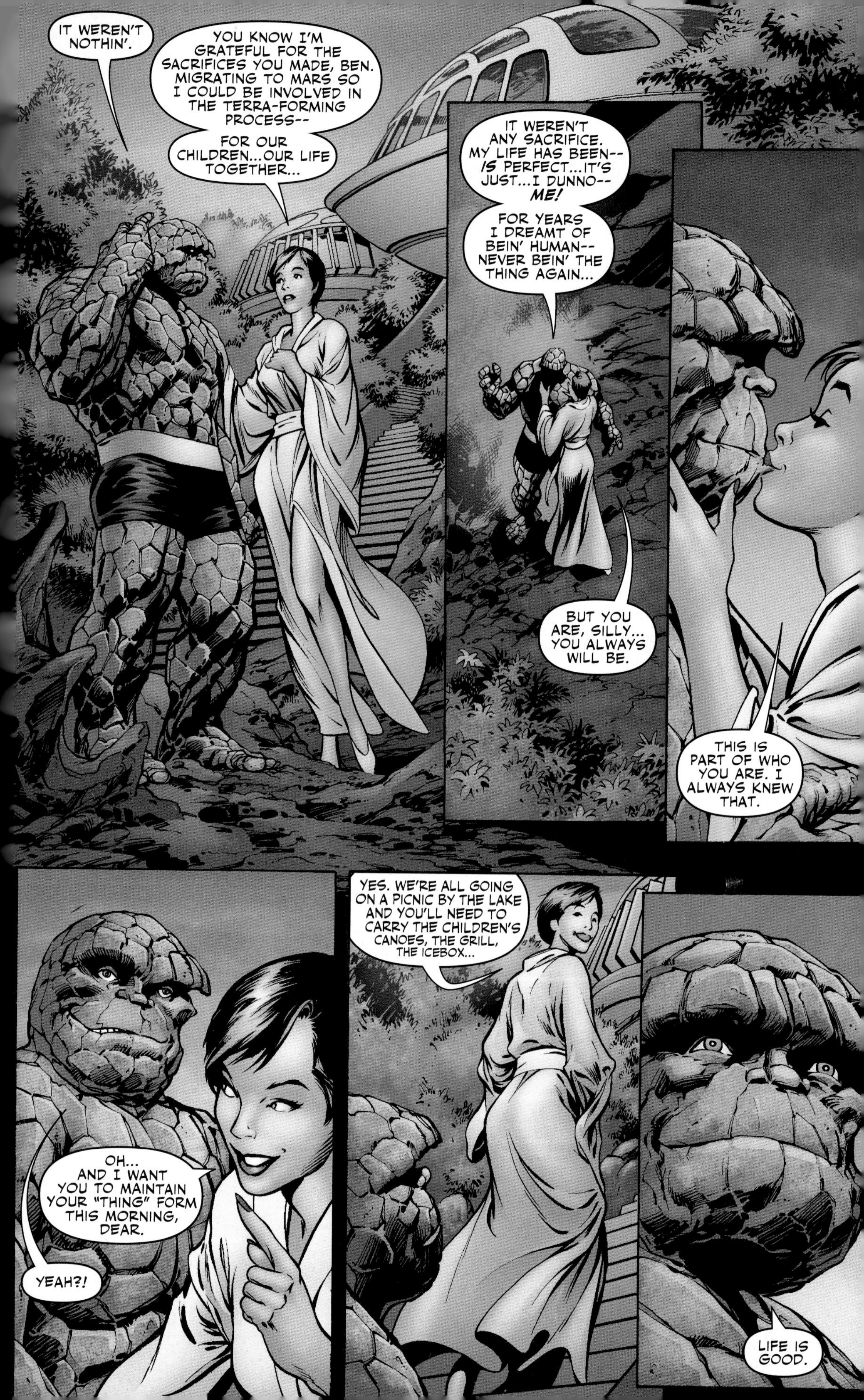

IT WEREN'T NOTHIN'.
YOU KNOW I'M GRATEFUL FOR THE SACRIFICES YOU MADE, BEN. MIGRATING TO MARS SO I COULD BE INVOLVED IN THE TERRA-FORMING PROCESS--
FOR OUR CHILDREN...OUR LIFE TOGETHER...
IT WEREN'T ANY SACRIFICE. MY LIFE HAS BEEN-- *IS* PERFECT...IT'S JUST...I DUNNO-- *ME!*
FOR YEARS I DREAMT OF BEIN' HUMAN-- NEVER BEIN' THE THING AGAIN...
BUT YOU ARE, SILLY... YOU ALWAYS WILL BE.
THIS IS PART OF WHO YOU ARE. I ALWAYS KNEW THAT.
OH... AND I WANT YOU TO MAINTAIN YOUR "THING" FORM THIS MORNING, DEAR.
YEAH?!
YES. WE'RE ALL GOING ON A PICNIC BY THE LAKE AND YOU'LL NEED TO CARRY THE CHILDREN'S CANOES, THE GRILL, THE ICEBOX...
LIFE IS GOOD.

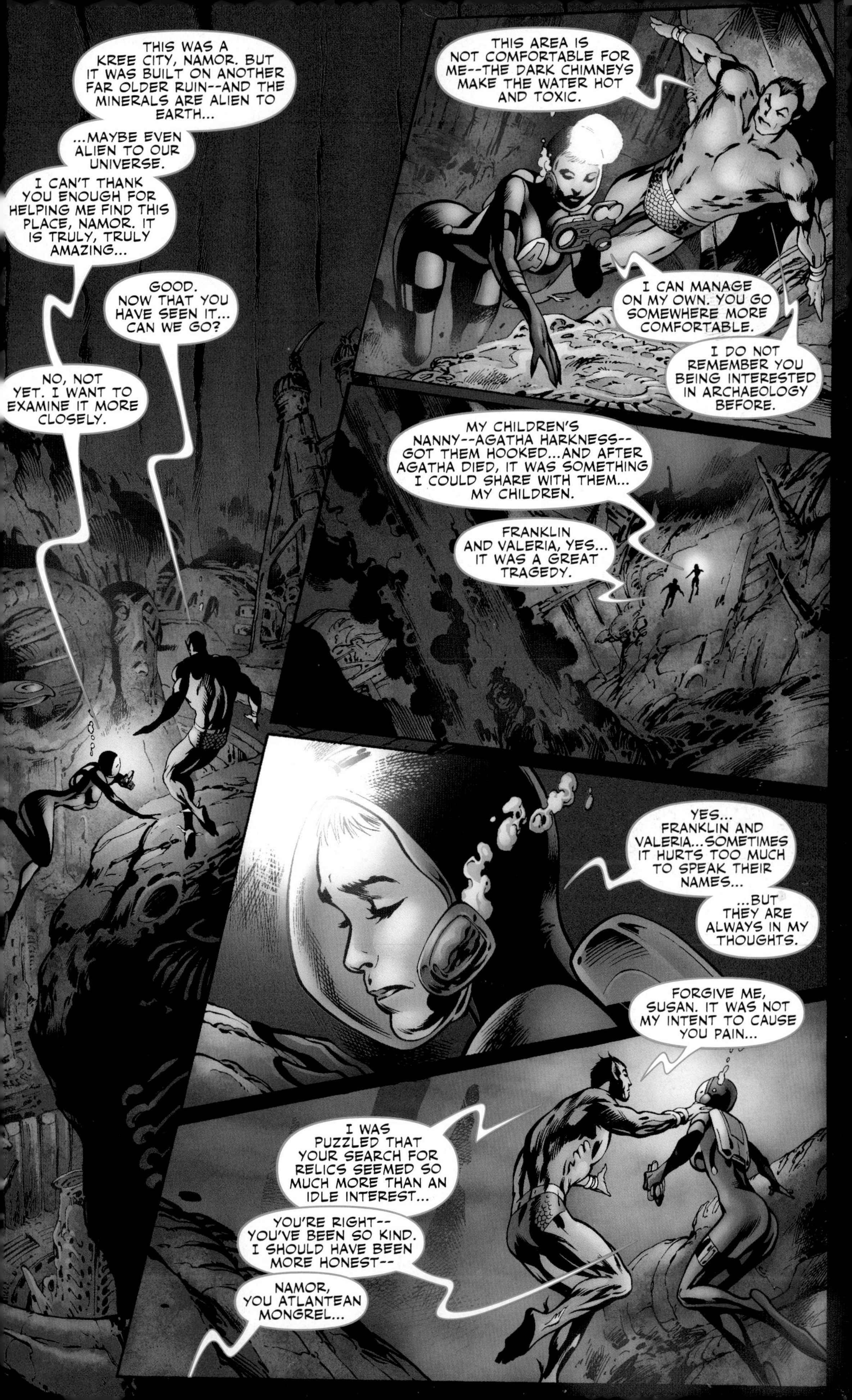
THIS WAS A KREE CITY, NAMOR. BUT IT WAS BUILT ON ANOTHER FAR OLDER RUIN--AND THE MINERALS ARE ALIEN TO EARTH...
...MAYBE EVEN ALIEN TO OUR UNIVERSE.
I CAN'T THANK YOU ENOUGH FOR HELPING ME FIND THIS PLACE, NAMOR. IT IS TRULY, TRULY AMAZING...
GOOD. NOW THAT YOU HAVE SEEN IT... CAN WE GO?
NO, NOT YET. I WANT TO EXAMINE IT MORE CLOSELY.
THIS AREA IS NOT COMFORTABLE FOR ME--THE DARK CHIMNEYS MAKE THE WATER HOT AND TOXIC.
I CAN MANAGE ON MY OWN. YOU GO SOMEWHERE MORE COMFORTABLE.
I DO NOT REMEMBER YOU BEING INTERESTED IN ARCHAEOLOGY BEFORE.
MY CHILDREN'S NANNY--AGATHA HARKNESS--GOT THEM HOOKED...AND AFTER AGATHA DIED, IT WAS SOMETHING I COULD SHARE WITH THEM... MY CHILDREN.
FRANKLIN AND VALERIA, YES... IT WAS A GREAT TRAGEDY.
YES... FRANKLIN AND VALERIA...SOMETIMES IT HURTS TOO MUCH TO SPEAK THEIR NAMES...
...BUT THEY ARE ALWAYS IN MY THOUGHTS.
FORGIVE ME, SUSAN. IT WAS NOT MY INTENT TO CAUSE YOU PAIN...
I WAS PUZZLED THAT YOUR SEARCH FOR RELICS SEEMED SO MUCH MORE THAN AN IDLE INTEREST...
YOU'RE RIGHT-- YOU'VE BEEN SO KIND. I SHOULD HAVE BEEN MORE HONEST--
NAMOR, YOU ATLANTEAN MONGREL...

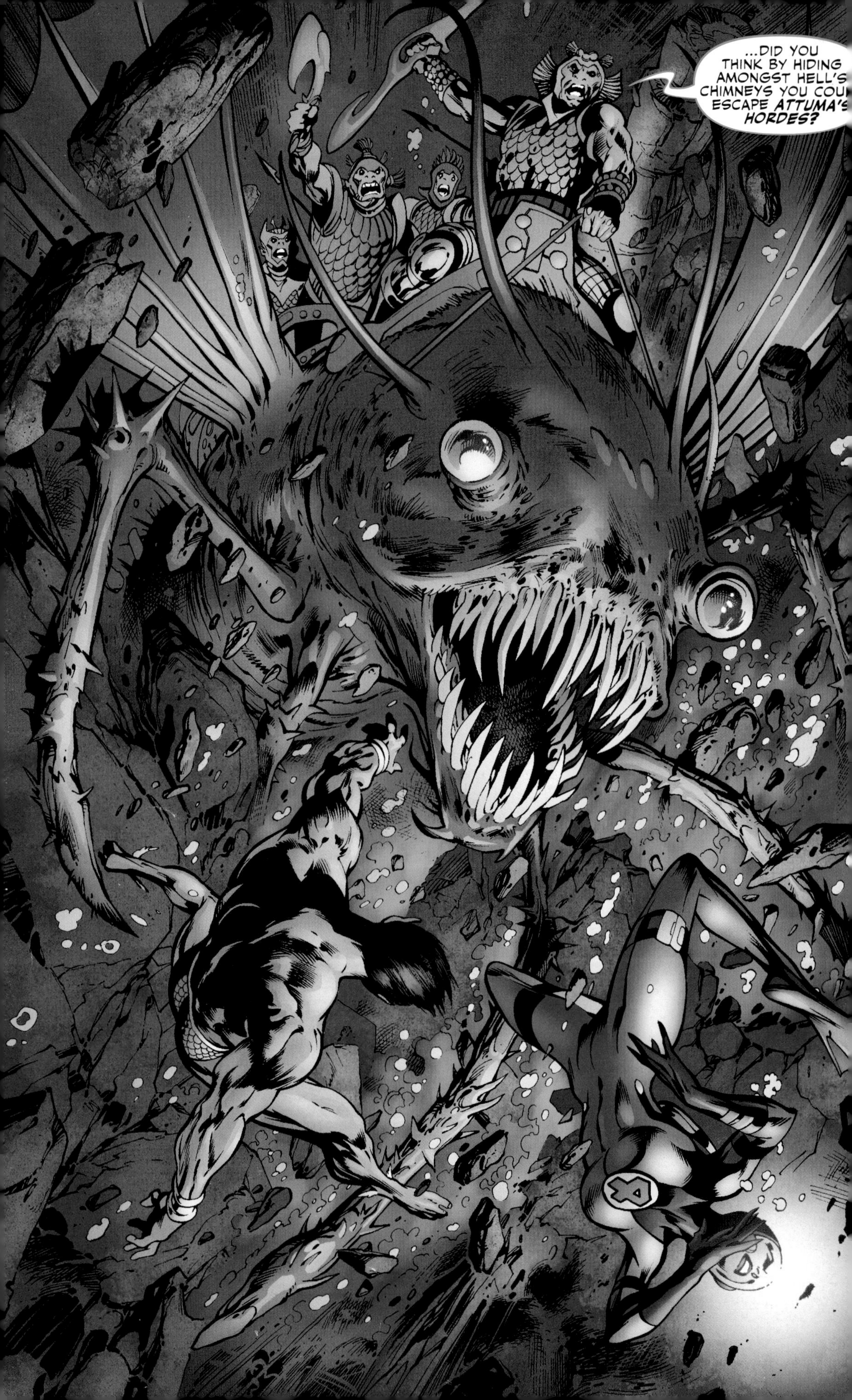
...DID YOU THINK BY HIDING AMONGST HELL'S CHIMNEYS YOU COU ESCAPE ATTUMA'S HORDES?

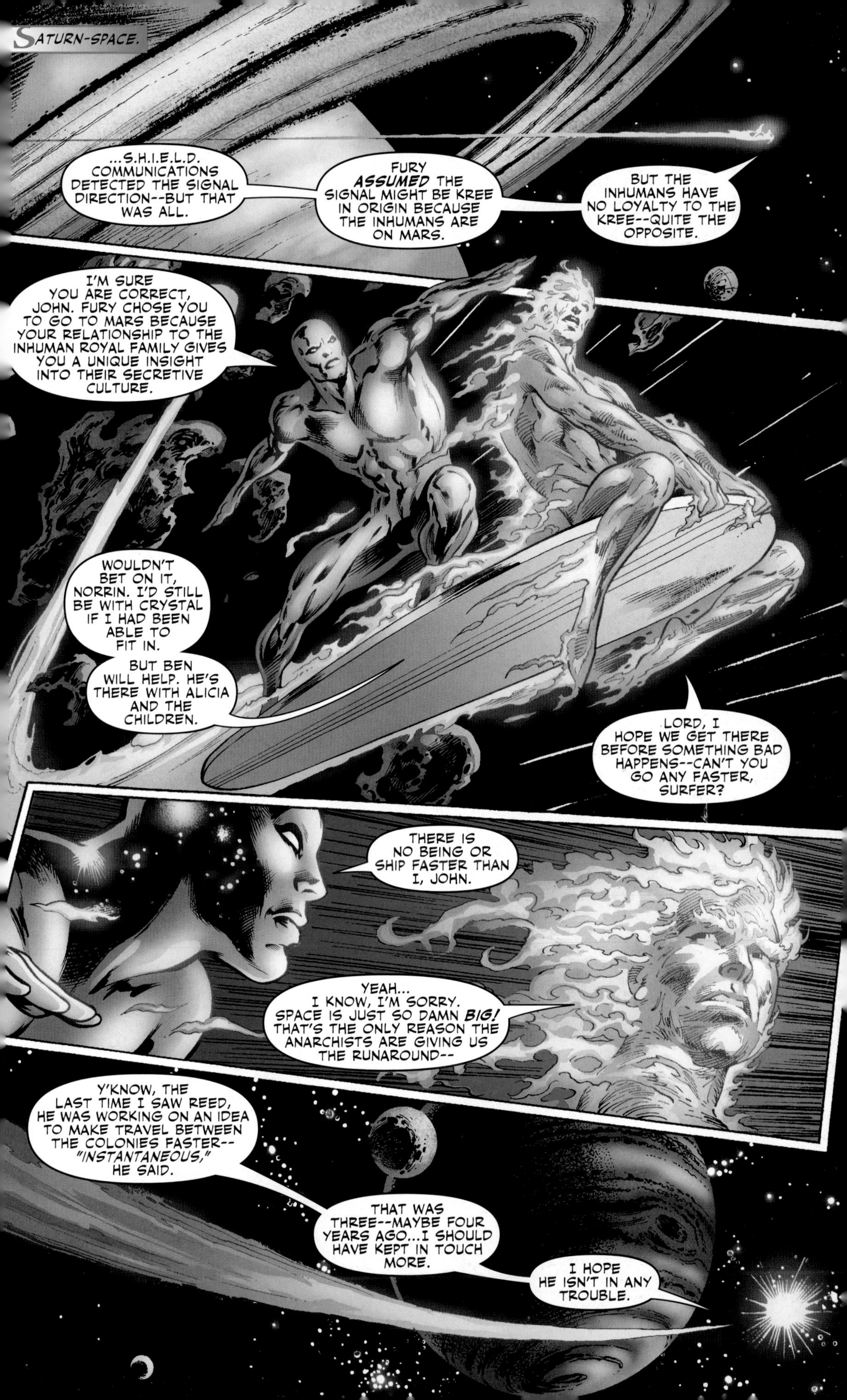
SATURN-SPACE.
...S.H.I.E.L.D. COMMUNICATIONS DETECTED THE SIGNAL DIRECTION--BUT THAT WAS ALL.
FURY ASSUMED THE SIGNAL MIGHT BE KREE IN ORIGIN BECAUSE THE INHUMANS ARE ON MARS.
BUT THE INHUMANS HAVE NO LOYALTY TO THE KREE--QUITE THE OPPOSITE.
I'M SURE YOU ARE CORRECT, JOHN. FURY CHOSE YOU TO GO TO MARS BECAUSE YOUR RELATIONSHIP TO THE INHUMAN ROYAL FAMILY GIVES YOU A UNIQUE INSIGHT INTO THEIR SECRETIVE CULTURE.
WOULDN'T BET ON IT, NORRIN. I'D STILL BE WITH CRYSTAL IF I HAD BEEN ABLE TO FIT IN.
BUT BEN WILL HELP. HE'S THERE WITH ALICIA AND THE CHILDREN.
LORD, I HOPE WE GET THERE BEFORE SOMETHING BAD HAPPENS--CAN'T YOU GO ANY FASTER, SURFER?
THERE IS NO BEING OR SHIP FASTER THAN I, JOHN.
YEAH... I KNOW, I'M SORRY. SPACE IS JUST SO DAMN BIG! THAT'S THE ONLY REASON THE ANARCHISTS ARE GIVING US THE RUNAROUND--
Y'KNOW, THE LAST TIME I SAW REED, HE WAS WORKING ON AN IDEA TO MAKE TRAVEL BETWEEN THE COLONIES FASTER-- "INSTANTANEOUS," HE SAID.
THAT WAS THREE--MAYBE FOUR YEARS AGO...I SHOULD HAVE KEPT IN TOUCH MORE.
I HOPE HE ISN'T IN ANY TROUBLE.

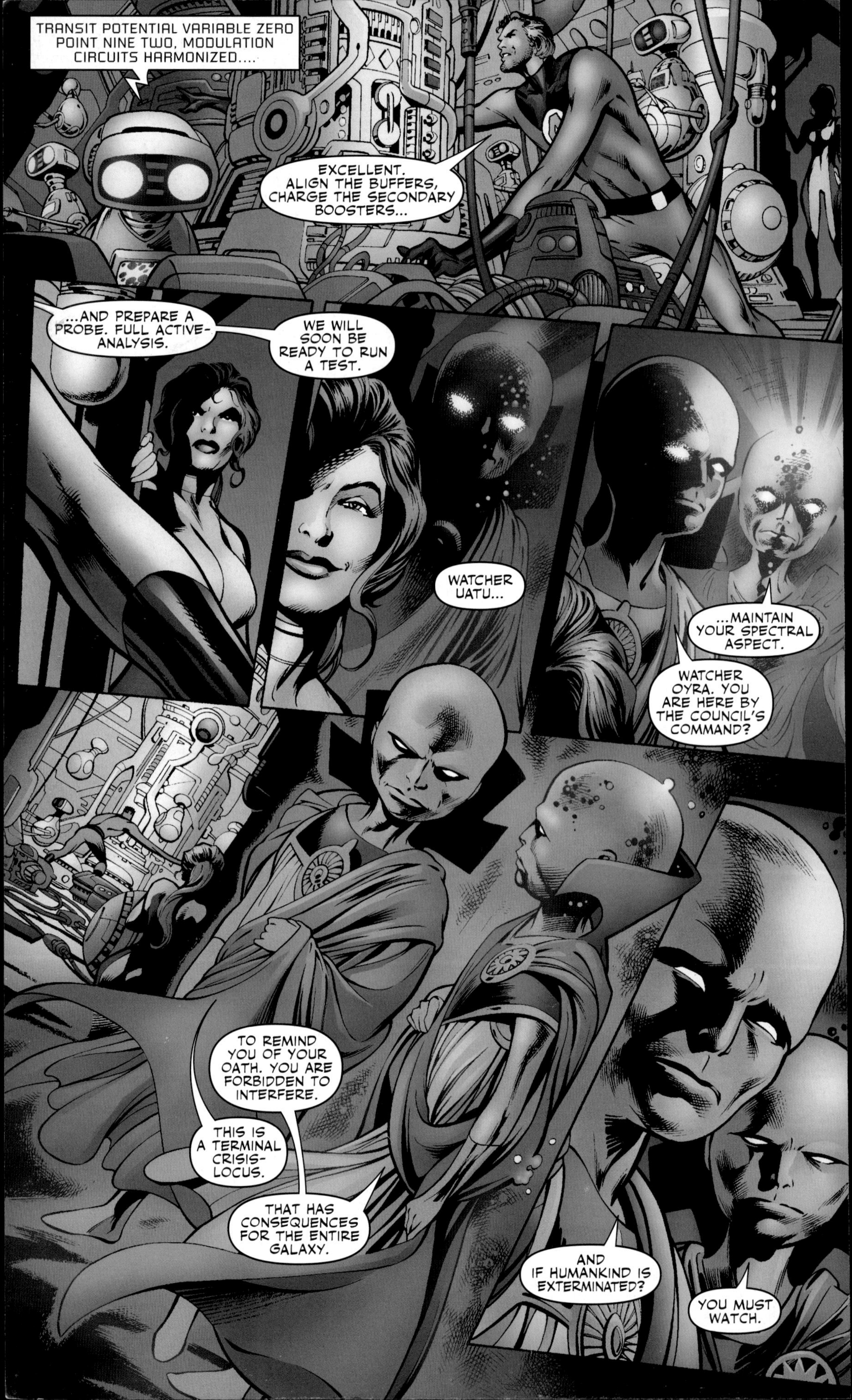
TRANSIT POTENTIAL VARIABLE ZERO POINT NINE TWO, MODULATION CIRCUITS HARMONIZED....
EXCELLENT. ALIGN THE BUFFERS, CHARGE THE SECONDARY BOOSTERS...
...AND PREPARE A PROBE. FULL ACTIVE-ANALYSIS.
WE WILL SOON BE READY TO RUN A TEST.
WATCHER UATU...
...MAINTAIN YOUR SPECTRAL ASPECT.
WATCHER OYRA. YOU ARE HERE BY THE COUNCIL'S COMMAND?
TO REMIND YOU OF YOUR OATH. YOU ARE FORBIDDEN TO INTERFERE.
THIS IS A TERMINAL CRISIS-LOCUS.
THAT HAS CONSEQUENCES FOR THE ENTIRE GALAXY.
AND IF HUMANKIND IS EXTERMINATED?
YOU MUST WATCH.

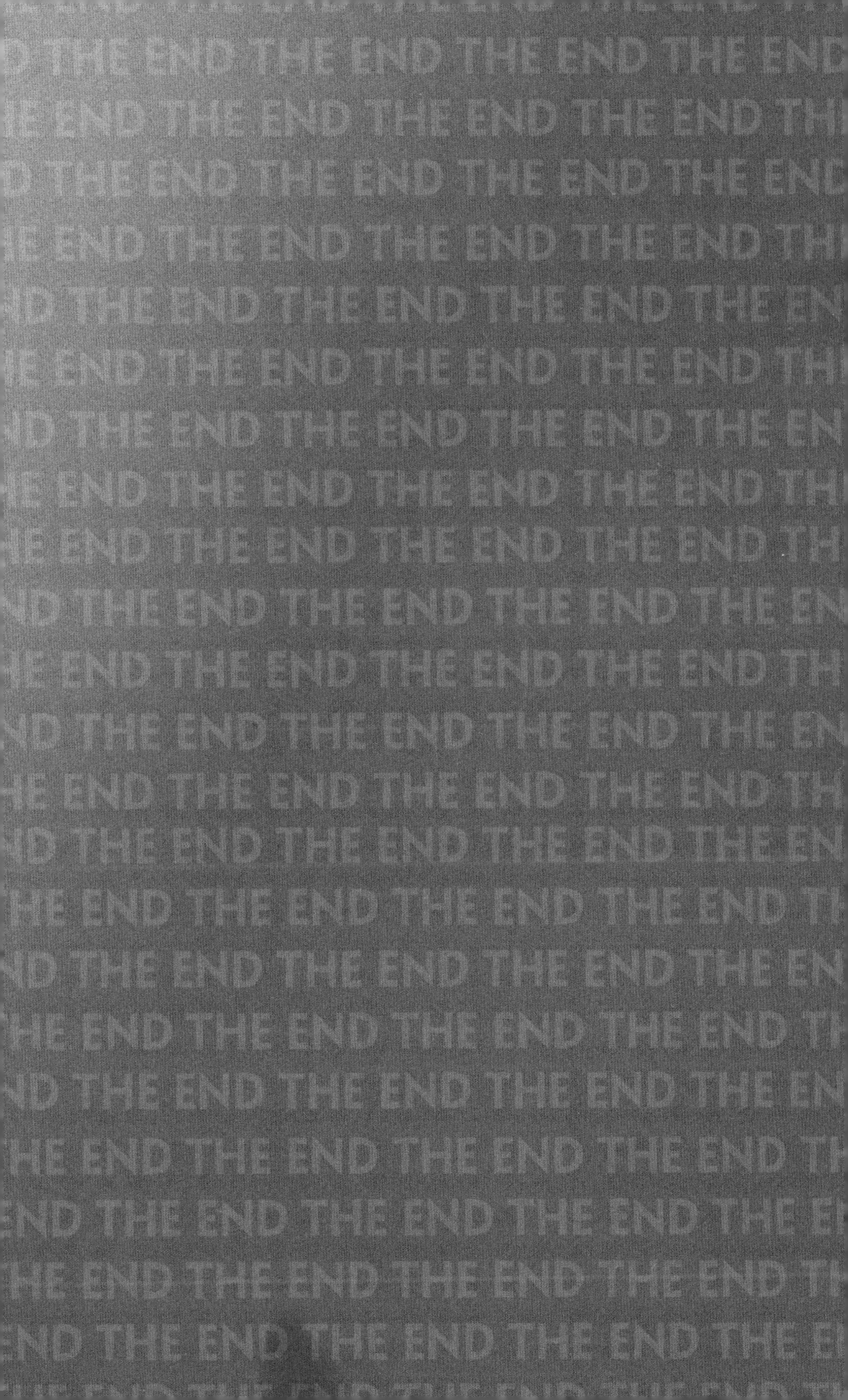
THE END

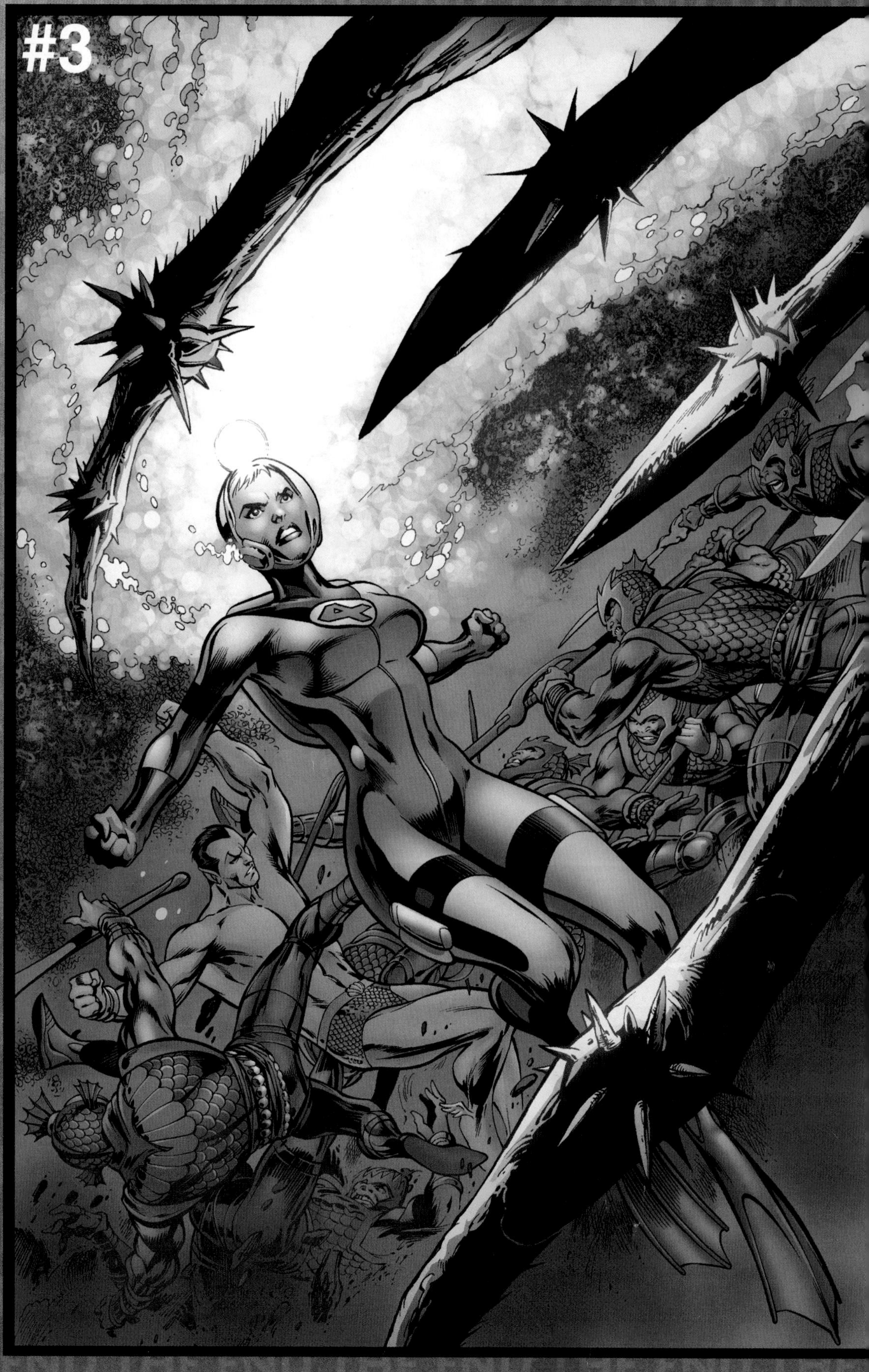
#3

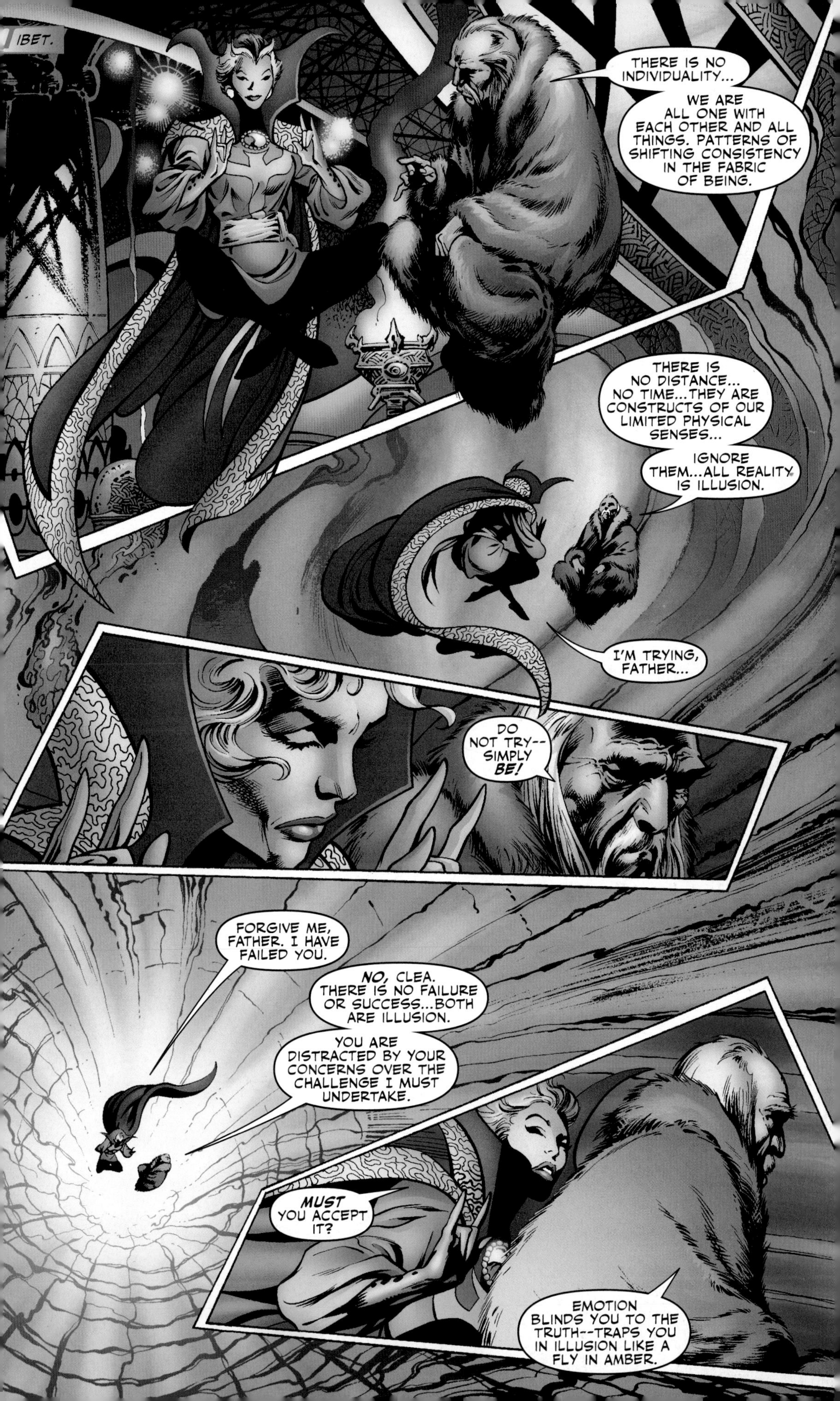
IBET.
THERE IS NO INDIVIDUALITY...
WE ARE ALL ONE WITH EACH OTHER AND ALL THINGS. PATTERNS OF SHIFTING CONSISTENCY IN THE FABRIC OF BEING.
THERE IS NO DISTANCE... NO TIME...THEY ARE CONSTRUCTS OF OUR LIMITED PHYSICAL SENSES...
IGNORE THEM...ALL REALITY IS ILLUSION.
I'M TRYING, FATHER...
DO NOT TRY-- SIMPLY *BE!*
FORGIVE ME, FATHER. I HAVE FAILED YOU.
NO, CLEA. THERE IS NO FAILURE OR SUCCESS...BOTH ARE ILLUSION.
YOU ARE DISTRACTED BY YOUR CONCERNS OVER THE CHALLENGE I MUST UNDERTAKE.
MUST YOU ACCEPT IT?
EMOTION BLINDS YOU TO THE TRUTH--TRAPS YOU IN ILLUSION LIKE A FLY IN AMBER.

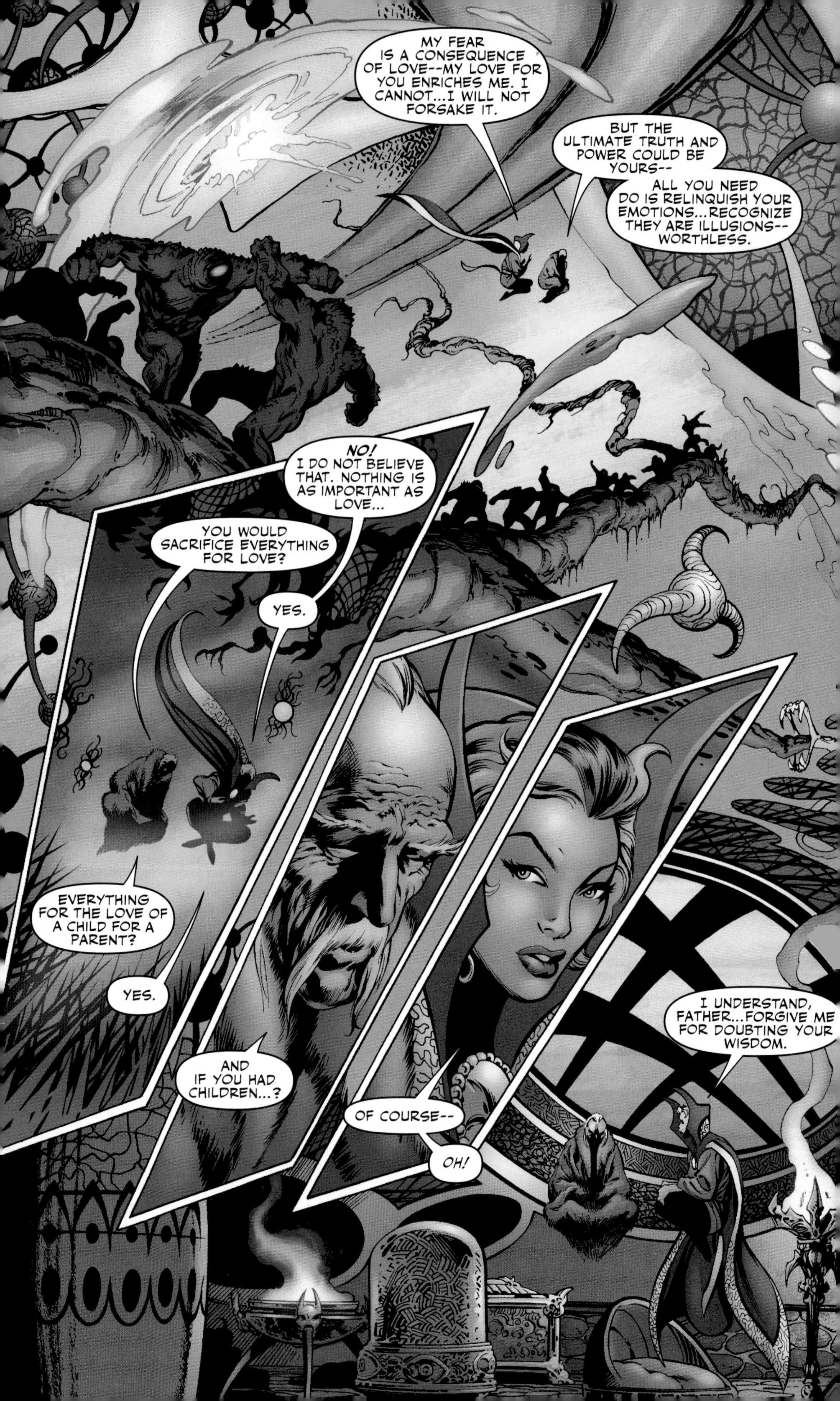
MY FEAR IS A CONSEQUENCE OF LOVE--MY LOVE FOR YOU ENRICHES ME. I CANNOT...I WILL NOT FORSAKE IT.
BUT THE ULTIMATE TRUTH AND POWER COULD BE YOURS--
ALL YOU NEED DO IS RELINQUISH YOUR EMOTIONS...RECOGNIZE THEY ARE ILLUSIONS--WORTHLESS.
NO! I DO NOT BELIEVE THAT. NOTHING IS AS IMPORTANT AS LOVE...
YOU WOULD SACRIFICE EVERYTHING FOR LOVE?
YES.
EVERYTHING FOR THE LOVE OF A CHILD FOR A PARENT?
YES.
AND IF YOU HAD CHILDREN...?
OF COURSE--
OH!
I UNDERSTAND, FATHER...FORGIVE ME FOR DOUBTING YOUR WISDOM.

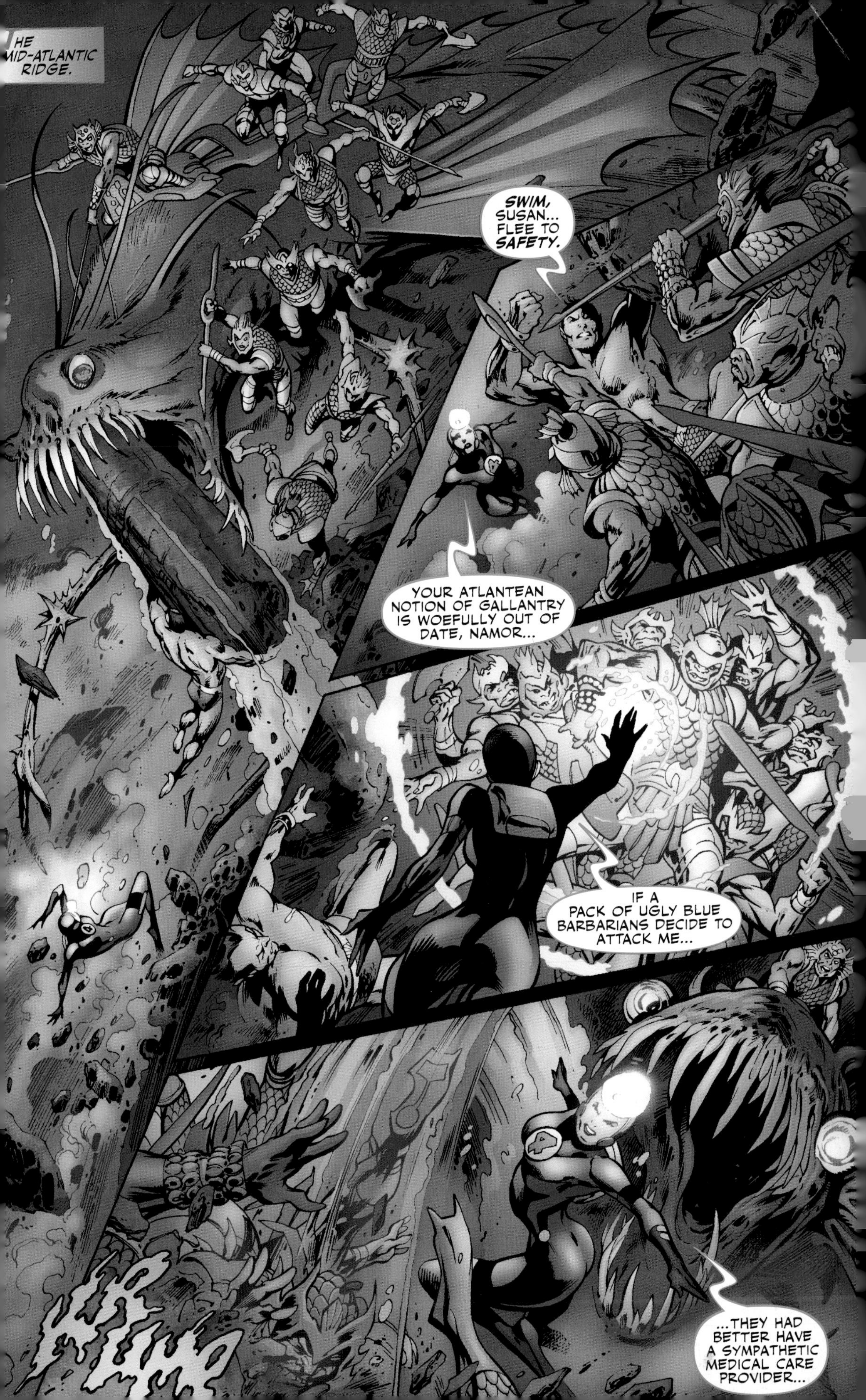
HE MID-ATLANTIC RIDGE.
SWIM, SUSAN... FLEE TO SAFETY.
YOUR ATLANTEAN NOTION OF GALLANTRY IS WOEFULLY OUT OF DATE, NAMOR...
IF A PACK OF UGLY BLUE BARBARIANS DECIDE TO ATTACK ME...
...THEY HAD BETTER HAVE A SYMPATHETIC MEDICAL CARE PROVIDER...

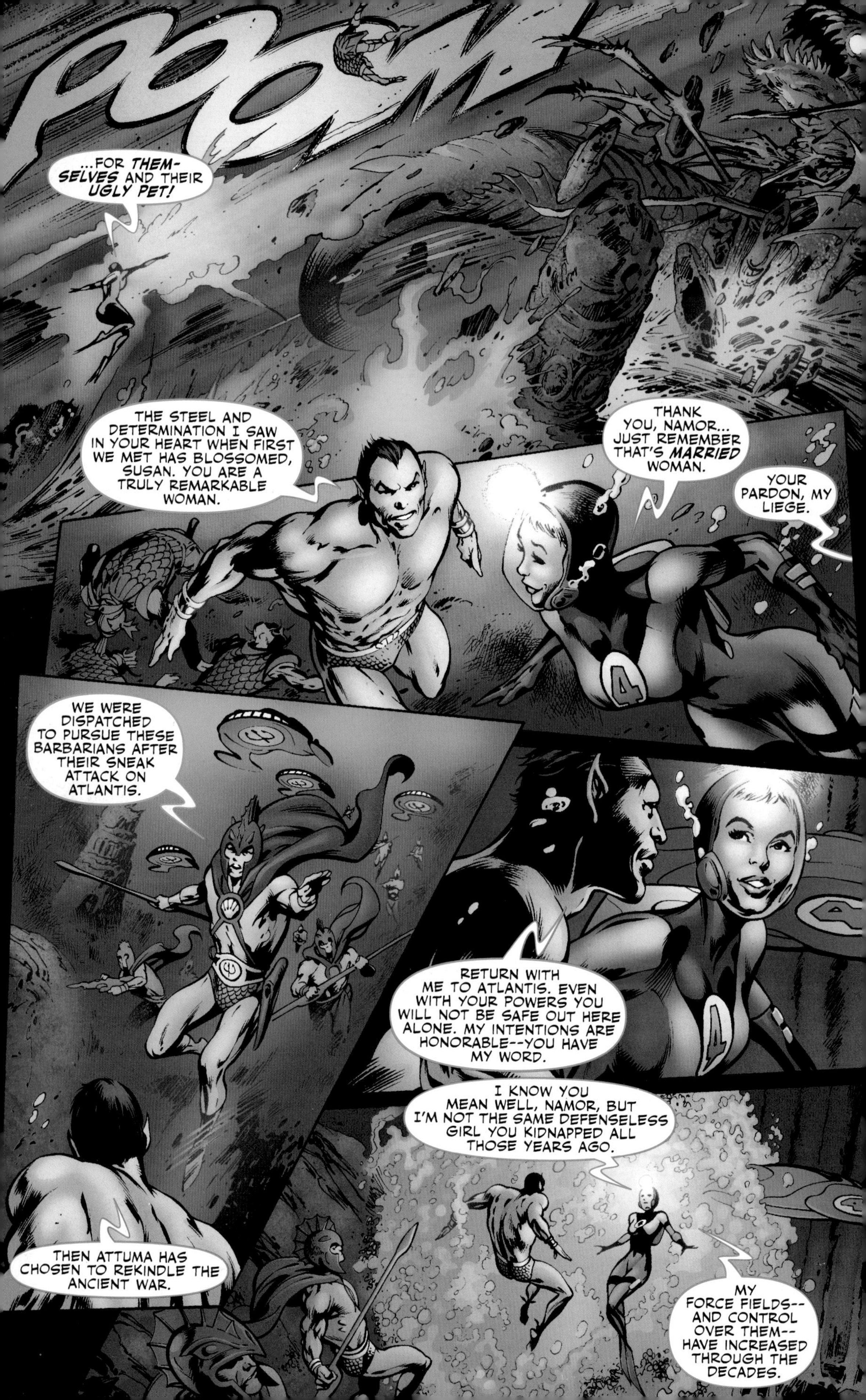
BOOOM!
...FOR THEMSELVES AND THEIR UGLY PET!
THE STEEL AND DETERMINATION I SAW IN YOUR HEART WHEN FIRST WE MET HAS BLOSSOMED, SUSAN. YOU ARE A TRULY REMARKABLE WOMAN.
THANK YOU, NAMOR... JUST REMEMBER THAT'S MARRIED WOMAN.
YOUR PARDON, MY LIEGE.
WE WERE DISPATCHED TO PURSUE THESE BARBARIANS AFTER THEIR SNEAK ATTACK ON ATLANTIS.
RETURN WITH ME TO ATLANTIS. EVEN WITH YOUR POWERS YOU WILL NOT BE SAFE OUT HERE ALONE. MY INTENTIONS ARE HONORABLE--YOU HAVE MY WORD.
THEN ATTUMA HAS CHOSEN TO REKINDLE THE ANCIENT WAR.
I KNOW YOU MEAN WELL, NAMOR, BUT I'M NOT THE SAME DEFENSELESS GIRL YOU KIDNAPPED ALL THOSE YEARS AGO.
MY FORCE FIELDS--AND CONTROL OVER THEM--HAVE INCREASED THROUGH THE DECADES.

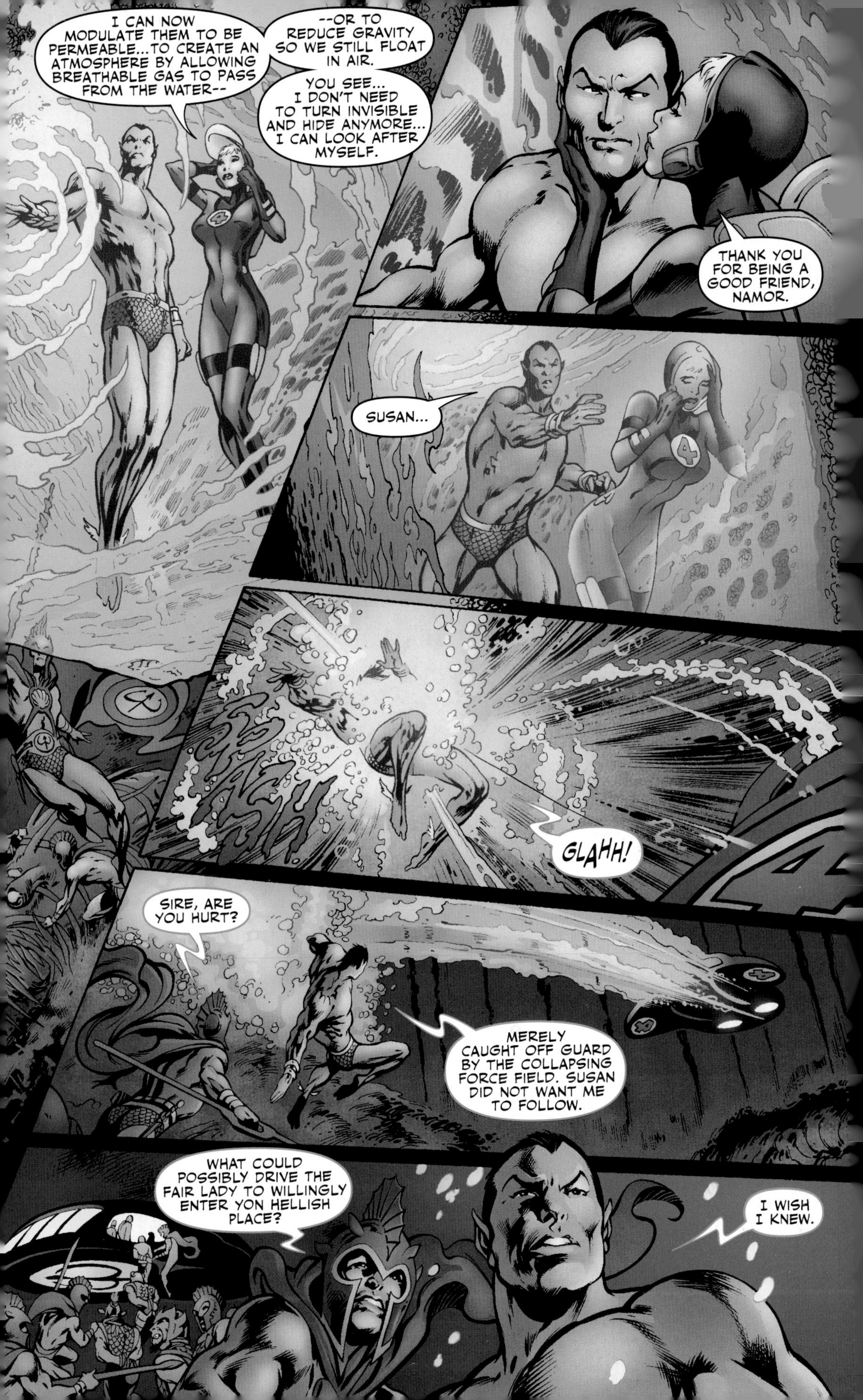
I CAN NOW MODULATE THEM TO BE PERMEABLE...TO CREATE AN ATMOSPHERE BY ALLOWING BREATHABLE GAS TO PASS FROM THE WATER--
--OR TO REDUCE GRAVITY SO WE STILL FLOAT IN AIR.
YOU SEE... I DON'T NEED TO TURN INVISIBLE AND HIDE ANYMORE... I CAN LOOK AFTER MYSELF.
THANK YOU FOR BEING A GOOD FRIEND, NAMOR.
SUSAN...
GLAHH!
SIRE, ARE YOU HURT?
MERELY CAUGHT OFF GUARD BY THE COLLAPSING FORCE FIELD. SUSAN DID NOT WANT ME TO FOLLOW.
WHAT COULD POSSIBLY DRIVE THE FAIR LADY TO WILLINGLY ENTER YON HELLISH PLACE?
I WISH I KNEW.

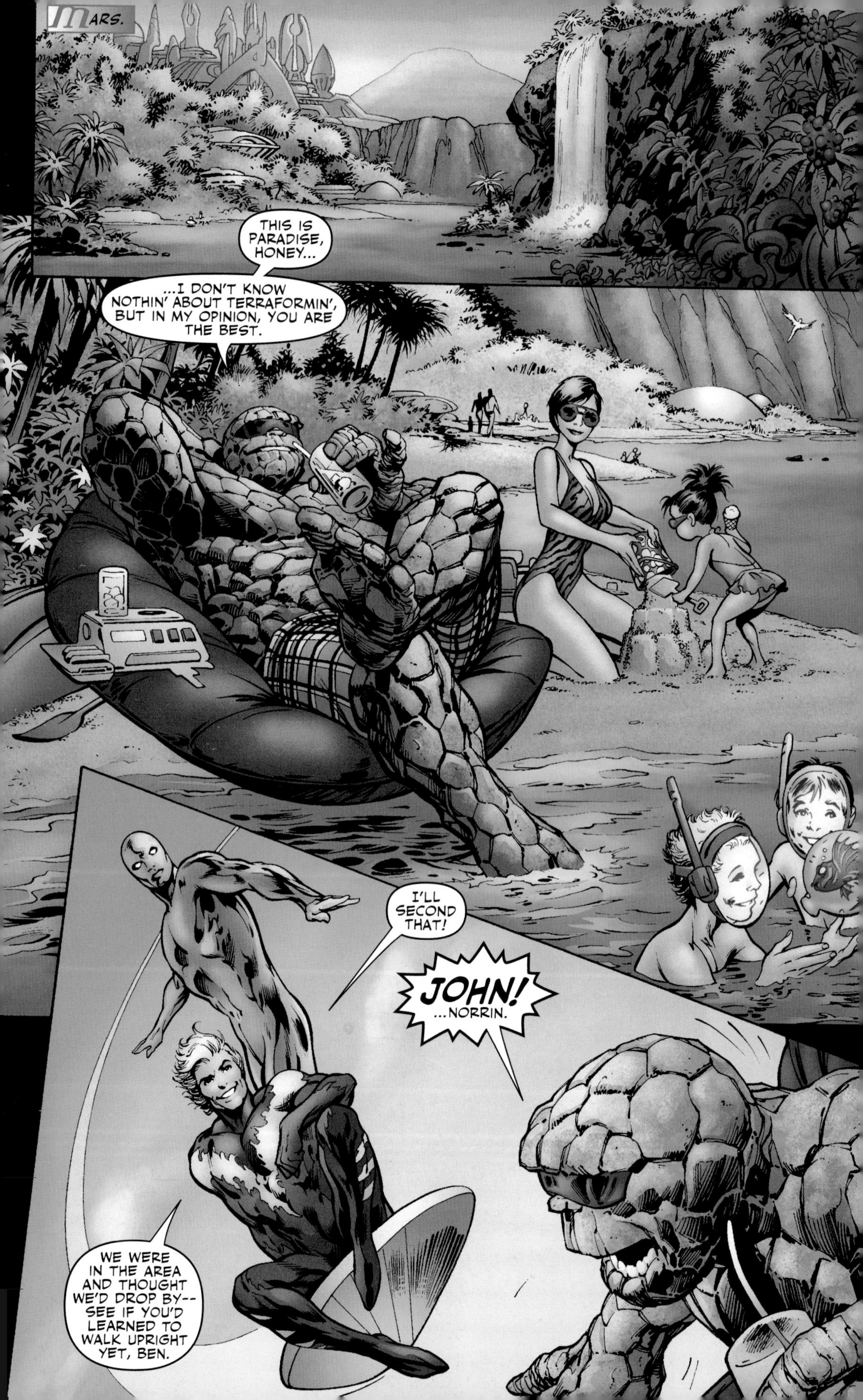
MARS.
THIS IS PARADISE, HONEY...
...I DON'T KNOW NOTHIN' ABOUT TERRAFORMIN', BUT IN MY OPINION, YOU ARE THE BEST.
I'LL SECOND THAT!
JOHN! ...NORRIN.
WE WERE IN THE AREA AND THOUGHT WE'D DROP BY-- SEE IF YOU'D LEARNED TO WALK UPRIGHT YET, BEN.

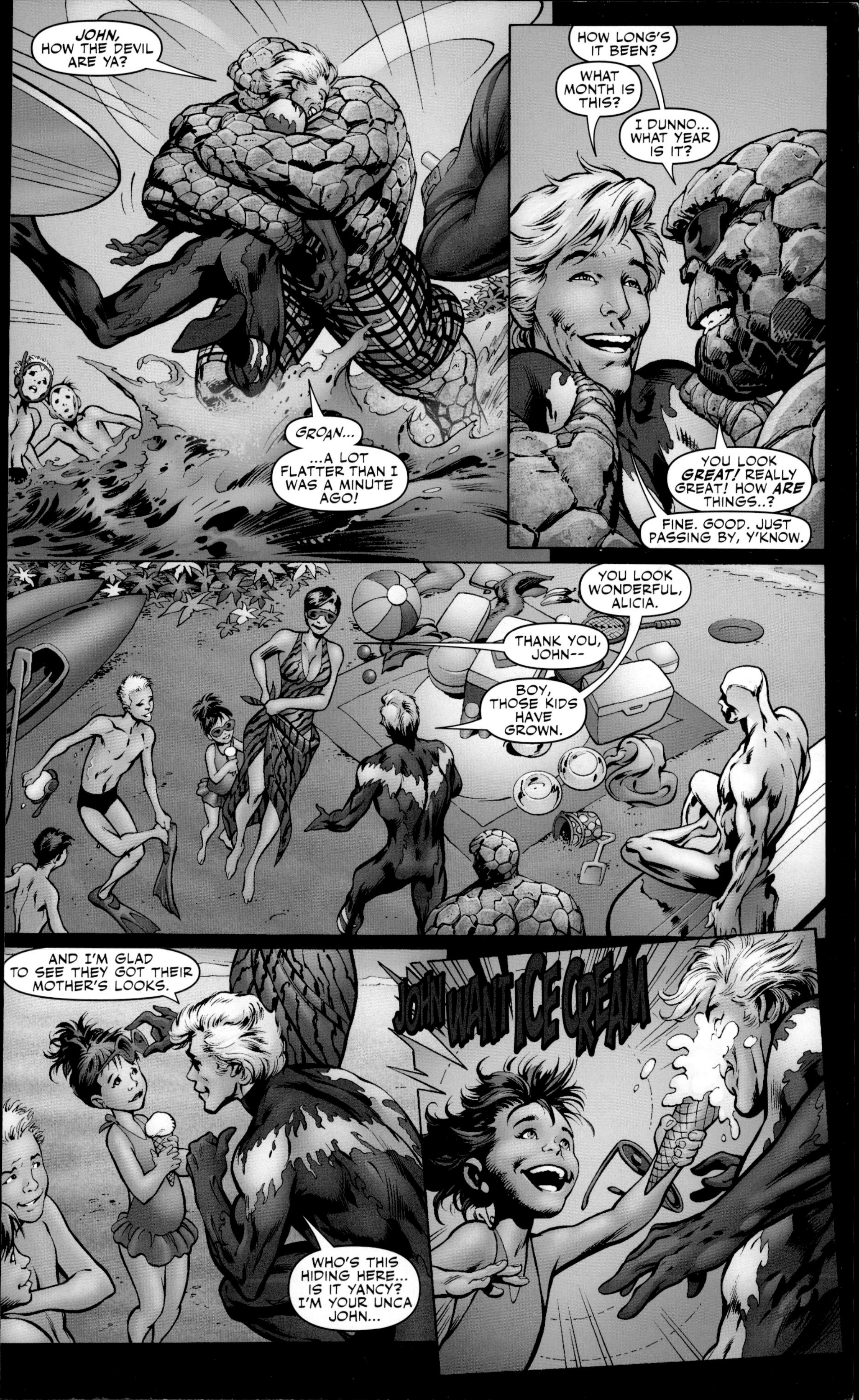
JOHN, HOW THE DEVIL ARE YA?
GROAN...
...A LOT FLATTER THAN I WAS A MINUTE AGO!
HOW LONG'S IT BEEN?
WHAT MONTH IS THIS?
I DUNNO... WHAT YEAR IS IT?
YOU LOOK GREAT! REALLY GREAT! HOW ARE THINGS..?
FINE. GOOD. JUST PASSING BY, Y'KNOW.
YOU LOOK WONDERFUL, ALICIA.
THANK YOU, JOHN--
BOY, THOSE KIDS HAVE GROWN.
AND I'M GLAD TO SEE THEY GOT THEIR MOTHER'S LOOKS.
WHO'S THIS HIDING HERE... IS IT YANCY? I'M YOUR UNCA JOHN...
JOHN WANT ICE CREAM

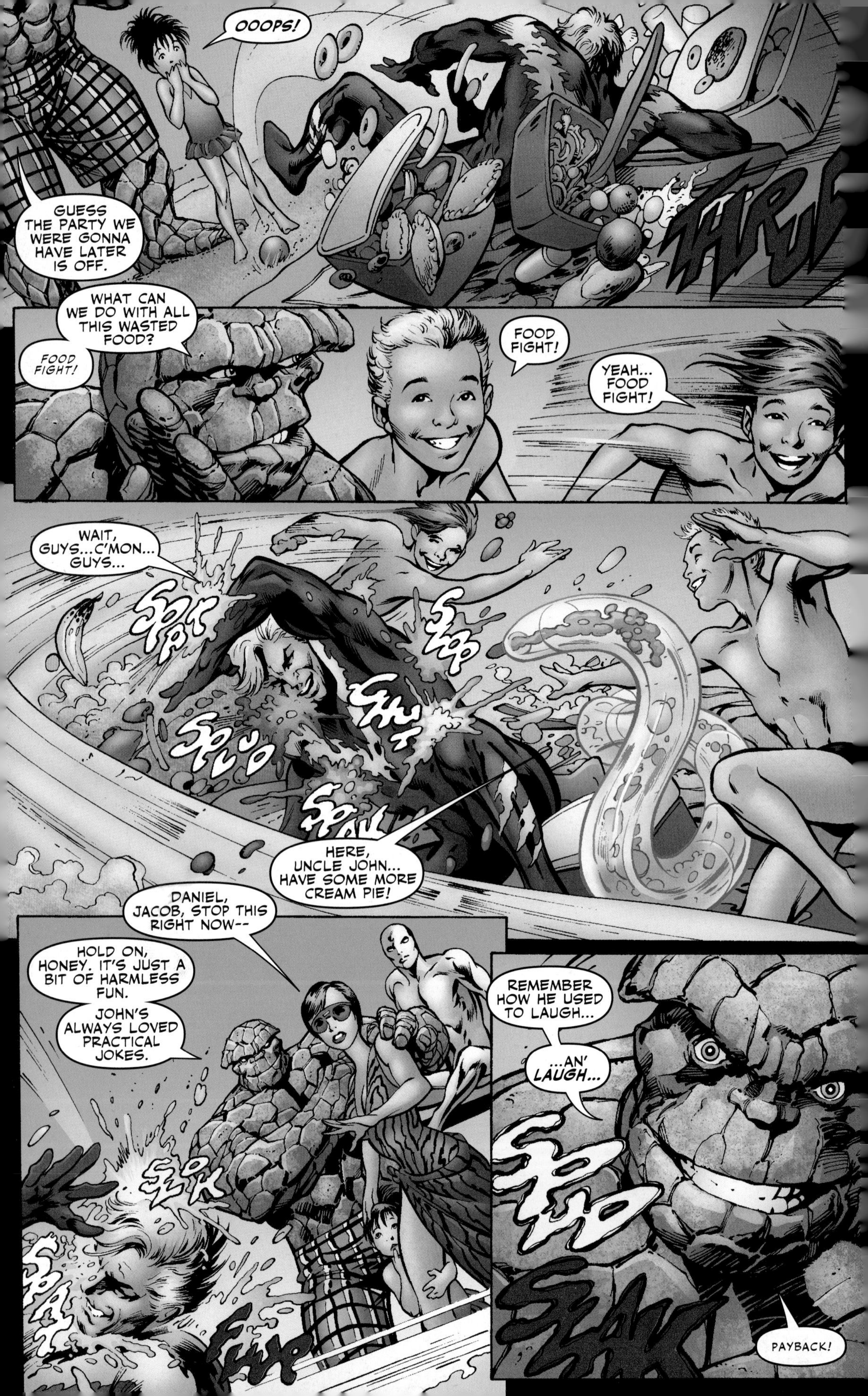
OOOPS!
GUESS THE PARTY WE WERE GONNA HAVE LATER IS OFF.
WHAT CAN WE DO WITH ALL THIS WASTED FOOD?
FOOD FIGHT!
FOOD FIGHT!
YEAH... FOOD FIGHT!
WAIT, GUYS...C'MON... GUYS...
HERE, UNCLE JOHN... HAVE SOME MORE CREAM PIE!
DANIEL, JACOB, STOP THIS RIGHT NOW--
HOLD ON, HONEY. IT'S JUST A BIT OF HARMLESS FUN.
JOHN'S ALWAYS LOVED PRACTICAL JOKES.
REMEMBER HOW HE USED TO LAUGH...
...AN' LAUGH...
PAYBACK!

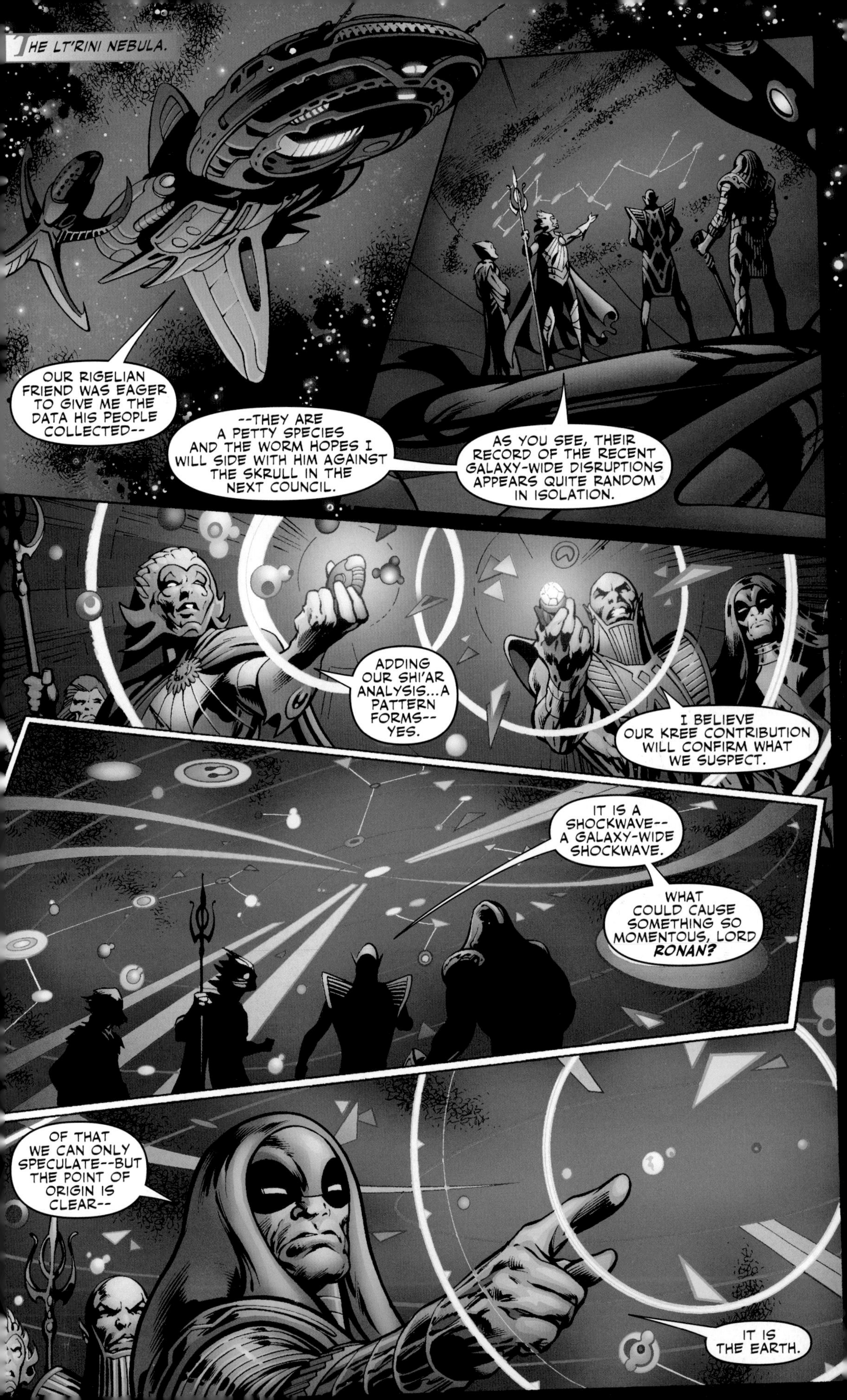
THE LT'RINI NEBULA.
OUR RIGELIAN FRIEND WAS EAGER TO GIVE ME THE DATA HIS PEOPLE COLLECTED--
--THEY ARE A PETTY SPECIES AND THE WORM HOPES I WILL SIDE WITH HIM AGAINST THE SKRULL IN THE NEXT COUNCIL.
AS YOU SEE, THEIR RECORD OF THE RECENT GALAXY-WIDE DISRUPTIONS APPEARS QUITE RANDOM IN ISOLATION.
ADDING OUR SHI'AR ANALYSIS...A PATTERN FORMS--YES.
I BELIEVE OUR KREE CONTRIBUTION WILL CONFIRM WHAT WE SUSPECT.
IT IS A SHOCKWAVE--A GALAXY-WIDE SHOCKWAVE.
WHAT COULD CAUSE SOMETHING SO MOMENTOUS, LORD *RONAN?*
OF THAT WE CAN ONLY SPECULATE--BUT THE POINT OF ORIGIN IS CLEAR--
IT IS THE EARTH.

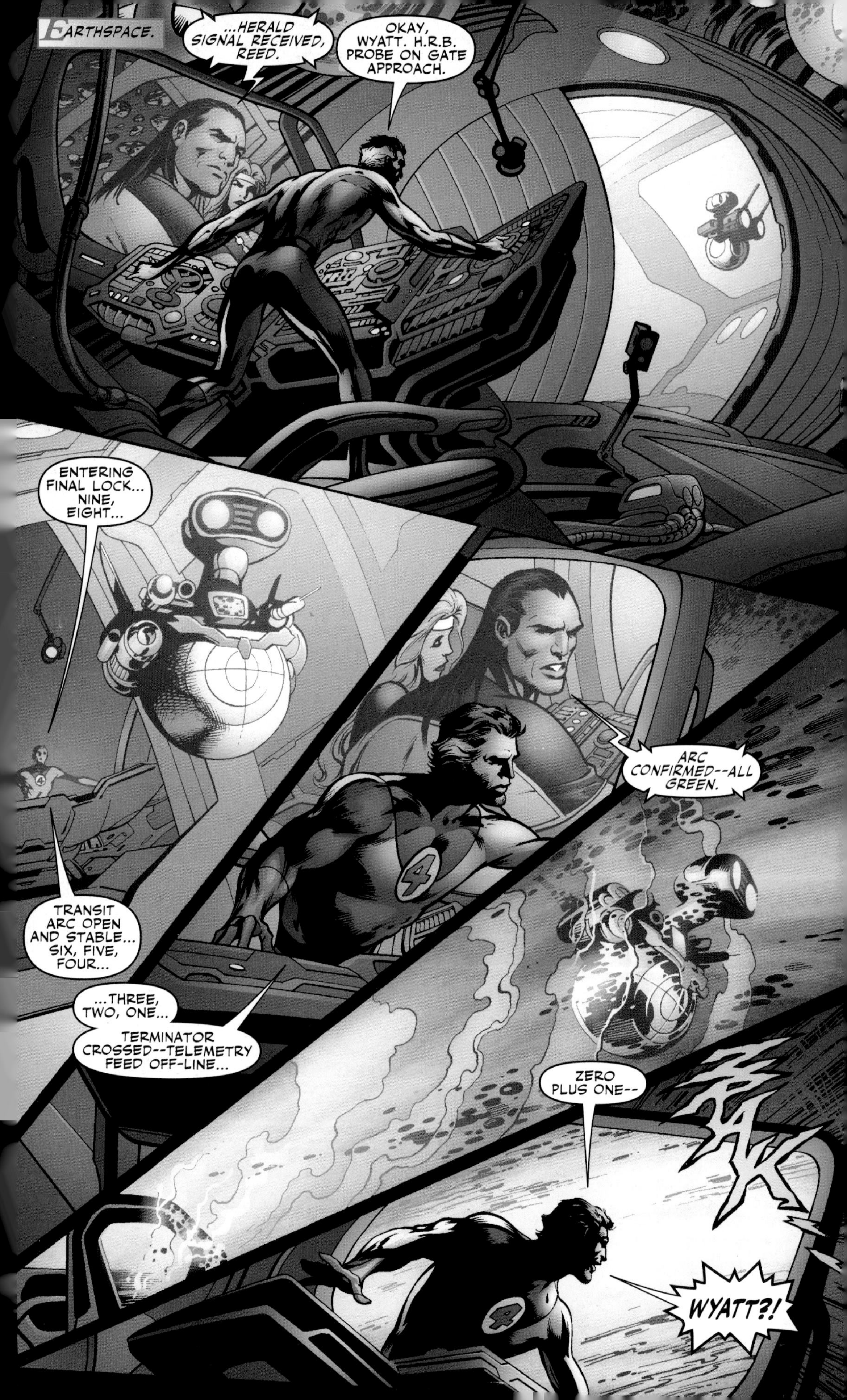
EARTHSPACE.
...HERALD SIGNAL RECEIVED, REED.
OKAY, WYATT. H.R.B. PROBE ON GATE APPROACH.
ENTERING FINAL LOCK... NINE, EIGHT...
ARC CONFIRMED--ALL GREEN.
TRANSIT ARC OPEN AND STABLE... SIX, FIVE, FOUR...
...THREE, TWO, ONE...
TERMINATOR CROSSED--TELEMETRY FEED OFF-LINE...
ZERO PLUS ONE--
ZAK
WYATT?!

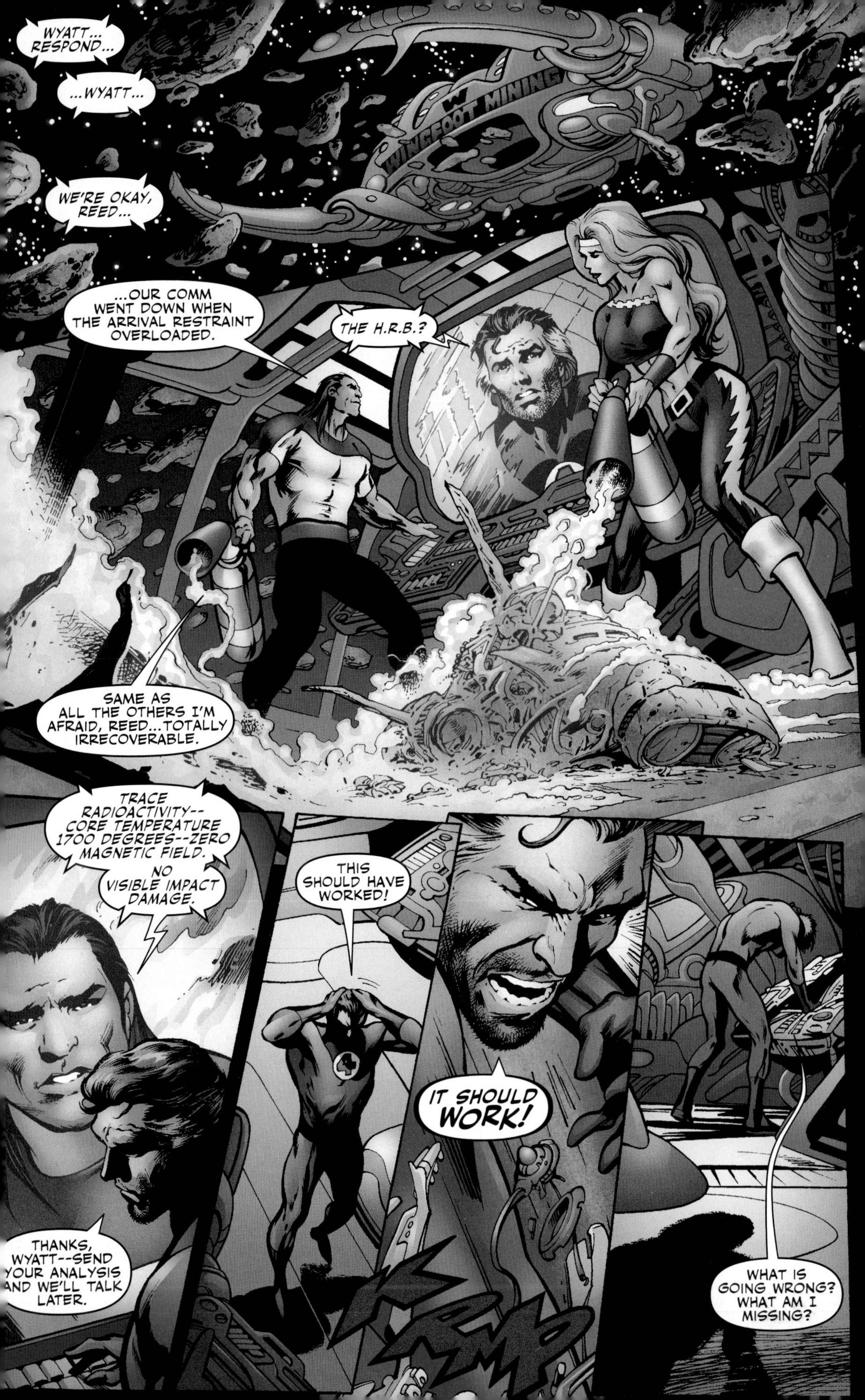
WYATT... RESPOND...
...WYATT...
WE'RE OKAY, REED...
...OUR COMM WENT DOWN WHEN THE ARRIVAL RESTRAINT OVERLOADED.
THE H.R.B.?
SAME AS ALL THE OTHERS I'M AFRAID, REED...TOTALLY IRRECOVERABLE.
TRACE RADIOACTIVITY--CORE TEMPERATURE 1700 DEGREES--ZERO MAGNETIC FIELD.
NO VISIBLE IMPACT DAMAGE.
THANKS, WYATT--SEND YOUR ANALYSIS AND WE'LL TALK LATER.
THIS SHOULD HAVE WORKED!
IT SHOULD WORK!
WHAT IS GOING WRONG? WHAT AM I MISSING?

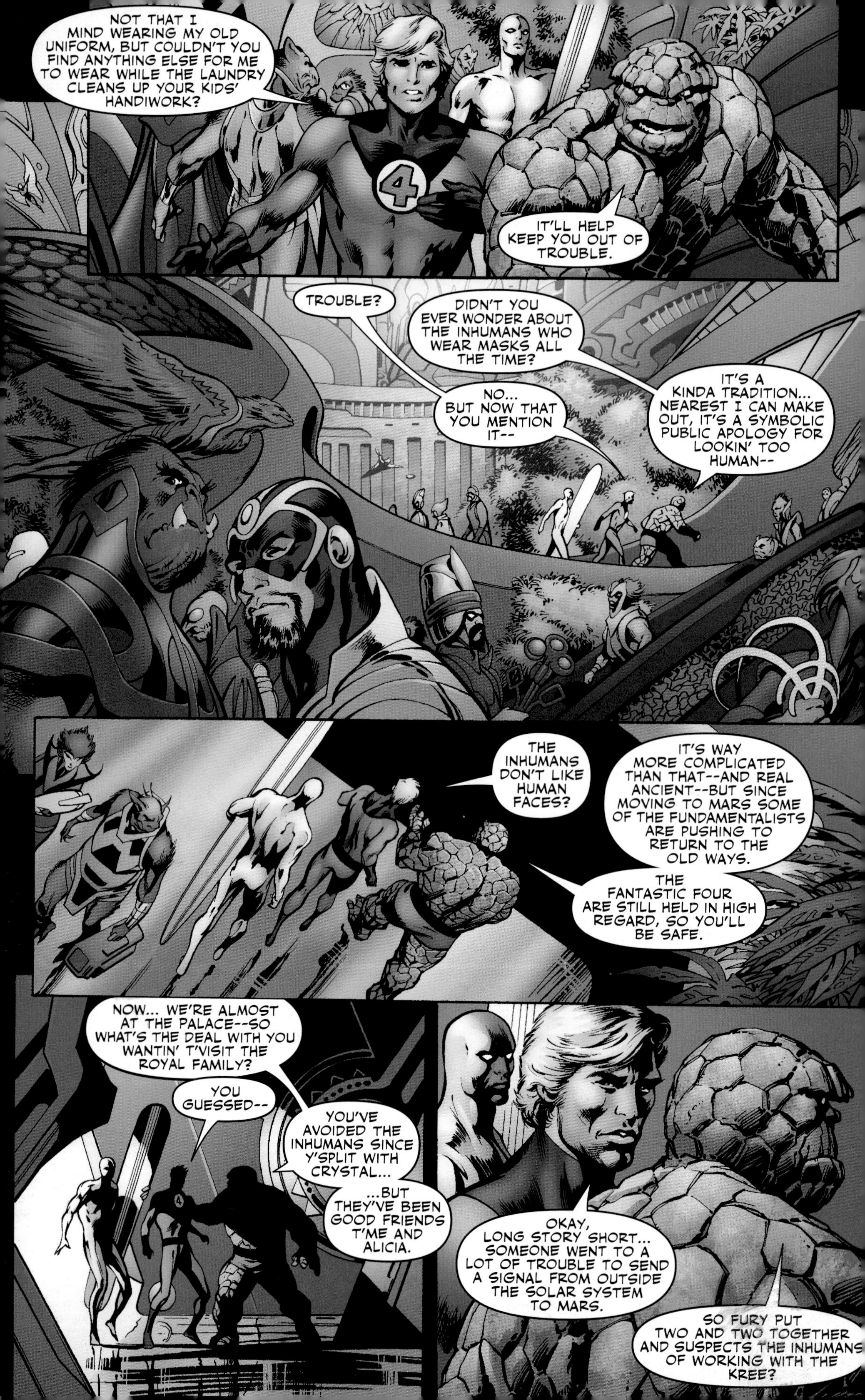
NOT THAT I MIND WEARING MY OLD UNIFORM, BUT COULDN'T YOU FIND ANYTHING ELSE FOR ME TO WEAR WHILE THE LAUNDRY CLEANS UP YOUR KIDS' HANDIWORK?
IT'LL HELP KEEP YOU OUT OF TROUBLE.
TROUBLE?
DIDN'T YOU EVER WONDER ABOUT THE INHUMANS WHO WEAR MASKS ALL THE TIME?
NO... BUT NOW THAT YOU MENTION IT--
IT'S A KINDA TRADITION... NEAREST I CAN MAKE OUT, IT'S A SYMBOLIC PUBLIC APOLOGY FOR LOOKIN' TOO HUMAN--
THE INHUMANS DON'T LIKE HUMAN FACES?
IT'S WAY MORE COMPLICATED THAN THAT--AND REAL ANCIENT--BUT SINCE MOVING TO MARS SOME OF THE FUNDAMENTALISTS ARE PUSHING TO RETURN TO THE OLD WAYS.
THE FANTASTIC FOUR ARE STILL HELD IN HIGH REGARD, SO YOU'LL BE SAFE.
NOW... WE'RE ALMOST AT THE PALACE--SO WHAT'S THE DEAL WITH YOU WANTIN' T'VISIT THE ROYAL FAMILY?
YOU GUESSED--
YOU'VE AVOIDED THE INHUMANS SINCE Y'SPLIT WITH CRYSTAL...
...BUT THEY'VE BEEN GOOD FRIENDS T'ME AND ALICIA.
OKAY, LONG STORY SHORT... SOMEONE WENT TO A LOT OF TROUBLE TO SEND A SIGNAL FROM OUTSIDE THE SOLAR SYSTEM TO MARS.
SO FURY PUT TWO AND TWO TOGETHER AND SUSPECTS THE INHUMANS OF WORKING WITH THE KREE?

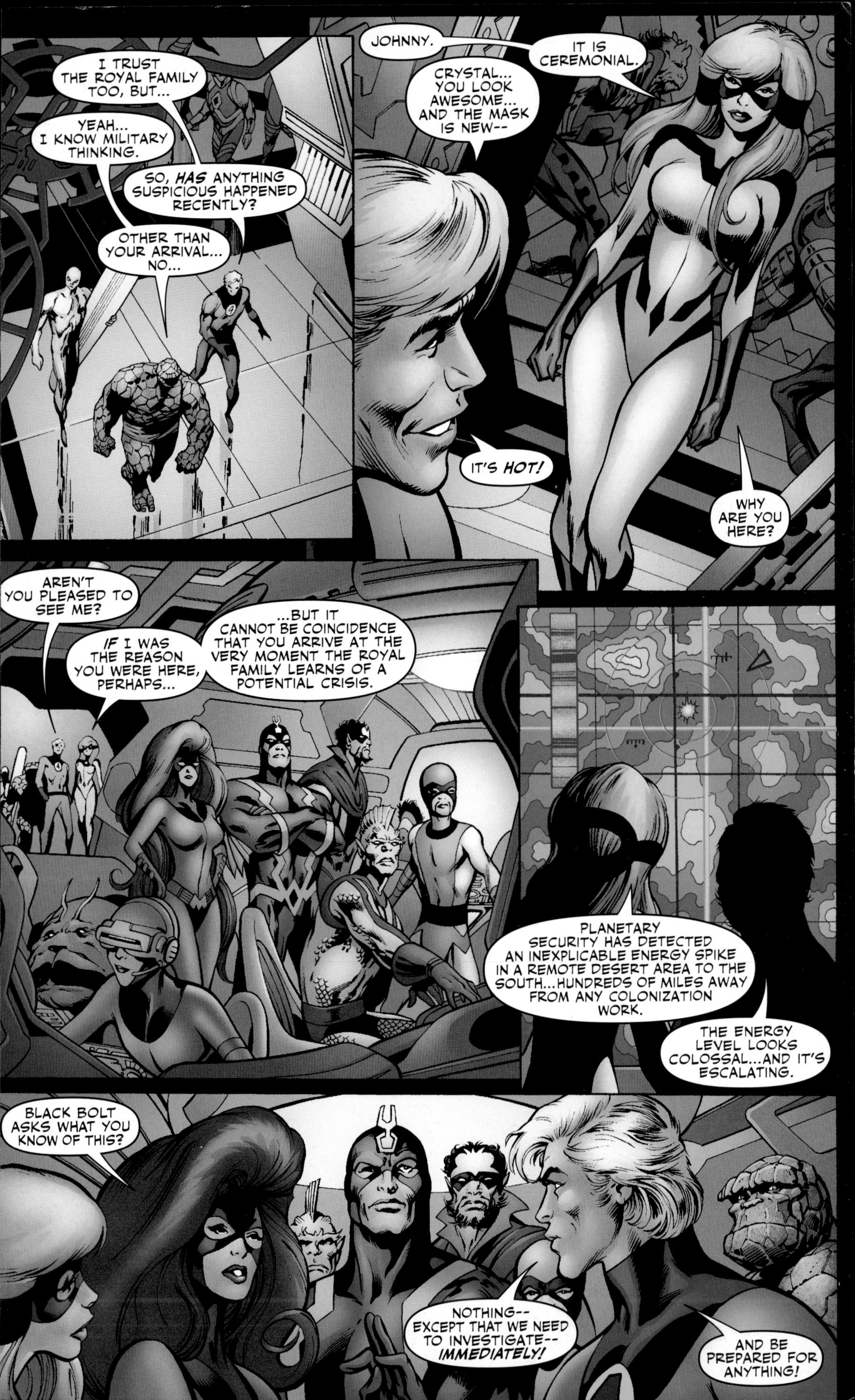
I TRUST THE ROYAL FAMILY TOO, BUT...
YEAH... I KNOW MILITARY THINKING.
SO, HAS ANYTHING SUSPICIOUS HAPPENED RECENTLY?
OTHER THAN YOUR ARRIVAL... NO...
JOHNNY.
IT IS CEREMONIAL.
CRYSTAL... YOU LOOK AWESOME... AND THE MASK IS NEW--
IT'S HOT!
WHY ARE YOU HERE?
AREN'T YOU PLEASED TO SEE ME?
IF I WAS THE REASON YOU WERE HERE, PERHAPS...
...BUT IT CANNOT BE COINCIDENCE THAT YOU ARRIVE AT THE VERY MOMENT THE ROYAL FAMILY LEARNS OF A POTENTIAL CRISIS.
PLANETARY SECURITY HAS DETECTED AN INEXPLICABLE ENERGY SPIKE IN A REMOTE DESERT AREA TO THE SOUTH...HUNDREDS OF MILES AWAY FROM ANY COLONIZATION WORK.
THE ENERGY LEVEL LOOKS COLOSSAL...AND IT'S ESCALATING.
BLACK BOLT ASKS WHAT YOU KNOW OF THIS?
NOTHING-- EXCEPT THAT WE NEED TO INVESTIGATE-- IMMEDIATELY!
AND BE PREPARED FOR ANYTHING!

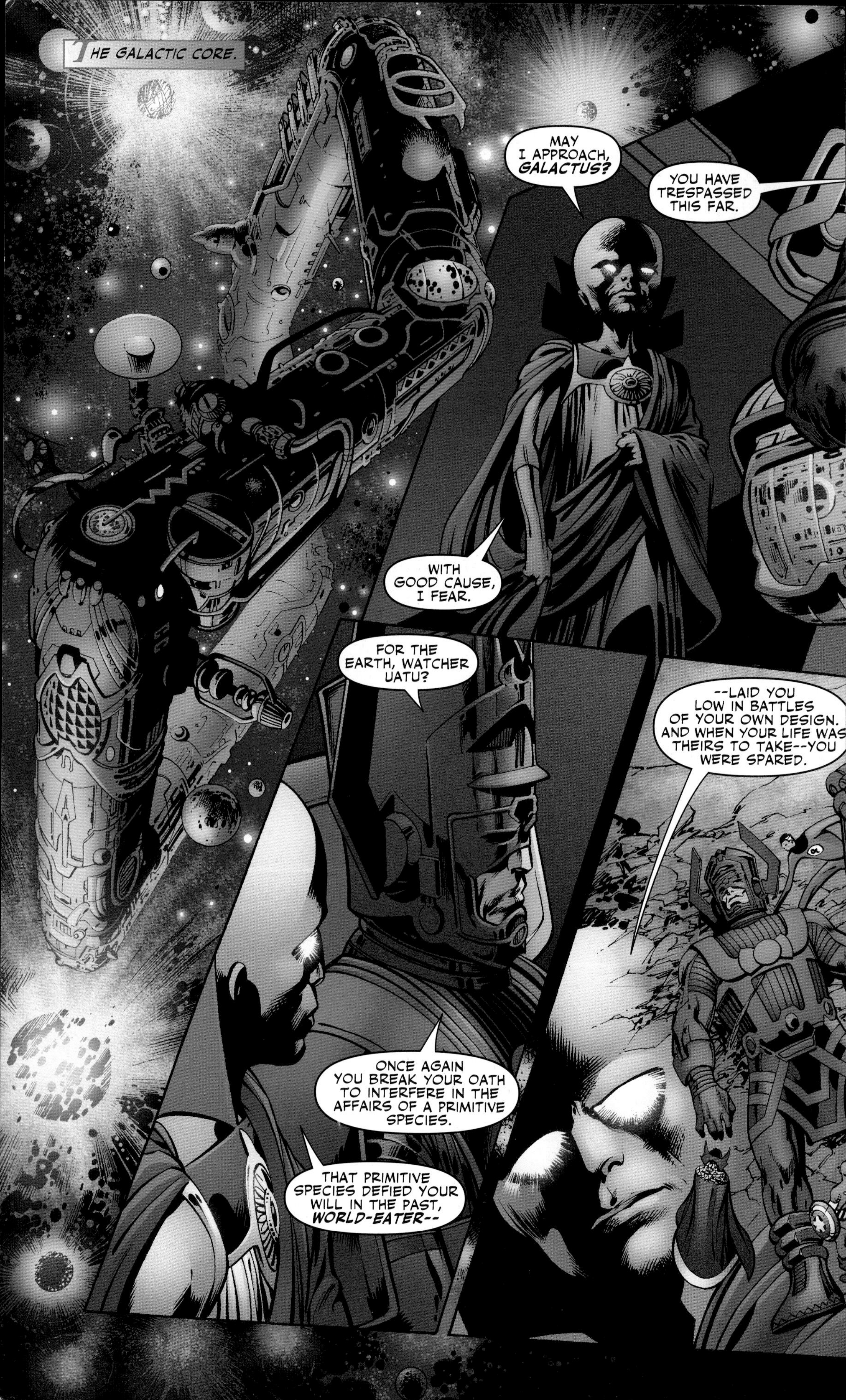
THE GALACTIC CORE.
MAY I APPROACH, GALACTUS?
YOU HAVE TRESPASSED THIS FAR.
WITH GOOD CAUSE, I FEAR.
FOR THE EARTH, WATCHER UATU?
ONCE AGAIN YOU BREAK YOUR OATH TO INTERFERE IN THE AFFAIRS OF A PRIMITIVE SPECIES.
THAT PRIMITIVE SPECIES DEFIED YOUR WILL IN THE PAST, WORLD-EATER--
--LAID YOU LOW IN BATTLES OF YOUR OWN DESIGN. AND WHEN YOUR LIFE WAS THEIRS TO TAKE--YOU WERE SPARED.

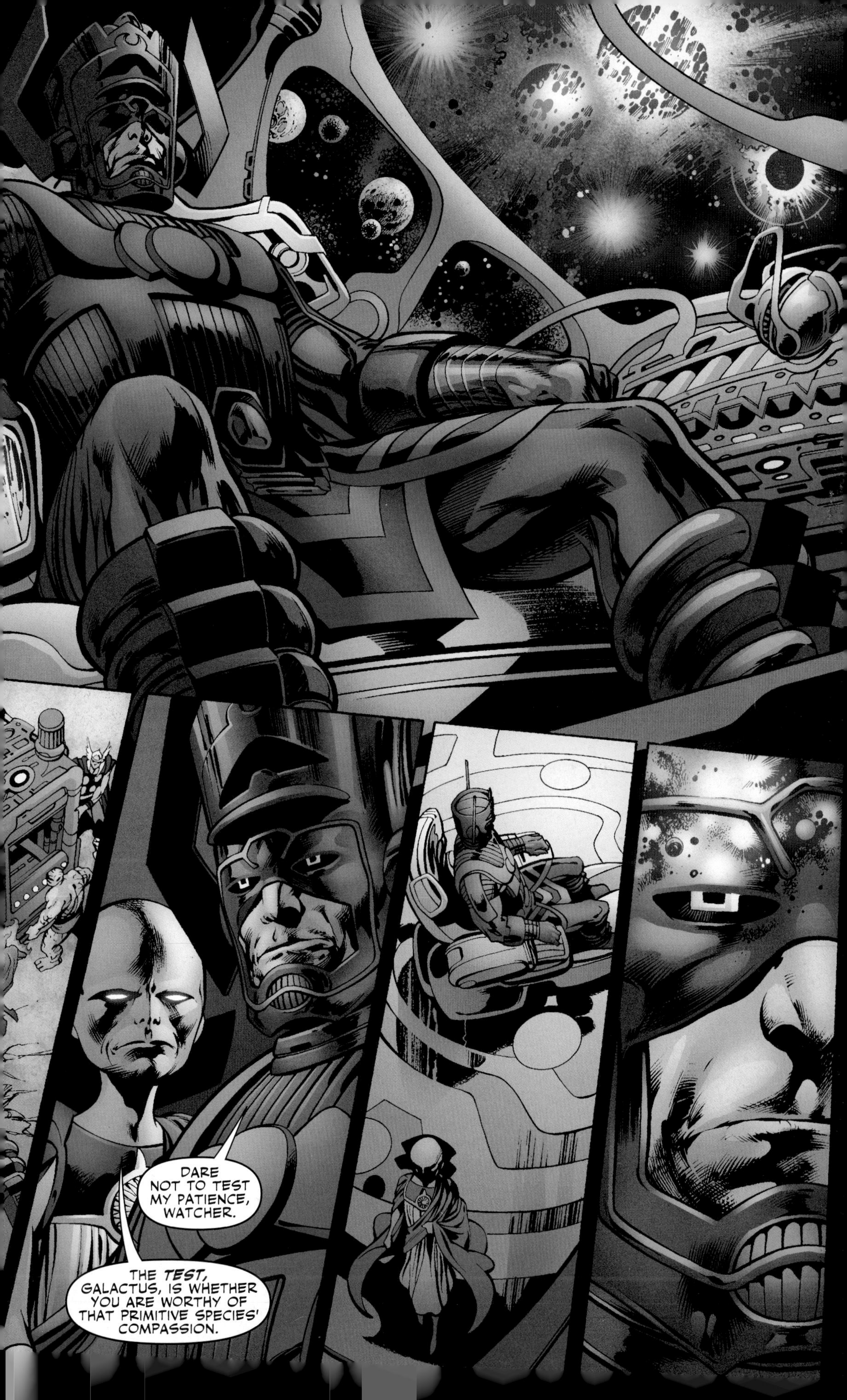
DARE NOT TO TEST MY PATIENCE, WATCHER.
THE *TEST*, GALACTUS, IS WHETHER YOU ARE WORTHY OF THAT PRIMITIVE SPECIES' COMPASSION.

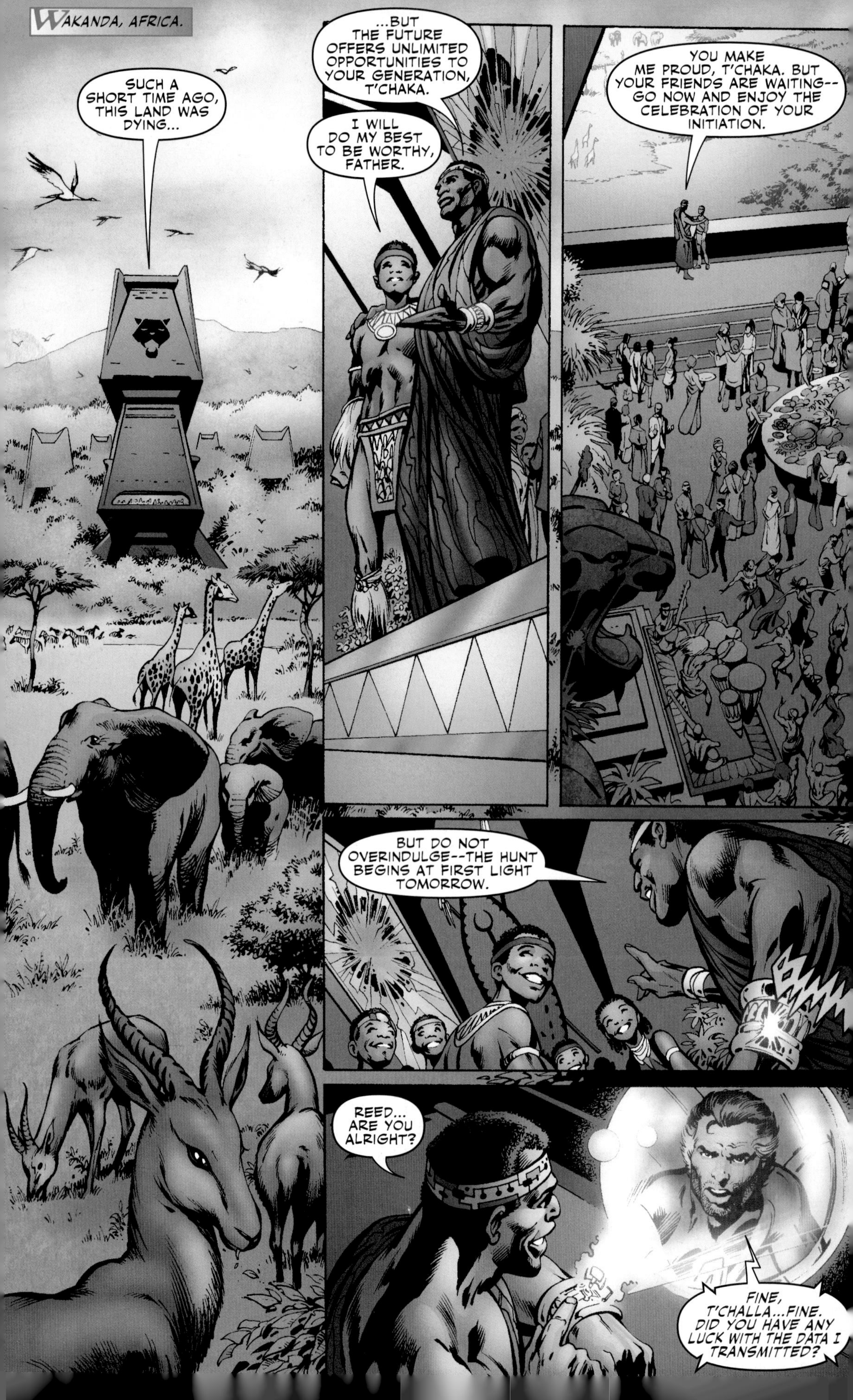
WAKANDA, AFRICA.
SUCH A SHORT TIME AGO, THIS LAND WAS DYING...
...BUT THE FUTURE OFFERS UNLIMITED OPPORTUNITIES TO YOUR GENERATION, T'CHAKA.
I WILL DO MY BEST TO BE WORTHY, FATHER.
YOU MAKE ME PROUD, T'CHAKA. BUT YOUR FRIENDS ARE WAITING--GO NOW AND ENJOY THE CELEBRATION OF YOUR INITIATION.
BUT DO NOT OVERINDULGE--THE HUNT BEGINS AT FIRST LIGHT TOMORROW.
REED... ARE YOU ALRIGHT?
FINE, T'CHALLA...FINE. DID YOU HAVE ANY LUCK WITH THE DATA I TRANSMITTED?

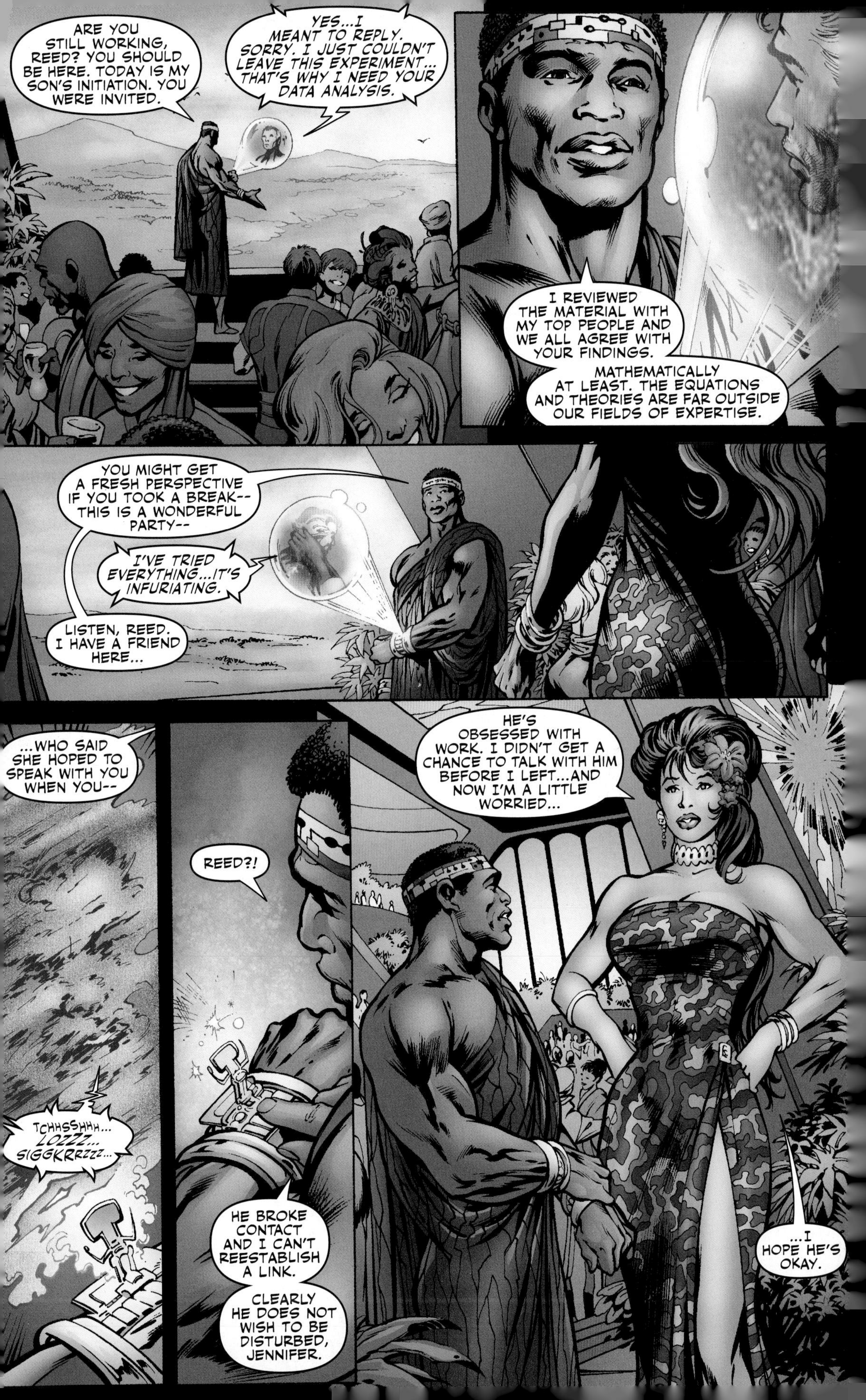
ARE YOU STILL WORKING, REED? YOU SHOULD BE HERE. TODAY IS MY SON'S INITIATION. YOU WERE INVITED.
YES...I MEANT TO REPLY. SORRY. I JUST COULDN'T LEAVE THIS EXPERIMENT... THAT'S WHY I NEED YOUR DATA ANALYSIS.
I REVIEWED THE MATERIAL WITH MY TOP PEOPLE AND WE ALL AGREE WITH YOUR FINDINGS.
MATHEMATICALLY AT LEAST. THE EQUATIONS AND THEORIES ARE FAR OUTSIDE OUR FIELDS OF EXPERTISE.
YOU MIGHT GET A FRESH PERSPECTIVE IF YOU TOOK A BREAK-- THIS IS A WONDERFUL PARTY--
I'VE TRIED EVERYTHING...IT'S INFURIATING.
LISTEN, REED. I HAVE A FRIEND HERE...
...WHO SAID SHE HOPED TO SPEAK WITH YOU WHEN YOU--
TCHHSSHHH... LOZZZ... SIGGKRRZZZ...
REED?!
HE BROKE CONTACT AND I CAN'T REESTABLISH A LINK.
CLEARLY HE DOES NOT WISH TO BE DISTURBED, JENNIFER.
HE'S OBSESSED WITH WORK. I DIDN'T GET A CHANCE TO TALK WITH HIM BEFORE I LEFT...AND NOW I'M A LITTLE WORRIED...
...I HOPE HE'S OKAY.

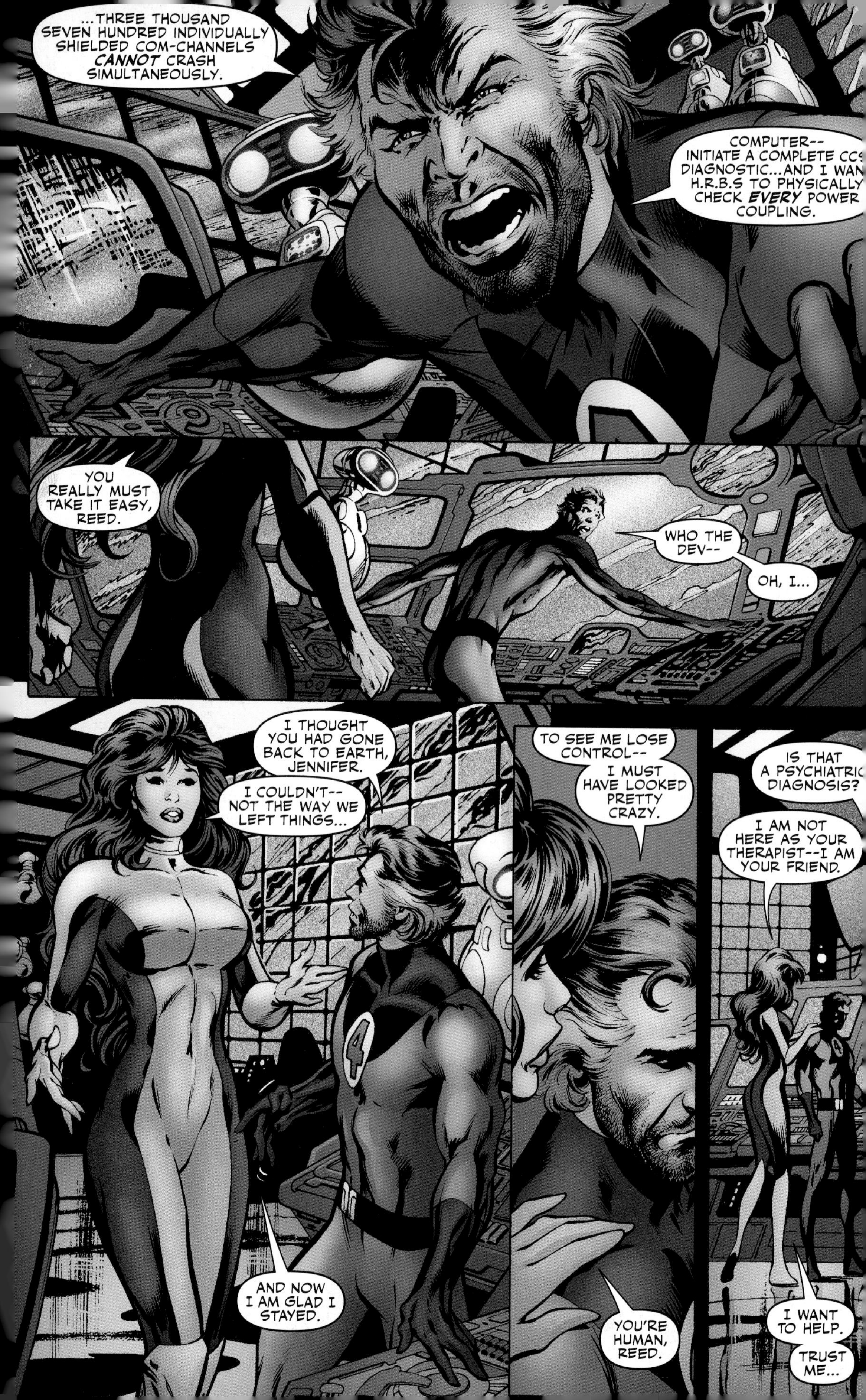
...THREE THOUSAND SEVEN HUNDRED INDIVIDUALLY SHIELDED COM-CHANNELS CANNOT CRASH SIMULTANEOUSLY.
COMPUTER-- INITIATE A COMPLETE CCS DIAGNOSTIC...AND I WANT H.R.B.S TO PHYSICALLY CHECK EVERY POWER COUPLING.
YOU REALLY MUST TAKE IT EASY, REED.
WHO THE DEV--
OH, I...
I THOUGHT YOU HAD GONE BACK TO EARTH, JENNIFER.
I COULDN'T-- NOT THE WAY WE LEFT THINGS...
AND NOW I AM GLAD I STAYED.
TO SEE ME LOSE CONTROL--
I MUST HAVE LOOKED PRETTY CRAZY.
YOU'RE HUMAN, REED.
IS THAT A PSYCHIATRIC DIAGNOSIS?
I AM NOT HERE AS YOUR THERAPIST--I AM YOUR FRIEND.
I WANT TO HELP.
TRUST ME...

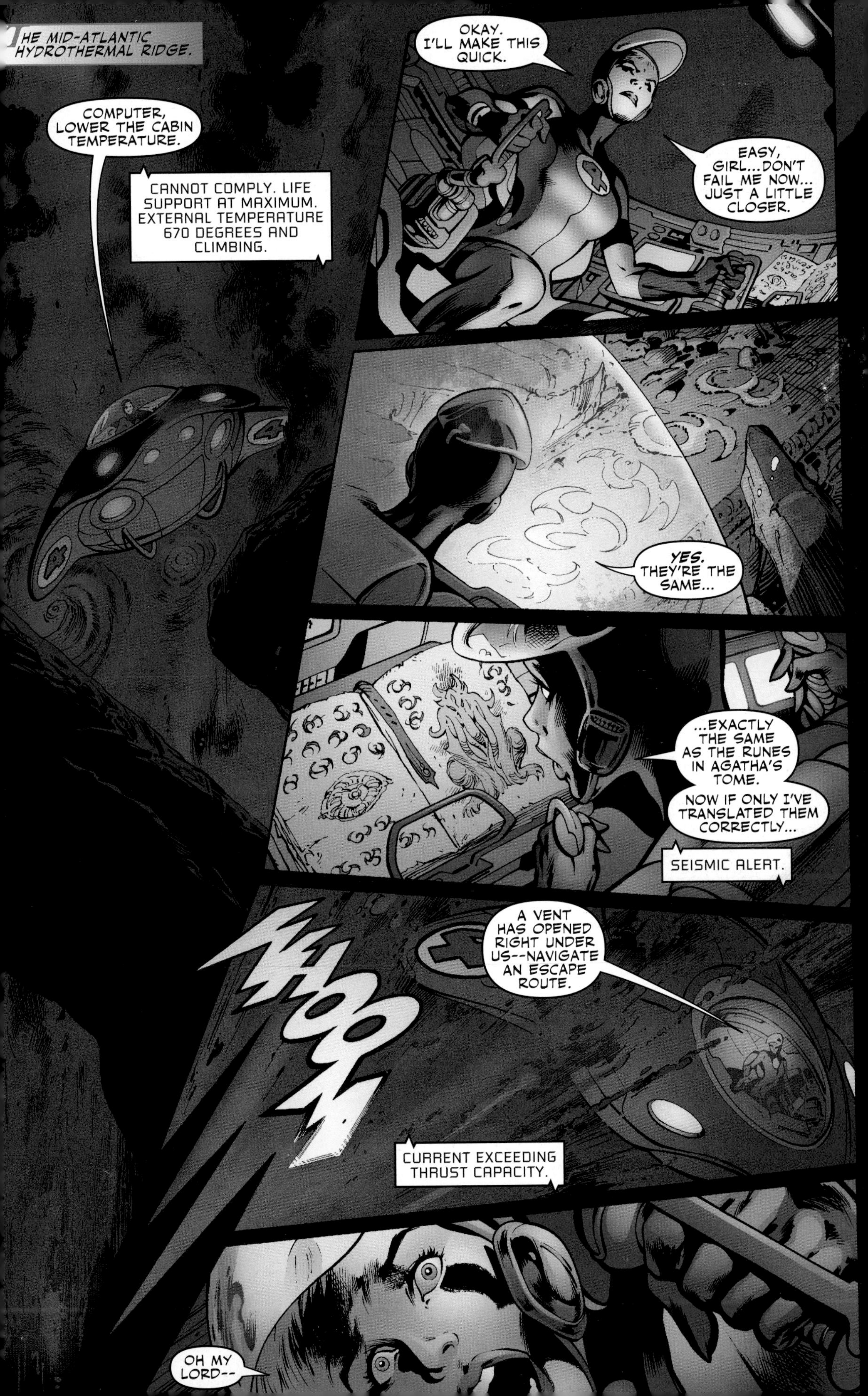
THE MID-ATLANTIC HYDROTHERMAL RIDGE.
COMPUTER, LOWER THE CABIN TEMPERATURE.
CANNOT COMPLY. LIFE SUPPORT AT MAXIMUM. EXTERNAL TEMPERATURE 670 DEGREES AND CLIMBING.
OKAY. I'LL MAKE THIS QUICK.
EASY, GIRL...DON'T FAIL ME NOW... JUST A LITTLE CLOSER.
YES. THEY'RE THE SAME...
...EXACTLY THE SAME AS THE RUNES IN AGATHA'S TOME.
NOW IF ONLY I'VE TRANSLATED THEM CORRECTLY...
SEISMIC ALERT.
WHOOM
A VENT HAS OPENED RIGHT UNDER US--NAVIGATE AN ESCAPE ROUTE.
CURRENT EXCEEDING THRUST CAPACITY.
OH MY LORD--

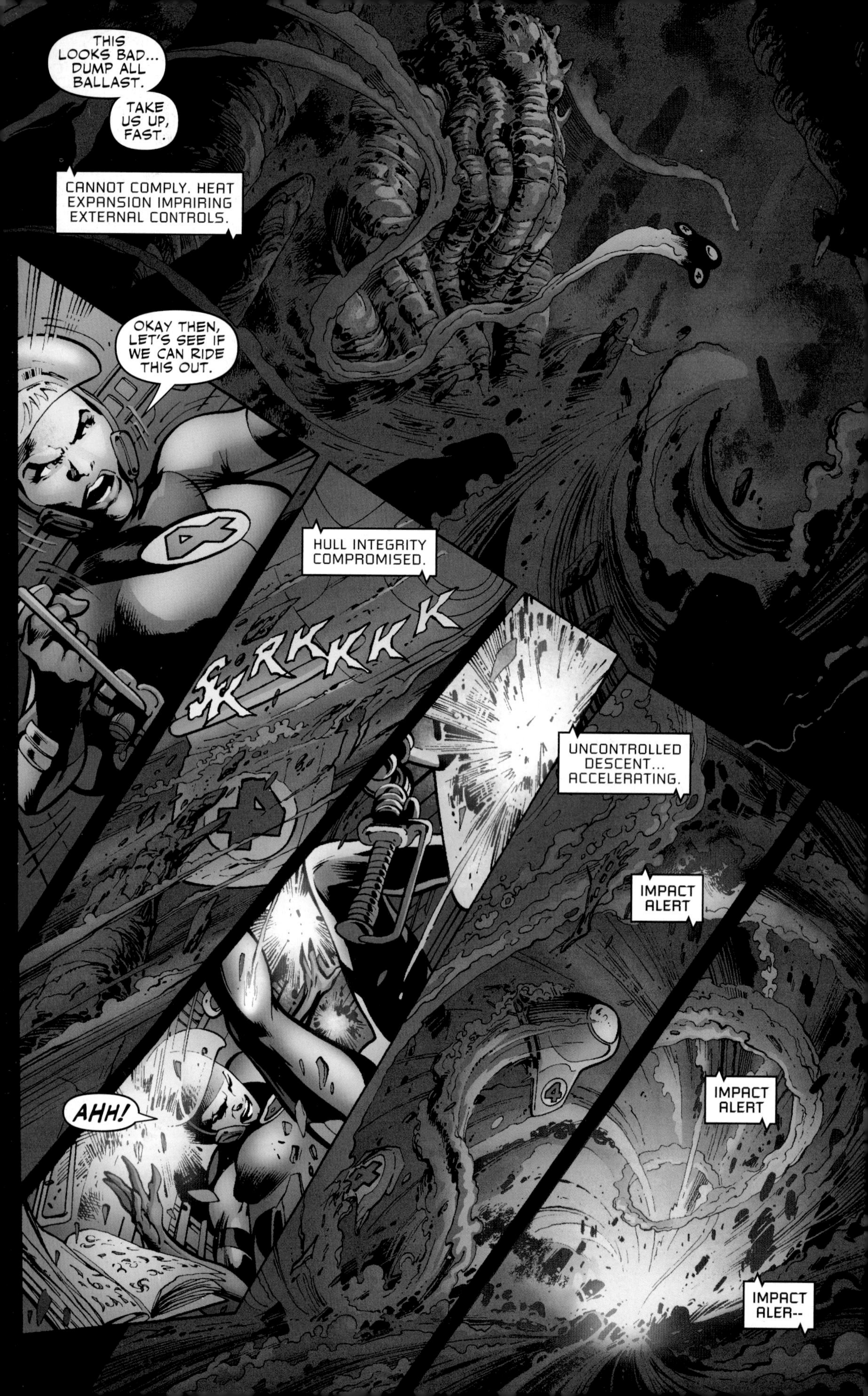
THIS LOOKS BAD... DUMP ALL BALLAST.
TAKE US UP, FAST.
CANNOT COMPLY. HEAT EXPANSION IMPAIRING EXTERNAL CONTROLS.
OKAY THEN, LET'S SEE IF WE CAN RIDE THIS OUT.
HULL INTEGRITY COMPROMISED.
SKRKKKK
UNCONTROLLED DESCENT... ACCELERATING.
IMPACT ALERT
AHH!
IMPACT ALERT
IMPACT ALER--

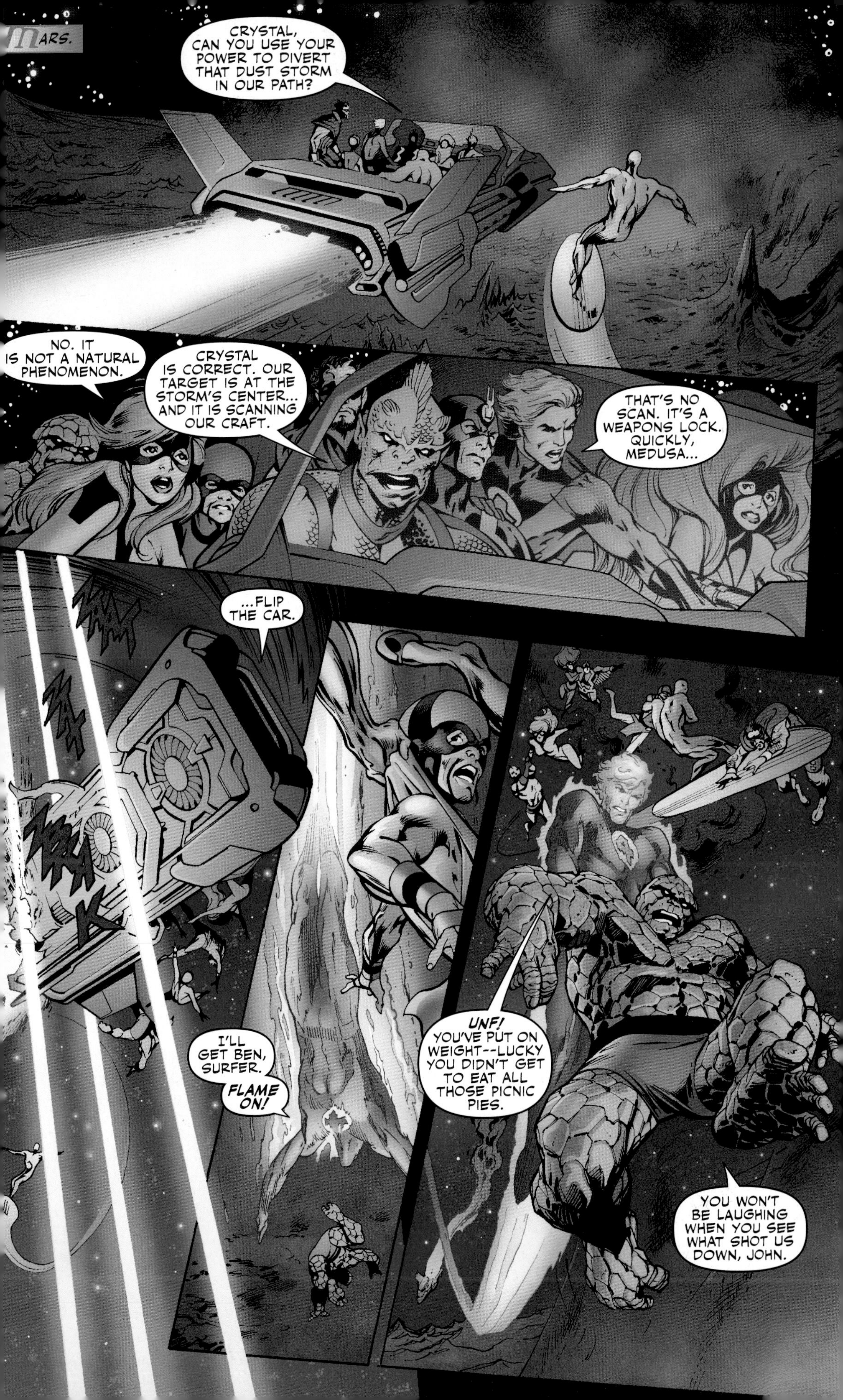
MARS.
CRYSTAL, CAN YOU USE YOUR POWER TO DIVERT THAT DUST STORM IN OUR PATH?
NO. IT IS NOT A NATURAL PHENOMENON.
CRYSTAL IS CORRECT. OUR TARGET IS AT THE STORM'S CENTER... AND IT IS SCANNING OUR CRAFT.
THAT'S NO SCAN. IT'S A WEAPONS LOCK. QUICKLY, MEDUSA...
...FLIP THE CAR.
I'LL GET BEN, SURFER. FLAME ON!
UNF! YOU'VE PUT ON WEIGHT--LUCKY YOU DIDN'T GET TO EAT ALL THOSE PICNIC PIES.
YOU WON'T BE LAUGHING WHEN YOU SEE WHAT SHOT US DOWN, JOHN.

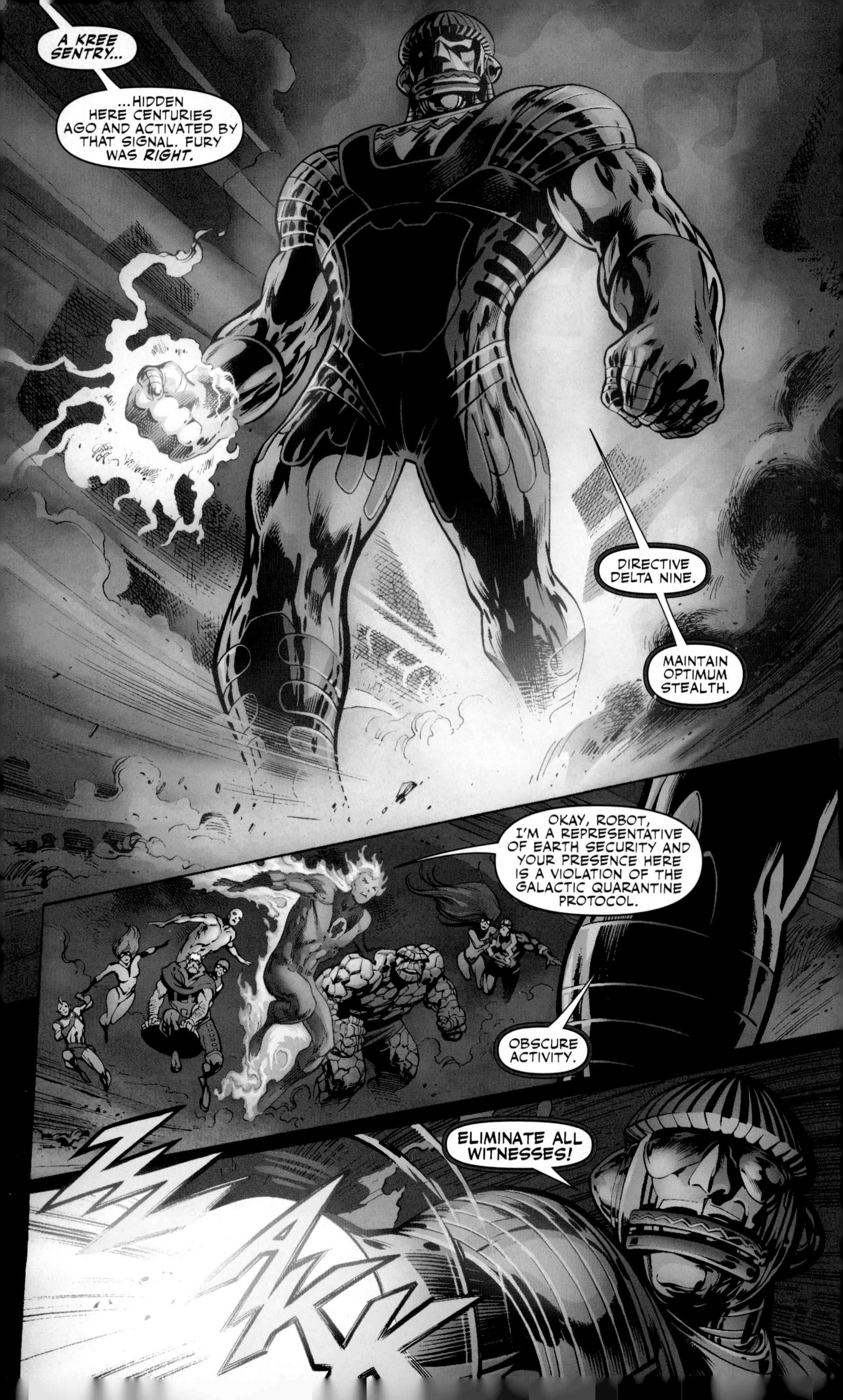
A KREE SENTRY...
...HIDDEN HERE CENTURIES AGO AND ACTIVATED BY THAT SIGNAL. FURY WAS RIGHT.
DIRECTIVE DELTA NINE.
MAINTAIN OPTIMUM STEALTH.
OKAY, ROBOT, I'M A REPRESENTATIVE OF EARTH SECURITY AND YOUR PRESENCE HERE IS A VIOLATION OF THE GALACTIC QUARANTINE PROTOCOL.
OBSCURE ACTIVITY.
ELIMINATE ALL WITNESSES!

D THE END THE END THE END THE EN
E END THE END THE END THE END TH
D THE END THE END THE END THE EN
E END THE END THE END THE END T
D THE END THE END THE END THE E
E END THE END THE END THE END T
D THE END THE END THE END THE E
E END THE END THE END THE END T
HE END THE END THE END THE END T
D THE END THE END THE END THE E
E END THE END THE END THE END T
D THE END THE END THE END THE E
E END THE END THE END THE END T
D THE END THE END THE END THE E
E END THE END THE END THE END
D THE END THE END THE END THE E
E END THE END THE END THE END T
D THE END THE END THE END THE E
E END THE END THE END THE END T
END THE END THE END THE END THE
E END THE END THE END THE END T
END THE END THE END THE END THE

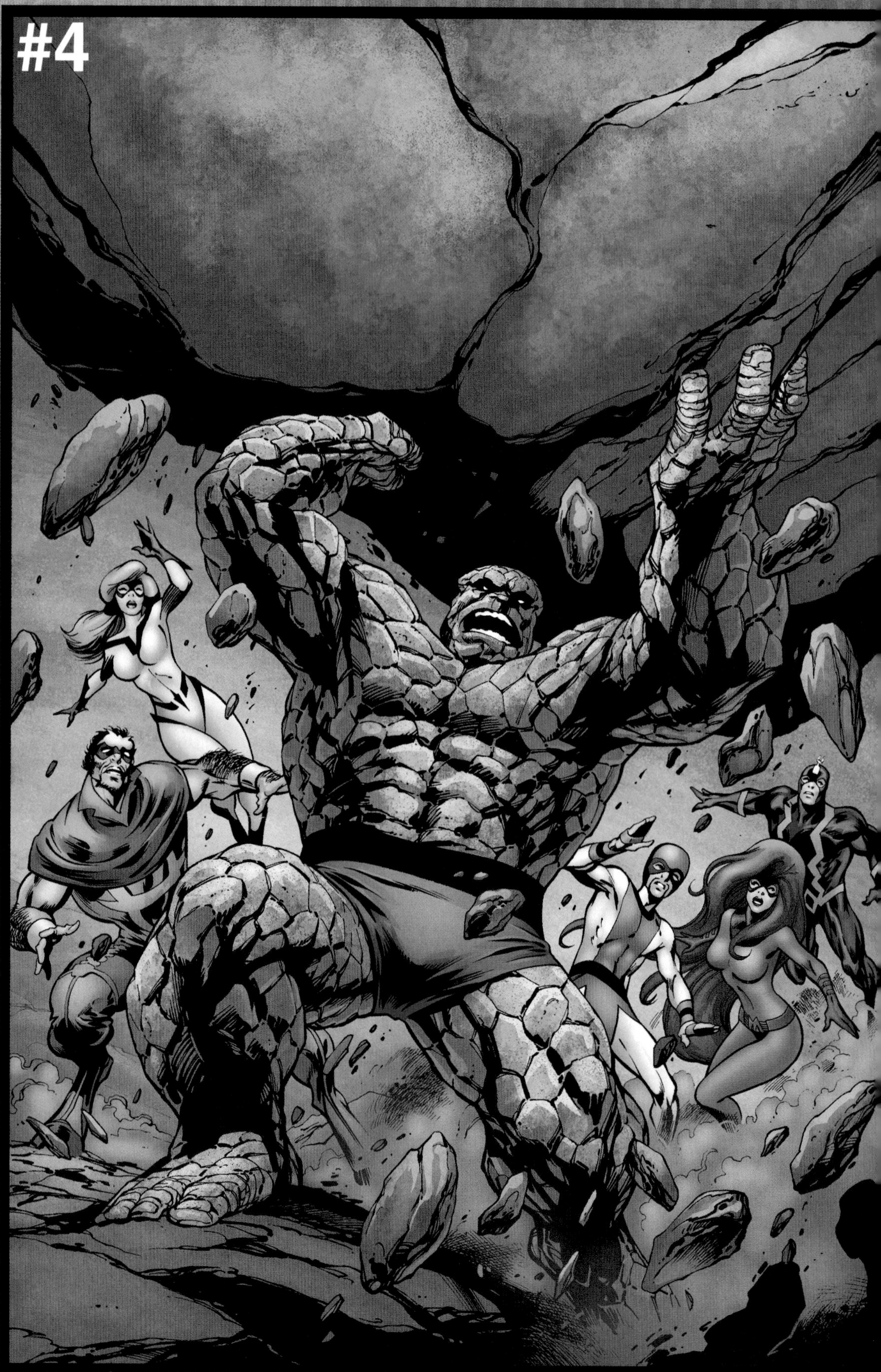
#4

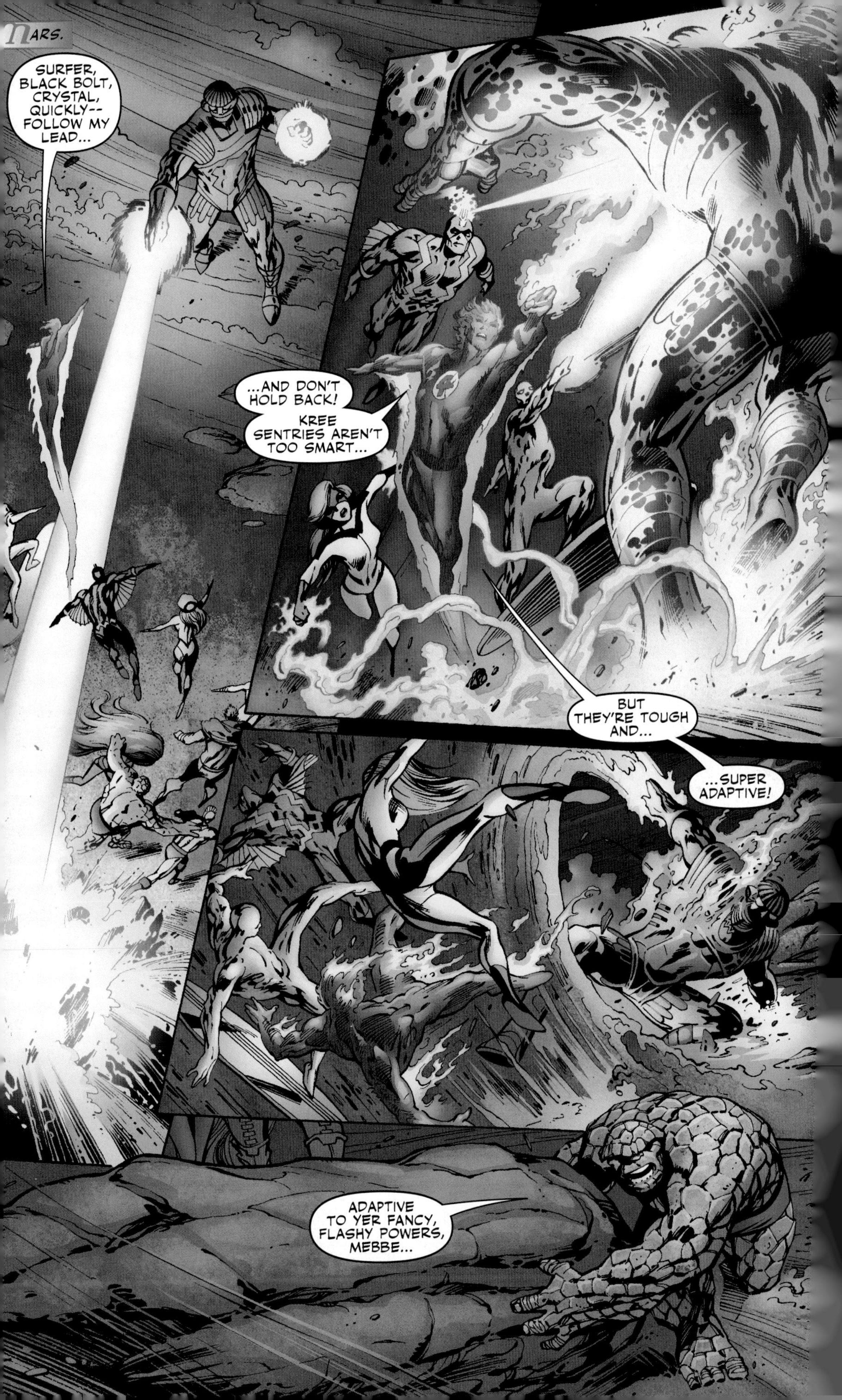
MARS.
SURFER, BLACK BOLT, CRYSTAL, QUICKLY-- FOLLOW MY LEAD...
...AND DON'T HOLD BACK!
KREE SENTRIES AREN'T TOO SMART...
BUT THEY'RE TOUGH AND...
...SUPER ADAPTIVE!
ADAPTIVE TO YER FANCY, FLASHY POWERS, MEBBE...

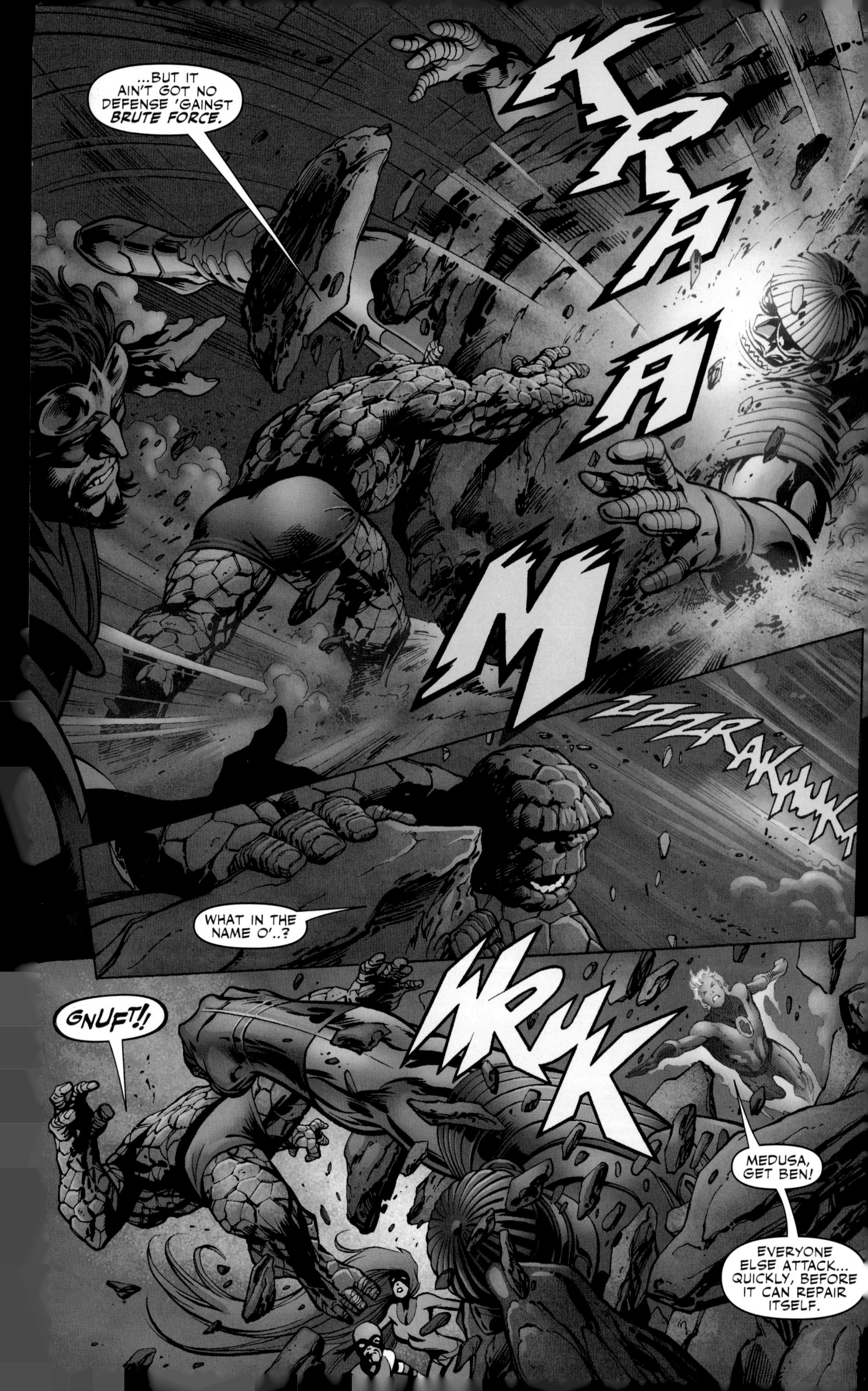

...BUT IT AIN'T GOT NO DEFENSE 'GAINST BRUTE FORCE.
KRRAAM
WHAT IN THE NAME O'..?
GNUFT!!
WRUK
MEDUSA, GET BEN!
EVERYONE ELSE ATTACK... QUICKLY, BEFORE IT CAN REPAIR ITSELF.

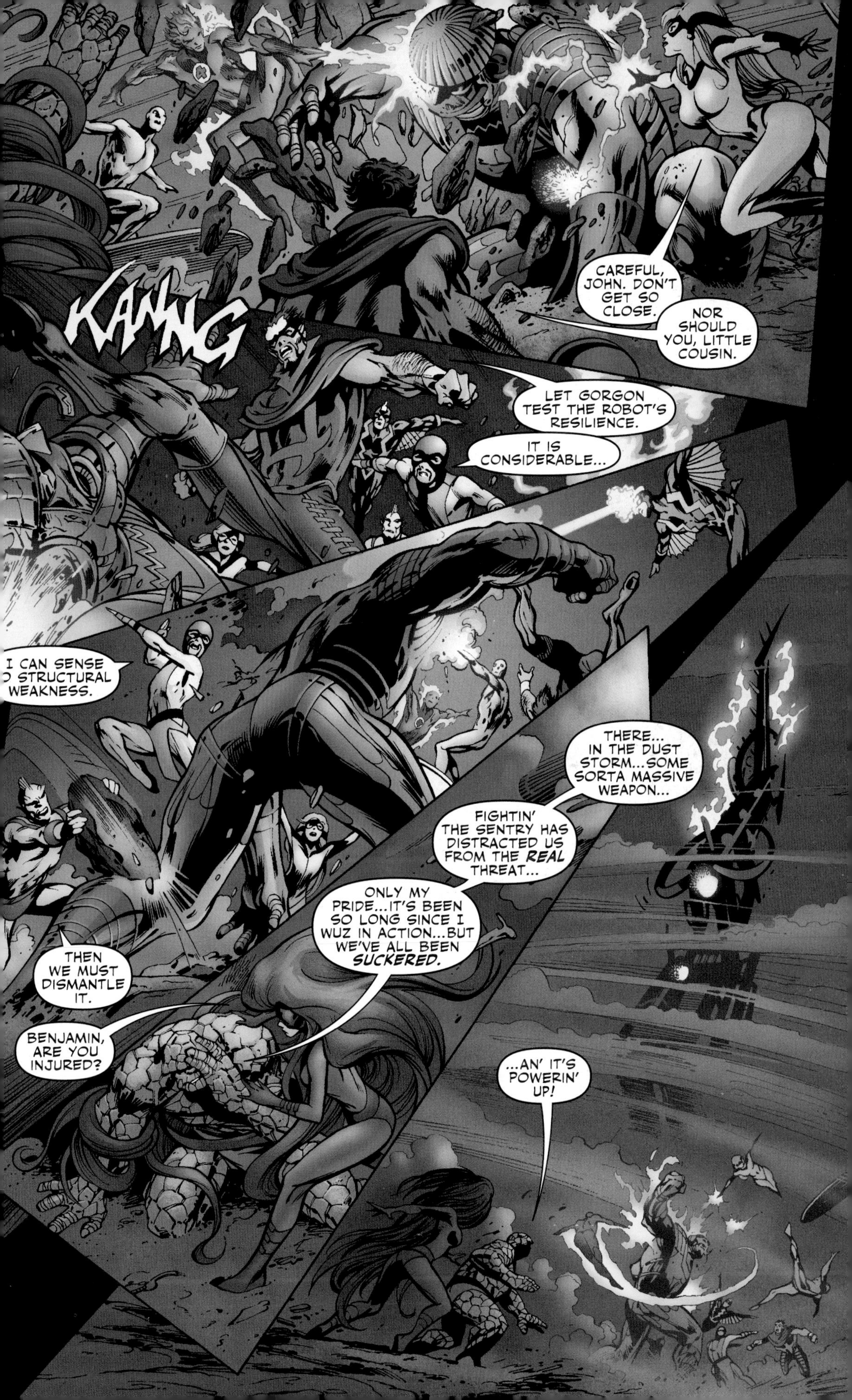
CAREFUL, JOHN. DON'T GET SO CLOSE.
NOR SHOULD YOU, LITTLE COUSIN.
KANNG
LET GORGON TEST THE ROBOT'S RESILIENCE.
IT IS CONSIDERABLE...
I CAN SENSE O STRUCTURAL WEAKNESS.
THEN WE MUST DISMANTLE IT.
BENJAMIN, ARE YOU INJURED?
ONLY MY PRIDE...IT'S BEEN SO LONG SINCE I WUZ IN ACTION...BUT WE'VE ALL BEEN ***SUCKERED.***
FIGHTIN' THE SENTRY HAS DISTRACTED US FROM THE ***REAL*** THREAT...
THERE... IN THE DUST STORM...SOME SORTA MASSIVE WEAPON...
...AN' IT'S POWERIN' UP!

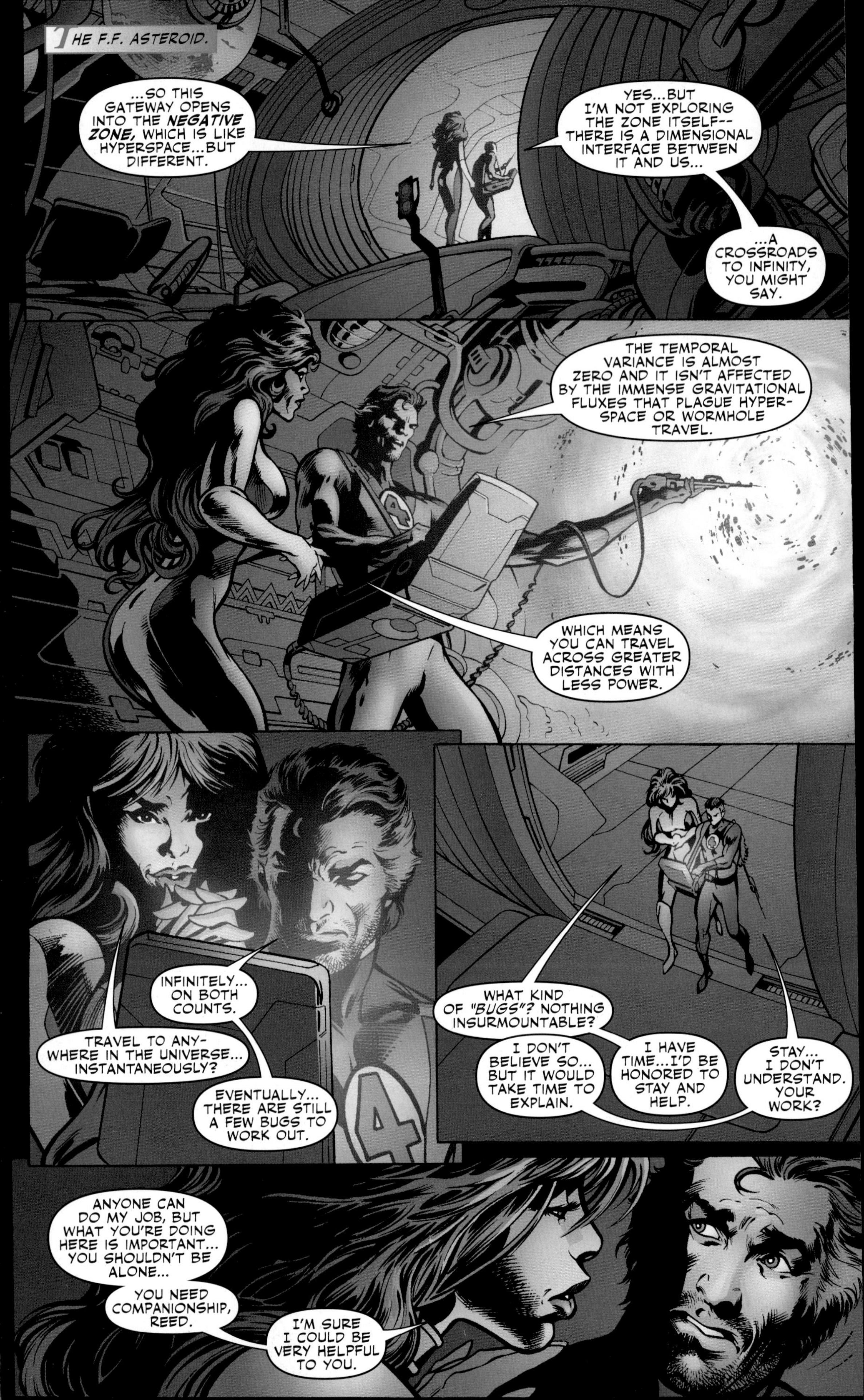
THE F.F. ASTEROID.
...SO THIS GATEWAY OPENS INTO THE NEGATIVE ZONE, WHICH IS LIKE HYPERSPACE...BUT DIFFERENT.
YES...BUT I'M NOT EXPLORING THE ZONE ITSELF-- THERE IS A DIMENSIONAL INTERFACE BETWEEN IT AND US...
...A CROSSROADS TO INFINITY, YOU MIGHT SAY.
THE TEMPORAL VARIANCE IS ALMOST ZERO AND IT ISN'T AFFECTED BY THE IMMENSE GRAVITATIONAL FLUXES THAT PLAGUE HYPER-SPACE OR WORMHOLE TRAVEL.
WHICH MEANS YOU CAN TRAVEL ACROSS GREATER DISTANCES WITH LESS POWER.
TRAVEL TO ANY-WHERE IN THE UNIVERSE... INSTANTANEOUSLY?
INFINITELY... ON BOTH COUNTS.
EVENTUALLY... THERE ARE STILL A FEW BUGS TO WORK OUT.
WHAT KIND OF "BUGS"? NOTHING INSURMOUNTABLE?
I DON'T BELIEVE SO... BUT IT WOULD TAKE TIME TO EXPLAIN.
I HAVE TIME...I'D BE HONORED TO STAY AND HELP.
STAY... I DON'T UNDERSTAND. YOUR WORK?
ANYONE CAN DO MY JOB, BUT WHAT YOU'RE DOING HERE IS IMPORTANT... YOU SHOULDN'T BE ALONE...
YOU NEED COMPANIONSHIP, REED.
I'M SURE I COULD BE VERY HELPFUL TO YOU.

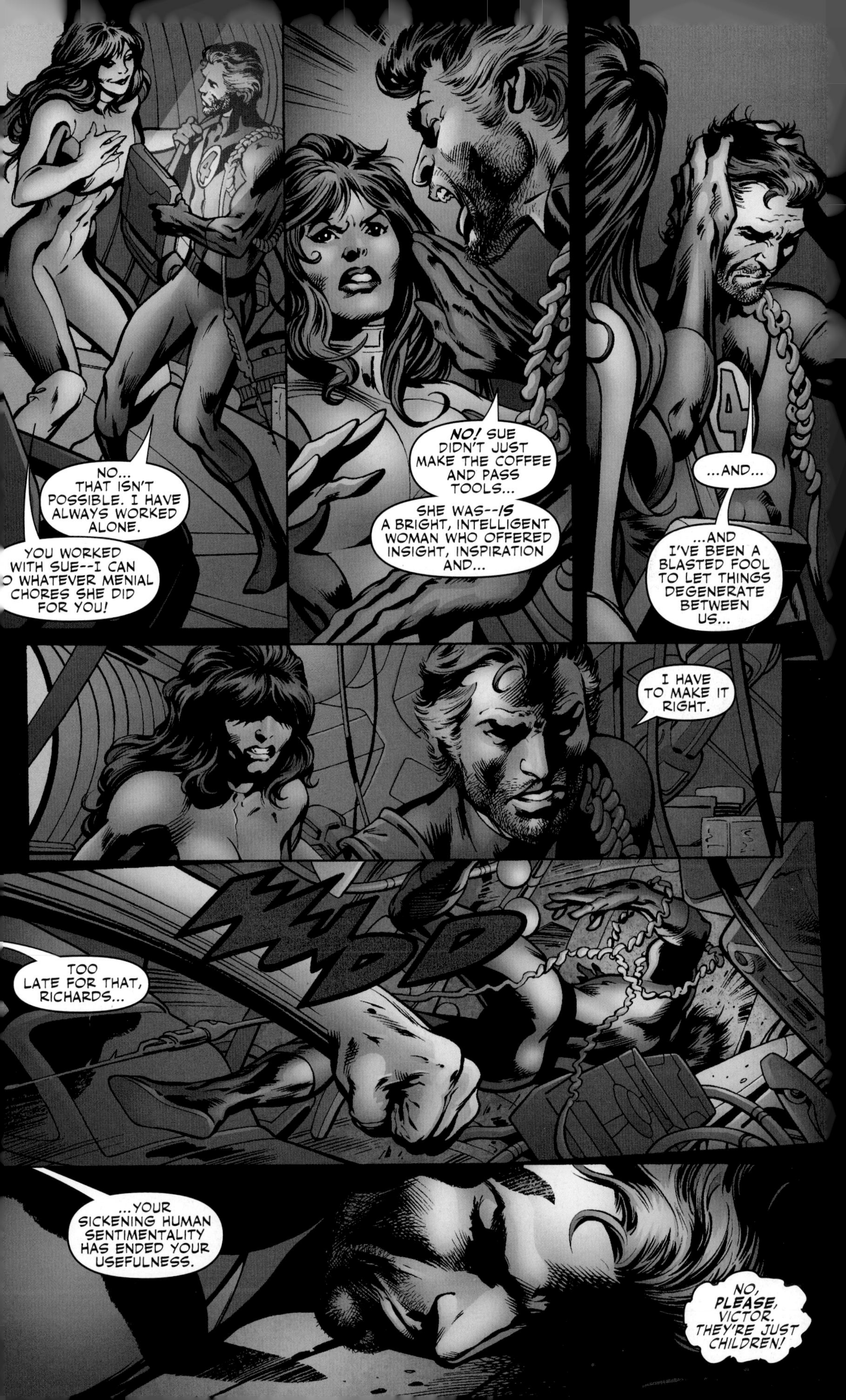
NO... THAT ISN'T POSSIBLE. I HAVE ALWAYS WORKED ALONE.
YOU WORKED WITH SUE--I CAN DO WHATEVER MENIAL CHORES SHE DID FOR YOU!
NO! SUE DIDN'T JUST MAKE THE COFFEE AND PASS TOOLS...
SHE WAS--IS A BRIGHT, INTELLIGENT WOMAN WHO OFFERED INSIGHT, INSPIRATION AND...
...AND...
...AND I'VE BEEN A BLASTED FOOL TO LET THINGS DEGENERATE BETWEEN US...
I HAVE TO MAKE IT RIGHT.
WHDD
TOO LATE FOR THAT, RICHARDS...
...YOUR SICKENING HUMAN SENTIMENTALITY HAS ENDED YOUR USEFULNESS.
NO, PLEASE, VICTOR. THEY'RE JUST CHILDREN!

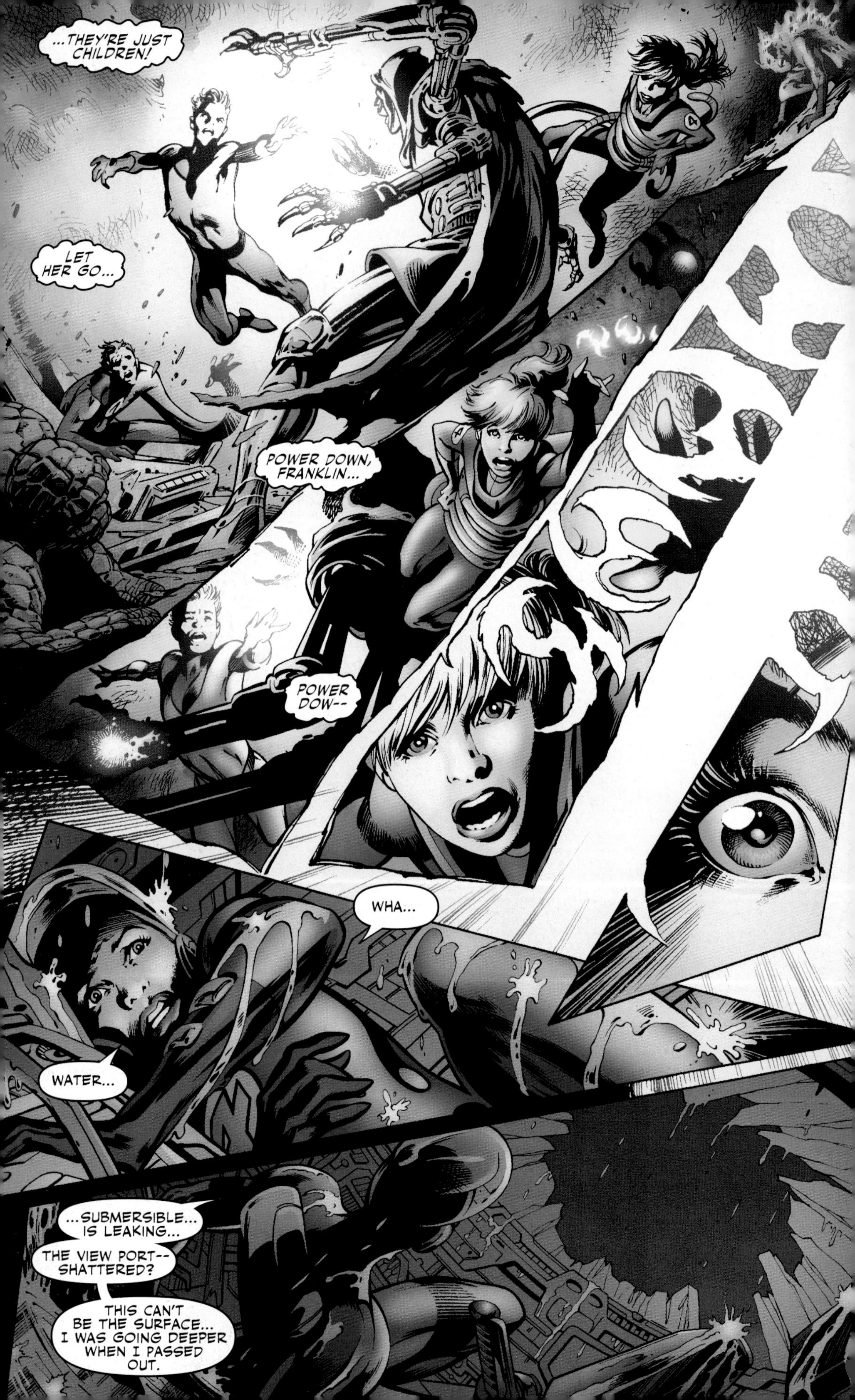
...THEY'RE JUST CHILDREN!
LET HER GO...
POWER DOWN, FRANKLIN...
POWER DOW--
WHA...
WATER...
...SUBMERSIBLE... IS LEAKING...
THE VIEW PORT-- SHATTERED?
THIS CAN'T BE THE SURFACE... I WAS GOING DEEPER WHEN I PASSED OUT.

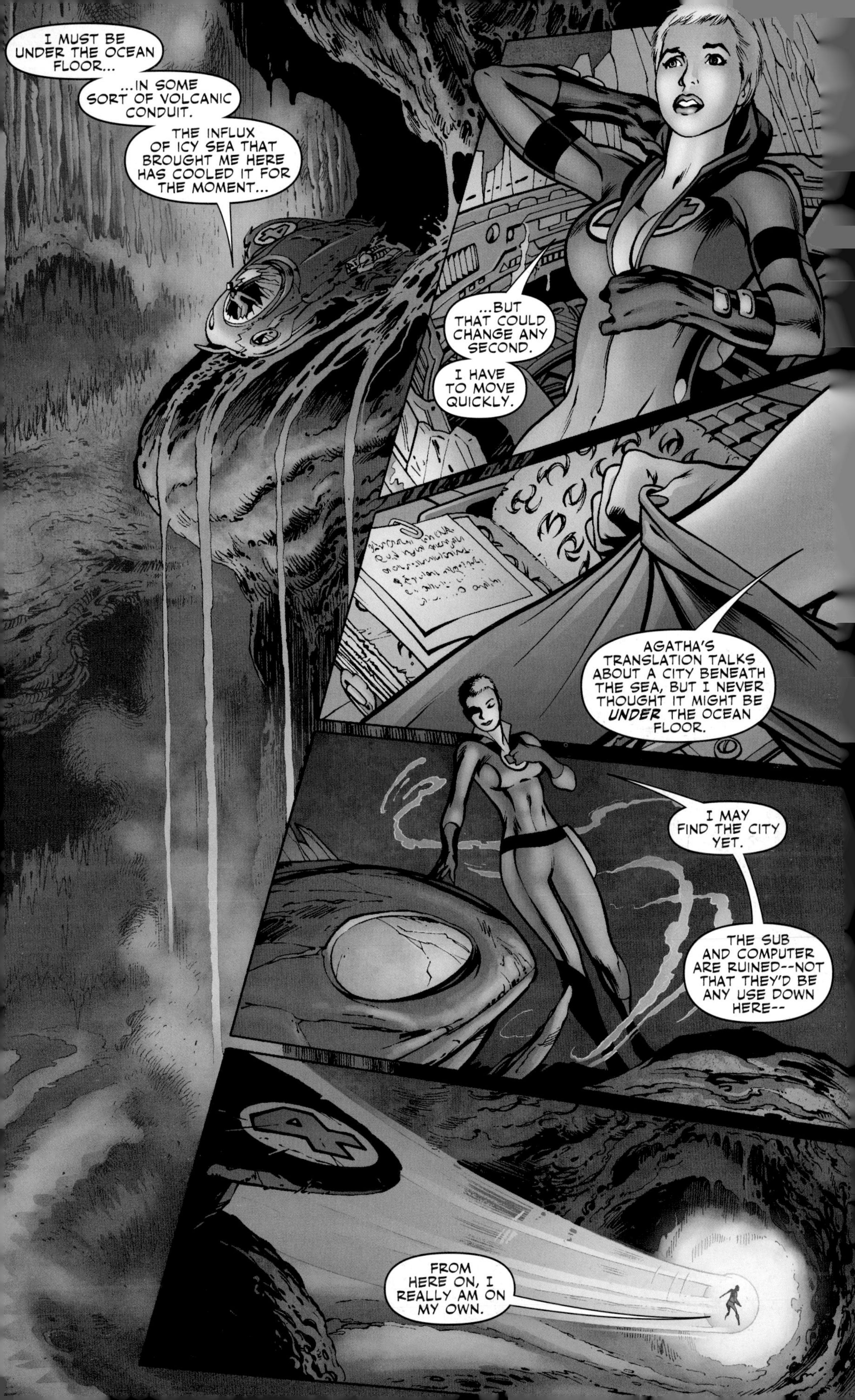

I MUST BE UNDER THE OCEAN FLOOR...
...IN SOME SORT OF VOLCANIC CONDUIT.
THE INFLUX OF ICY SEA THAT BROUGHT ME HERE HAS COOLED IT FOR THE MOMENT...
...BUT THAT COULD CHANGE ANY SECOND.
I HAVE TO MOVE QUICKLY.
AGATHA'S TRANSLATION TALKS ABOUT A CITY BENEATH THE SEA, BUT I NEVER THOUGHT IT MIGHT BE UNDER THE OCEAN FLOOR.
I MAY FIND THE CITY YET.
THE SUB AND COMPUTER ARE RUINED--NOT THAT THEY'D BE ANY USE DOWN HERE--
FROM HERE ON, I REALLY AM ON MY OWN.

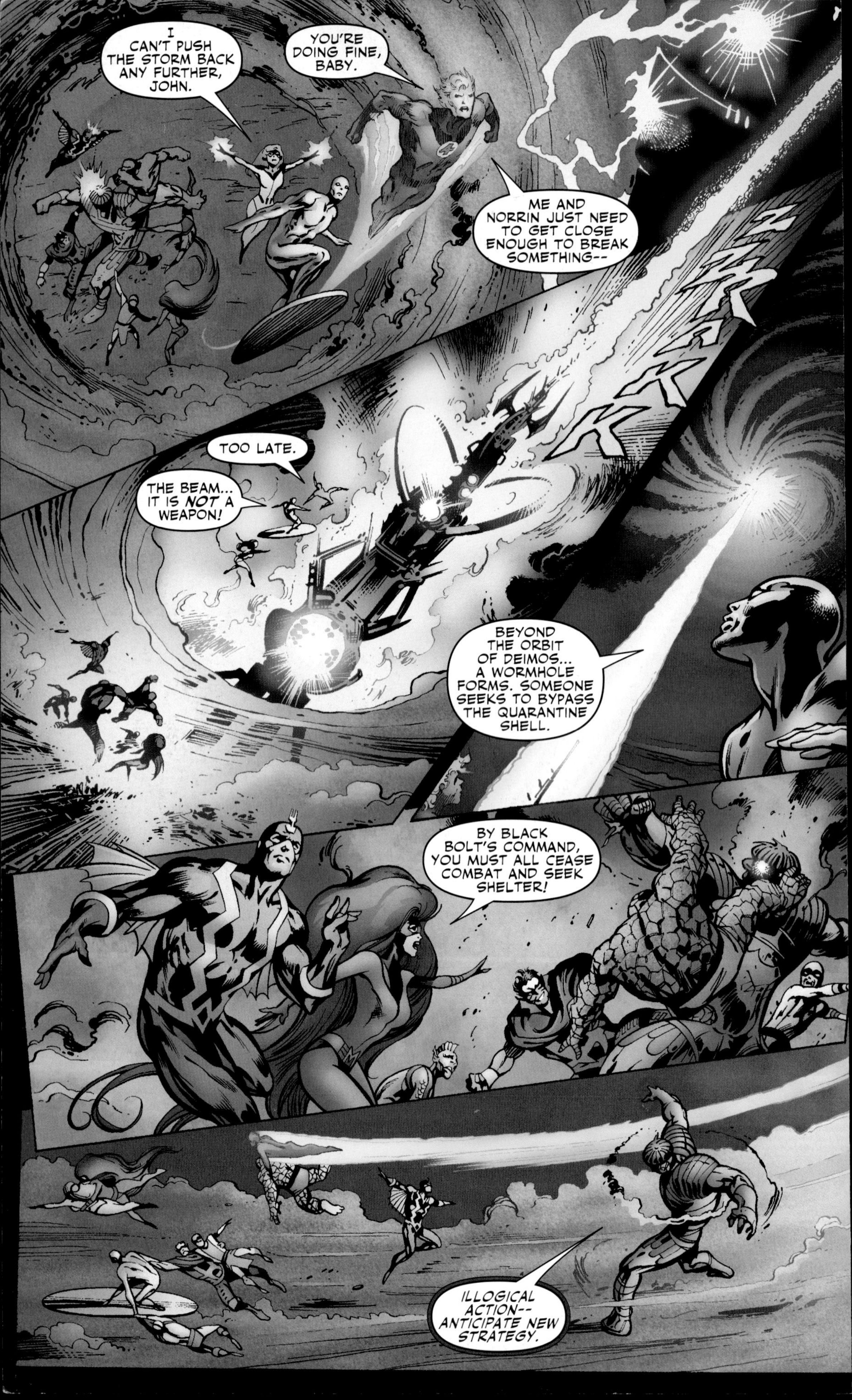

I CAN'T PUSH THE STORM BACK ANY FURTHER, JOHN.
YOU'RE DOING FINE, BABY.
ME AND NORRIN JUST NEED TO GET CLOSE ENOUGH TO BREAK SOMETHING--
KRRRAKK
TOO LATE.
THE BEAM... IT IS NOT A WEAPON!
BEYOND THE ORBIT OF DEIMOS... A WORMHOLE FORMS. SOMEONE SEEKS TO BYPASS THE QUARANTINE SHELL.
BY BLACK BOLT'S COMMAND, YOU MUST ALL CEASE COMBAT AND SEEK SHELTER!
ILLOGICAL ACTION-- ANTICIPATE NEW STRATEGY.

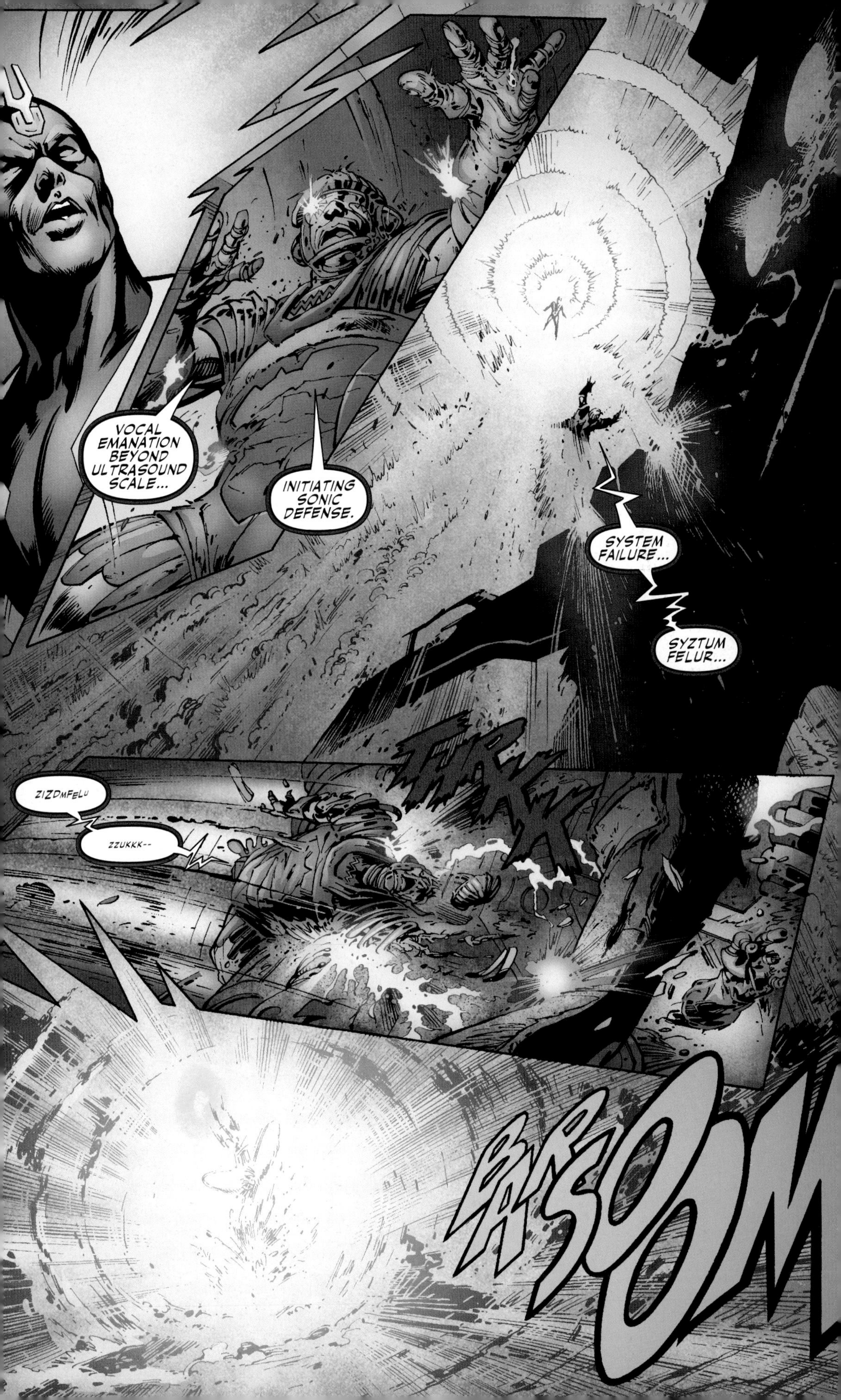
VOCAL EMANATION BEYOND ULTRASOUND SCALE...
INITIATING SONIC DEFENSE.
SYSTEM FAILURE...
SYZTUM FELUR...
FIRKK
ZIZDMFELU
ZZUKKK--
BRASOOM

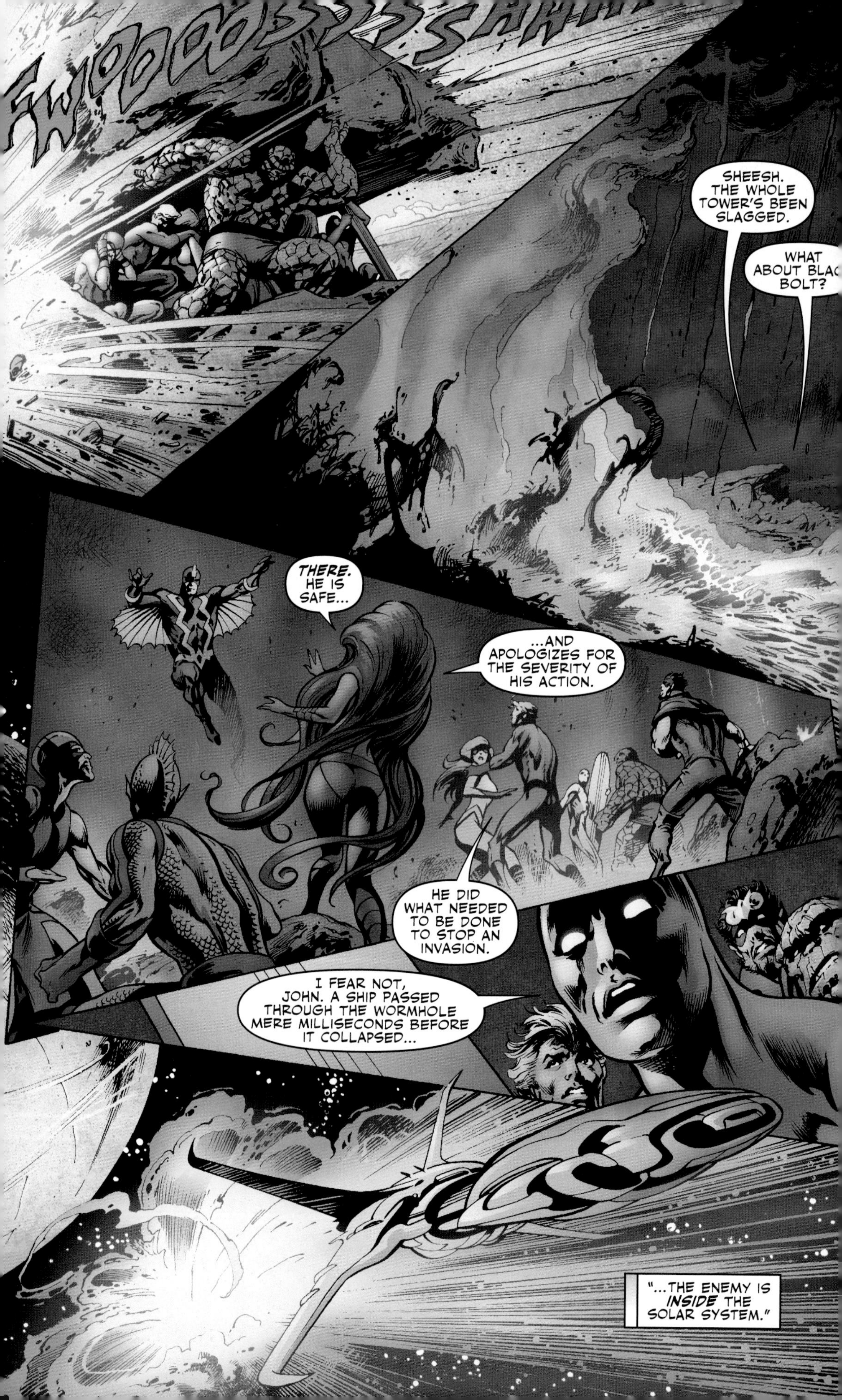
FWOOOSSHHH
SHEESH. THE WHOLE TOWER'S BEEN SLAGGED.
WHAT ABOUT BLAC BOLT?
THERE. HE IS SAFE...
...AND APOLOGIZES FOR THE SEVERITY OF HIS ACTION.
HE DID WHAT NEEDED TO BE DONE TO STOP AN INVASION.
I FEAR NOT, JOHN. A SHIP PASSED THROUGH THE WORMHOLE MERE MILLISECONDS BEFORE IT COLLAPSED...
"...THE ENEMY IS INSIDE THE SOLAR SYSTEM."

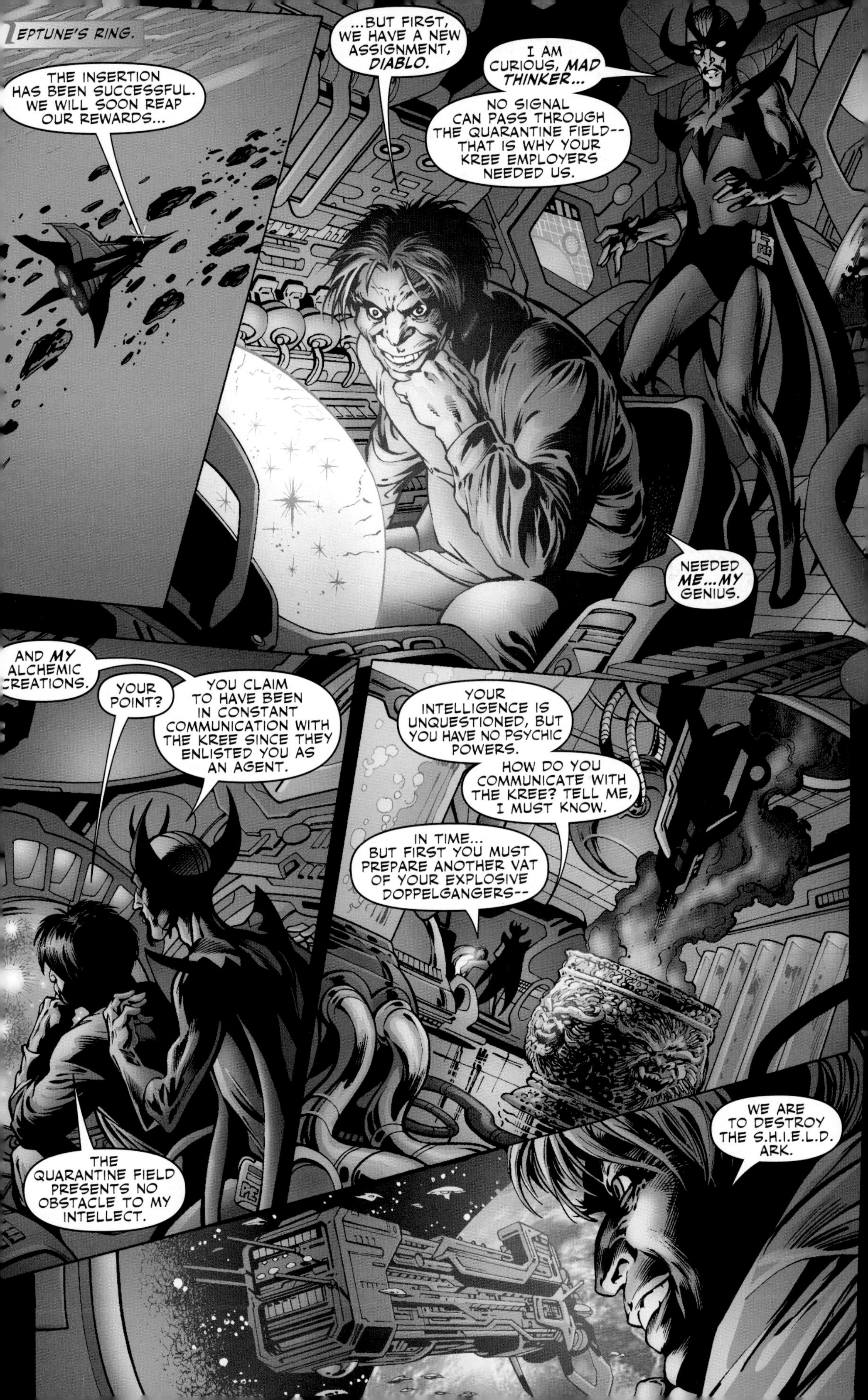
EPTUNE'S RING.
THE INSERTION HAS BEEN SUCCESSFUL. WE WILL SOON REAP OUR REWARDS...
...BUT FIRST, WE HAVE A NEW ASSIGNMENT, DIABLO.
I AM CURIOUS, MAD THINKER...
NO SIGNAL CAN PASS THROUGH THE QUARANTINE FIELD-- THAT IS WHY YOUR KREE EMPLOYERS NEEDED US.
NEEDED ME...MY GENIUS.
AND MY ALCHEMIC CREATIONS.
YOUR POINT?
YOU CLAIM TO HAVE BEEN IN CONSTANT COMMUNICATION WITH THE KREE SINCE THEY ENLISTED YOU AS AN AGENT.
THE QUARANTINE FIELD PRESENTS NO OBSTACLE TO MY INTELLECT.
YOUR INTELLIGENCE IS UNQUESTIONED, BUT YOU HAVE NO PSYCHIC POWERS.
HOW DO YOU COMMUNICATE WITH THE KREE? TELL ME, I MUST KNOW.
IN TIME... BUT FIRST YOU MUST PREPARE ANOTHER VAT OF YOUR EXPLOSIVE DOPPELGANGERS--
WE ARE TO DESTROY THE S.H.I.E.L.D. ARK.

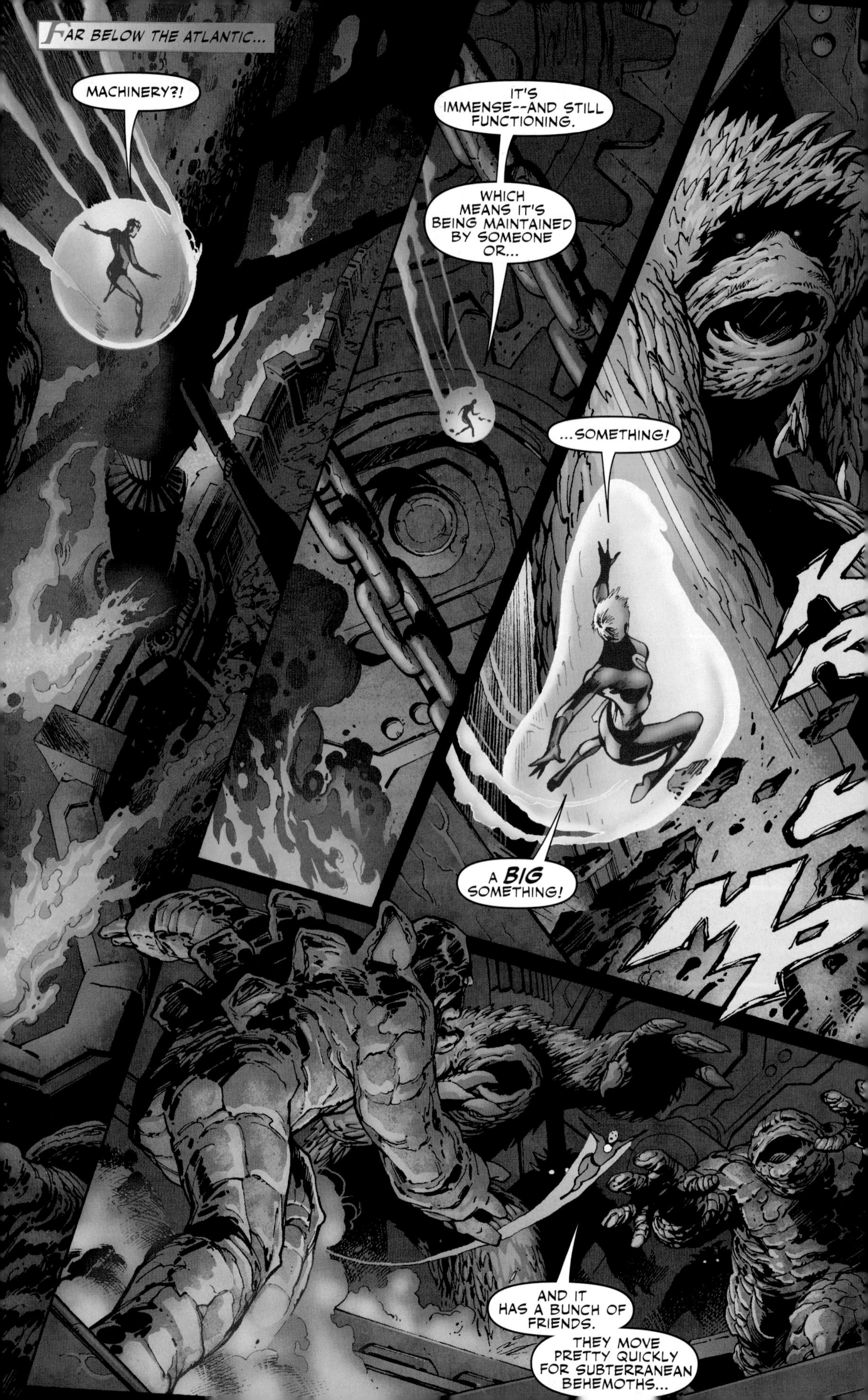
FAR BELOW THE ATLANTIC...
MACHINERY?!
IT'S IMMENSE--AND STILL FUNCTIONING.
WHICH MEANS IT'S BEING MAINTAINED BY SOMEONE OR...
...SOMETHING!
A BIG SOMETHING!
AND IT HAS A BUNCH OF FRIENDS.
THEY MOVE PRETTY QUICKLY FOR SUBTERRANEAN BEHEMOTHS...

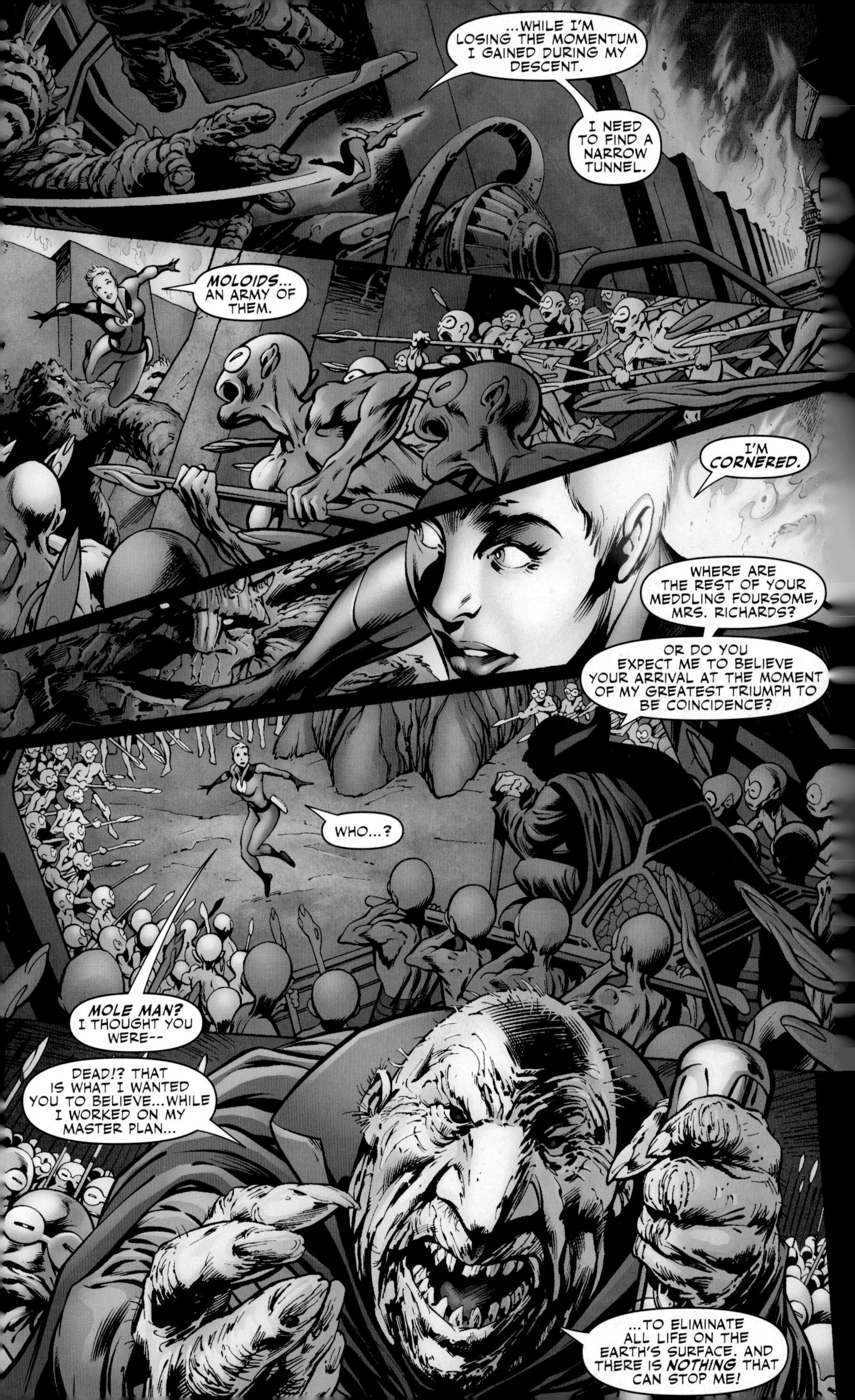
...WHILE I'M LOSING THE MOMENTUM I GAINED DURING MY DESCENT.
I NEED TO FIND A NARROW TUNNEL.
MOLOIDS... AN ARMY OF THEM.
I'M CORNERED.
WHERE ARE THE REST OF YOUR MEDDLING FOURSOME, MRS. RICHARDS?
OR DO YOU EXPECT ME TO BELIEVE YOUR ARRIVAL AT THE MOMENT OF MY GREATEST TRIUMPH TO BE COINCIDENCE?
WHO...?
MOLE MAN? I THOUGHT YOU WERE--
DEAD!? THAT IS WHAT I WANTED YOU TO BELIEVE...WHILE I WORKED ON MY MASTER PLAN...
...TO ELIMINATE ALL LIFE ON THE EARTH'S SURFACE. AND THERE IS NOTHING THAT CAN STOP ME!

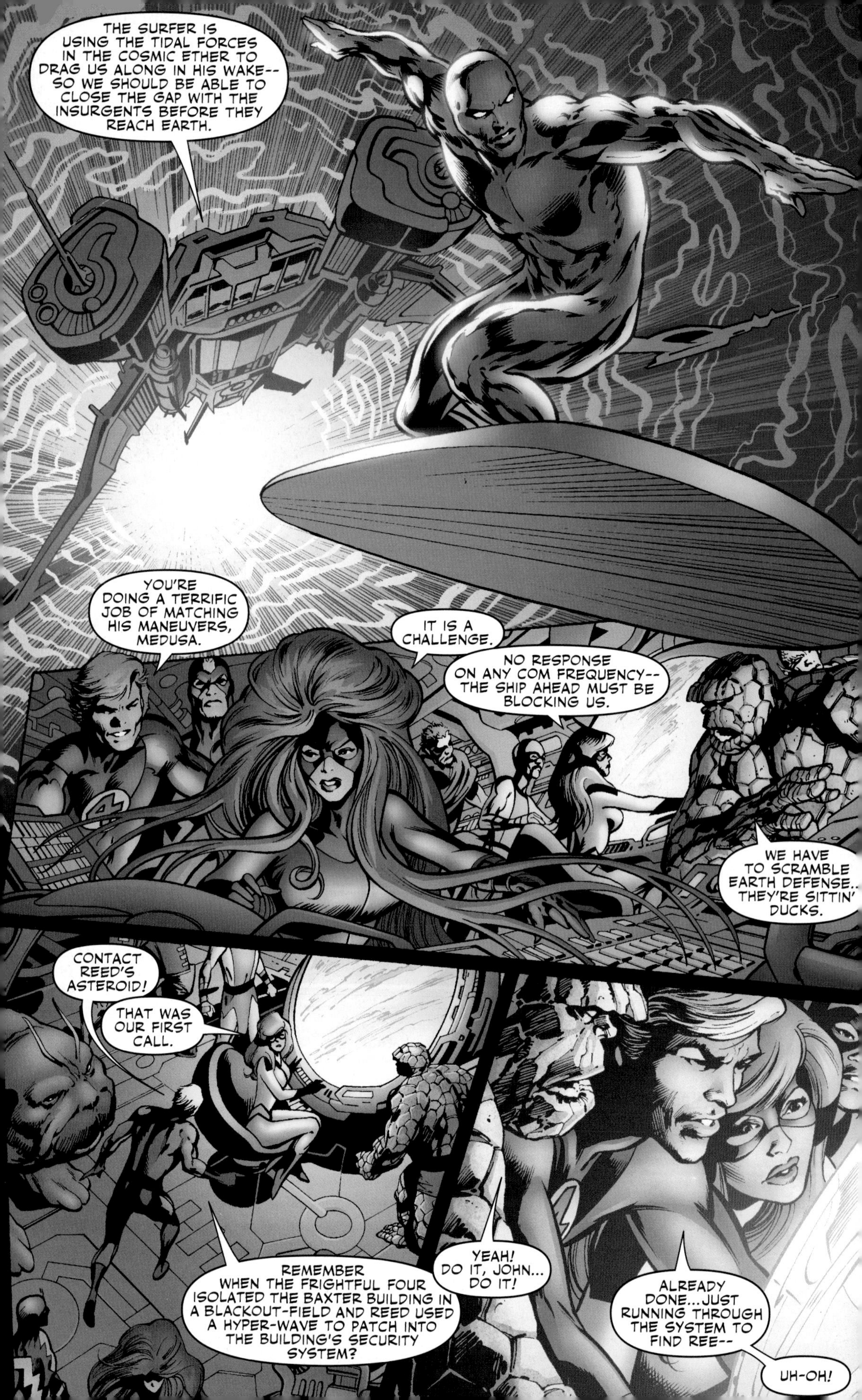
THE SURFER IS USING THE TIDAL FORCES IN THE COSMIC ETHER TO DRAG US ALONG IN HIS WAKE-- SO WE SHOULD BE ABLE TO CLOSE THE GAP WITH THE INSURGENTS BEFORE THEY REACH EARTH.
YOU'RE DOING A TERRIFIC JOB OF MATCHING HIS MANEUVERS, MEDUSA.
IT IS A CHALLENGE.
NO RESPONSE ON ANY COM FREQUENCY-- THE SHIP AHEAD MUST BE BLOCKING US.
WE HAVE TO SCRAMBLE EARTH DEFENSE.. THEY'RE SITTIN' DUCKS.
CONTACT REED'S ASTEROID!
THAT WAS OUR FIRST CALL.
REMEMBER WHEN THE FRIGHTFUL FOUR ISOLATED THE BAXTER BUILDING IN A BLACKOUT-FIELD AND REED USED A HYPER-WAVE TO PATCH INTO THE BUILDING'S SECURITY SYSTEM?
YEAH! DO IT, JOHN... DO IT!
ALREADY DONE...JUST RUNNING THROUGH THE SYSTEM TO FIND REE--
UH-OH!

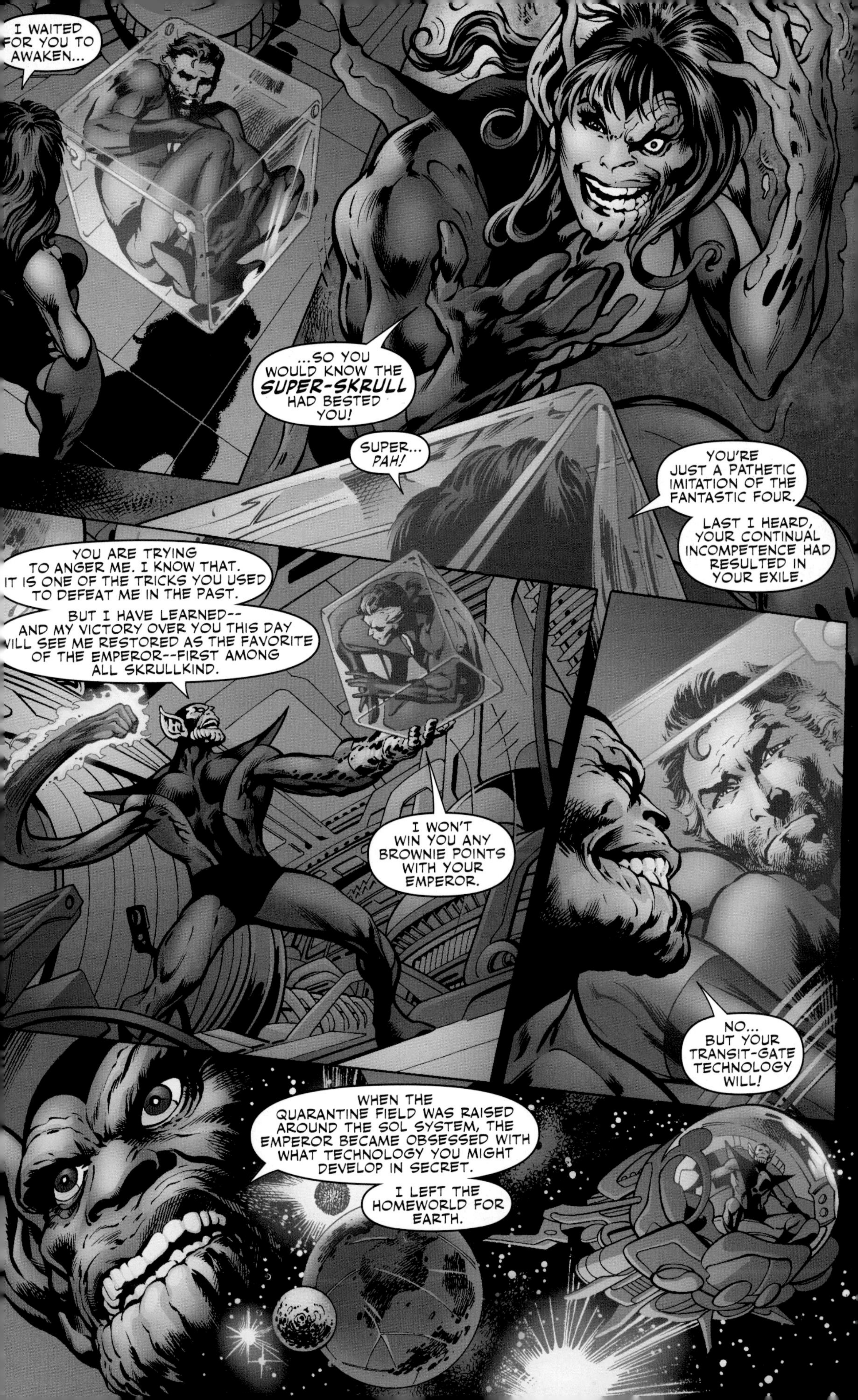
I WAITED FOR YOU TO AWAKEN...
...SO YOU WOULD KNOW THE SUPER-SKRULL HAD BESTED YOU!
SUPER... PAH!
YOU'RE JUST A PATHETIC IMITATION OF THE FANTASTIC FOUR.
LAST I HEARD, YOUR CONTINUAL INCOMPETENCE HAD RESULTED IN YOUR EXILE.
YOU ARE TRYING TO ANGER ME. I KNOW THAT. IT IS ONE OF THE TRICKS YOU USED TO DEFEAT ME IN THE PAST.
BUT I HAVE LEARNED-- AND MY VICTORY OVER YOU THIS DAY WILL SEE ME RESTORED AS THE FAVORITE OF THE EMPEROR--FIRST AMONG ALL SKRULLKIND.
I WON'T WIN YOU ANY BROWNIE POINTS WITH YOUR EMPEROR.
NO... BUT YOUR TRANSIT-GATE TECHNOLOGY WILL!
WHEN THE QUARANTINE FIELD WAS RAISED AROUND THE SOL SYSTEM, THE EMPEROR BECAME OBSESSED WITH WHAT TECHNOLOGY YOU MIGHT DEVELOP IN SECRET.
I LEFT THE HOMEWORLD FOR EARTH.

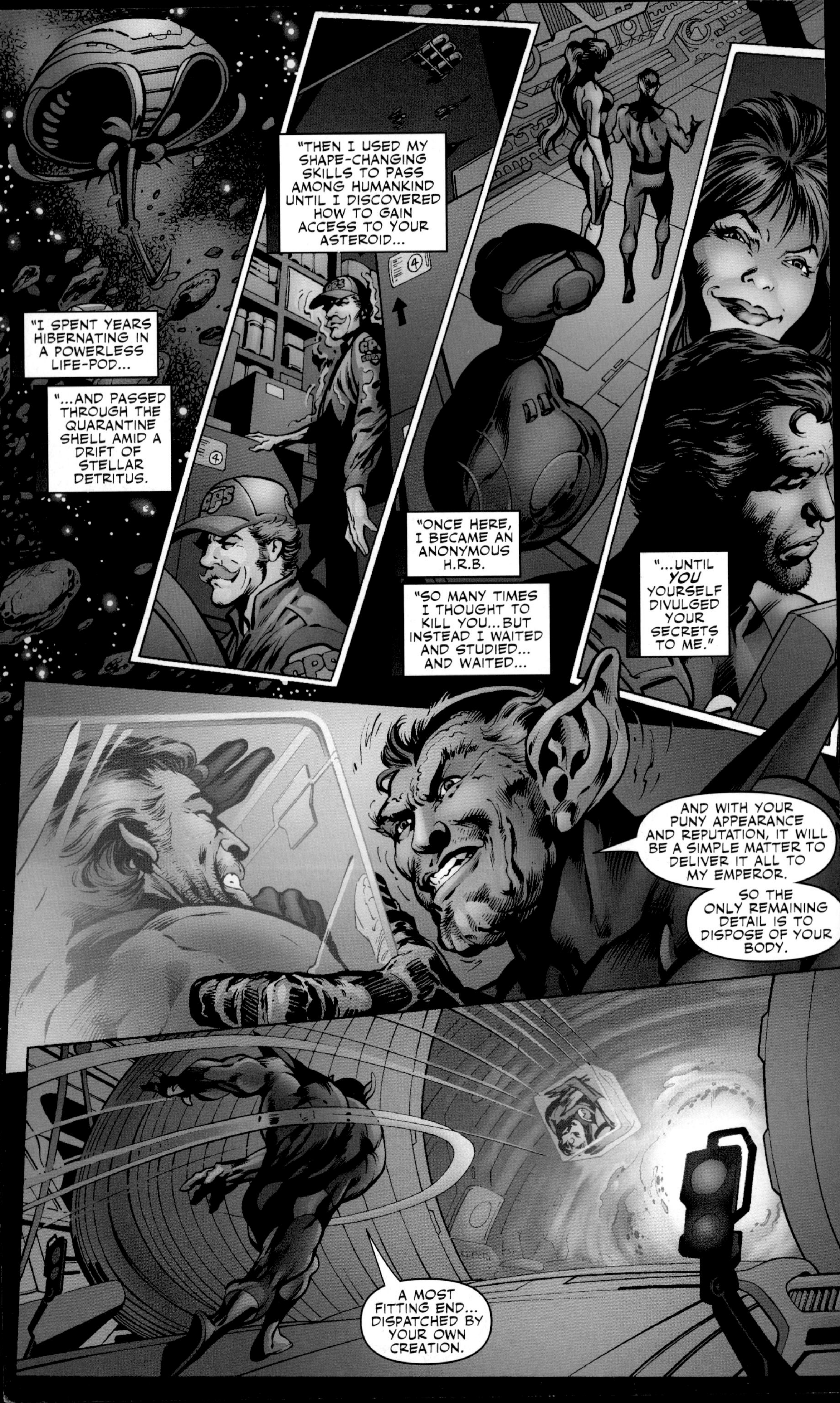
"I SPENT YEARS HIBERNATING IN A POWERLESS LIFE-POD...
"...AND PASSED THROUGH THE QUARANTINE SHELL AMID A DRIFT OF STELLAR DETRITUS.
"THEN I USED MY SHAPE-CHANGING SKILLS TO PASS AMONG HUMANKIND UNTIL I DISCOVERED HOW TO GAIN ACCESS TO YOUR ASTEROID...
"ONCE HERE, I BECAME AN ANONYMOUS H.R.B.
"SO MANY TIMES I THOUGHT TO KILL YOU...BUT INSTEAD I WAITED AND STUDIED... AND WAITED...
"...UNTIL *YOU* YOURSELF DIVULGED YOUR SECRETS TO ME."
AND WITH YOUR PUNY APPEARANCE AND REPUTATION, IT WILL BE A SIMPLE MATTER TO DELIVER IT ALL TO MY EMPEROR.
SO THE ONLY REMAINING DETAIL IS TO DISPOSE OF YOUR BODY.
A MOST FITTING END... DISPATCHED BY YOUR OWN CREATION.

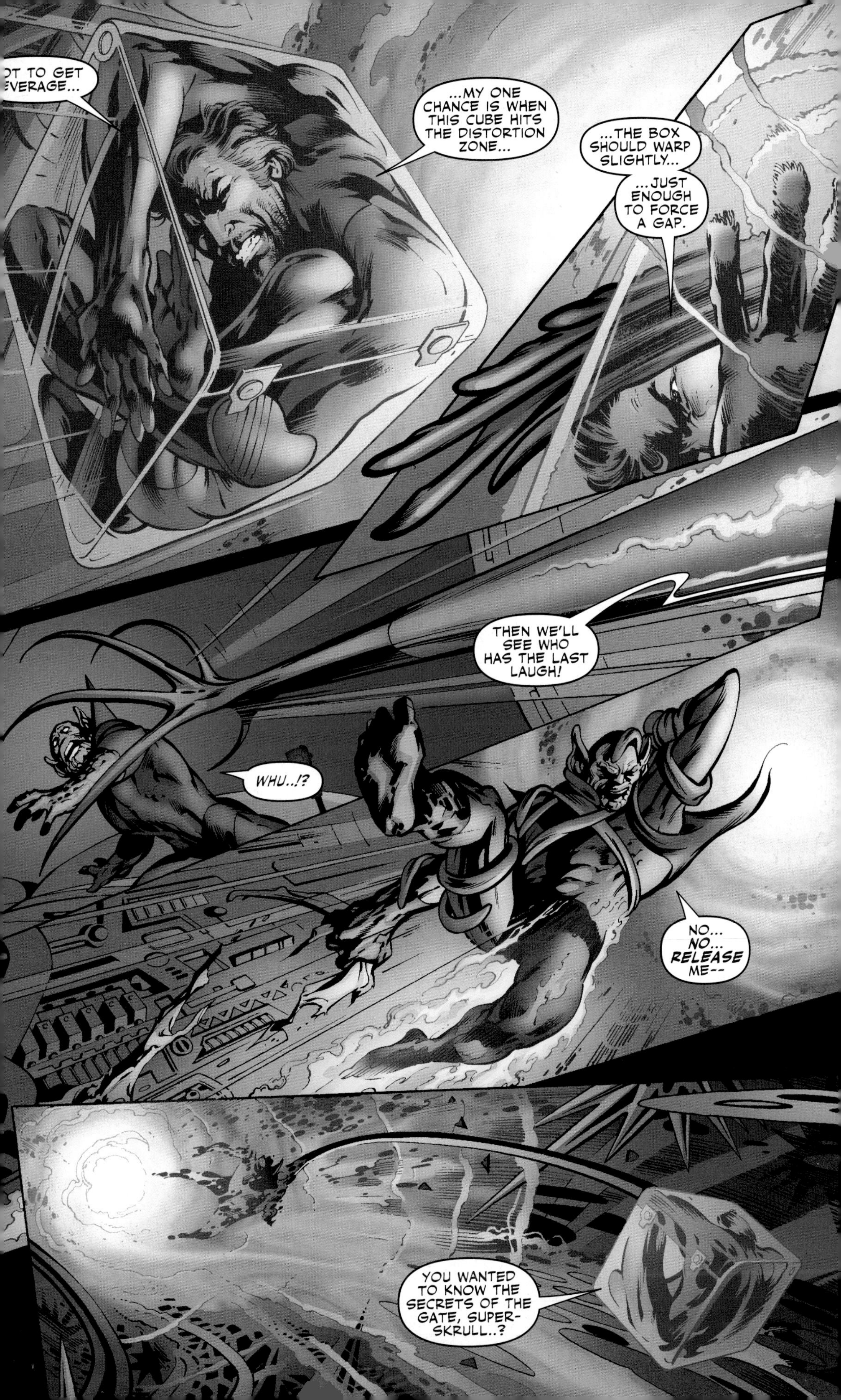

OT TO GET
EVERAGE...
...MY ONE CHANCE IS WHEN THIS CUBE HITS THE DISTORTION ZONE...
...THE BOX SHOULD WARP SLIGHTLY...
...JUST ENOUGH TO FORCE A GAP.
THEN WE'LL SEE WHO HAS THE LAST LAUGH!
WHU..!?
NO... NO... RELEASE ME--
YOU WANTED TO KNOW THE SECRETS OF THE GATE, SUPER-SKRULL..?

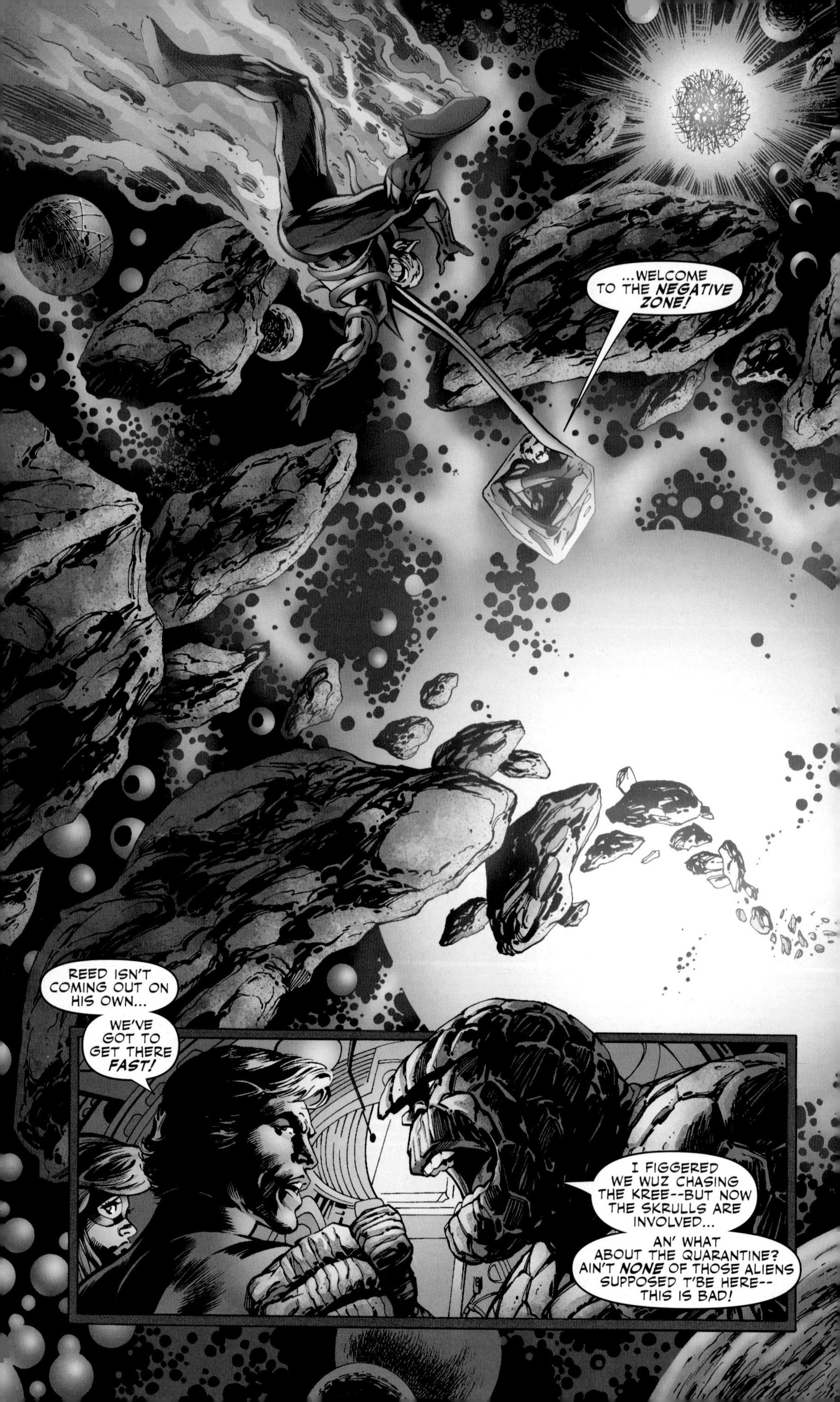
...WELCOME TO THE *NEGATIVE ZONE!*
REED ISN'T COMING OUT ON HIS OWN...
WE'VE GOT TO GET THERE *FAST!*
I FIGGERED WE WUZ CHASING THE KREE--BUT NOW THE SKRULLS ARE INVOLVED...
AN' WHAT ABOUT THE QUARANTINE? AIN'T *NONE* OF THOSE ALIENS SUPPOSED T'BE HERE-- THIS IS BAD!

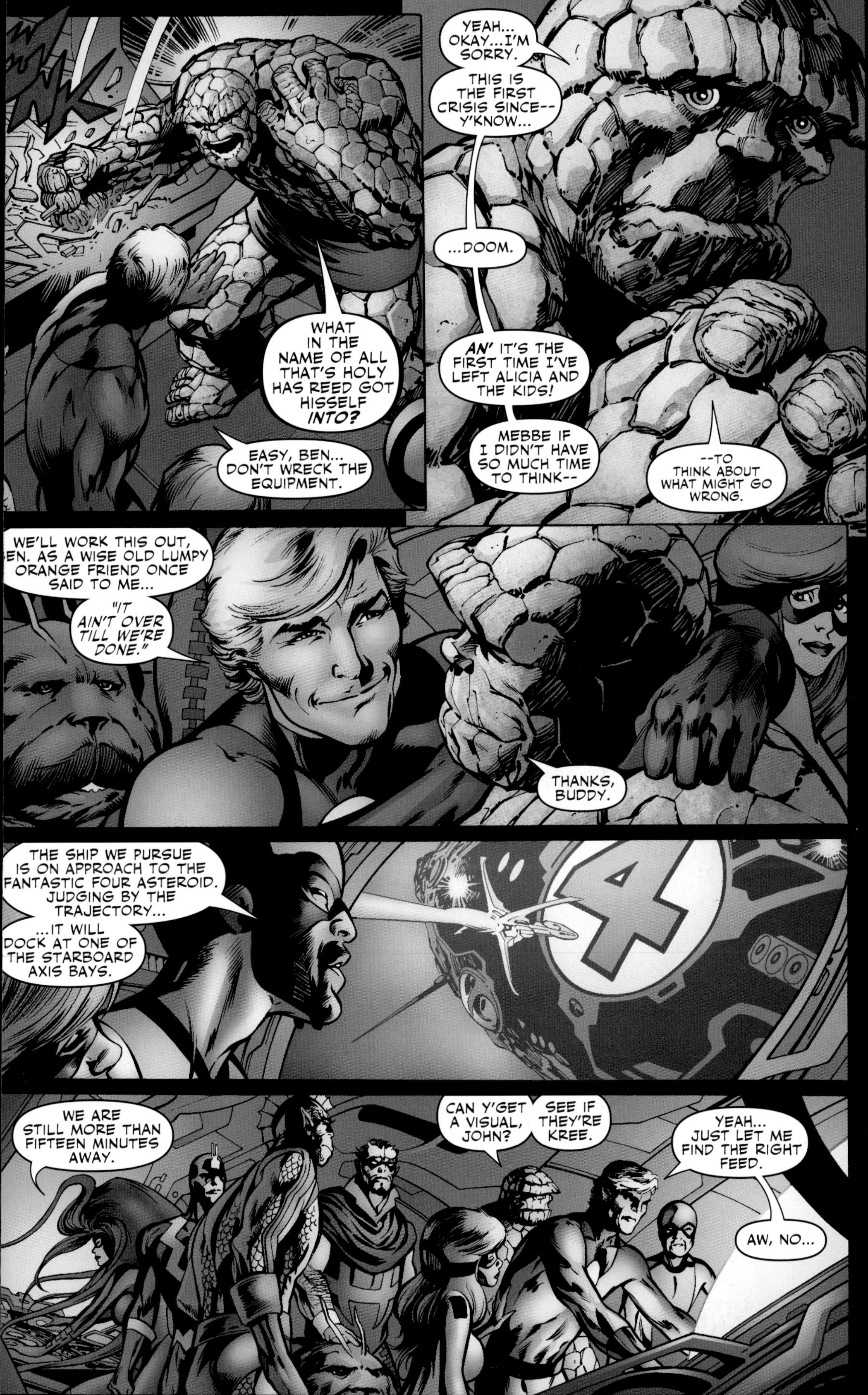
WHAT IN THE NAME OF ALL THAT'S HOLY HAS REED GOT HISSELF *INTO?*
EASY, BEN... DON'T WRECK THE EQUIPMENT.
YEAH... OKAY...I'M SORRY.
THIS IS THE FIRST CRISIS SINCE-- Y'KNOW...
...DOOM.
AN' IT'S THE FIRST TIME I'VE LEFT ALICIA AND THE KIDS!
MEBBE IF I DIDN'T HAVE SO MUCH TIME TO THINK--
--TO THINK ABOUT WHAT MIGHT GO WRONG.
WE'LL WORK THIS OUT, BEN. AS A WISE OLD LUMPY ORANGE FRIEND ONCE SAID TO ME...
"IT AIN'T OVER TILL WE'RE DONE."
THANKS, BUDDY.
THE SHIP WE PURSUE IS ON APPROACH TO THE FANTASTIC FOUR ASTEROID. JUDGING BY THE TRAJECTORY...
...IT WILL DOCK AT ONE OF THE STARBOARD AXIS BAYS.
WE ARE STILL MORE THAN FIFTEEN MINUTES AWAY.
CAN Y'GET A VISUAL, JOHN?
SEE IF THEY'RE KREE.
YEAH... JUST LET ME FIND THE RIGHT FEED.
AW, NO...

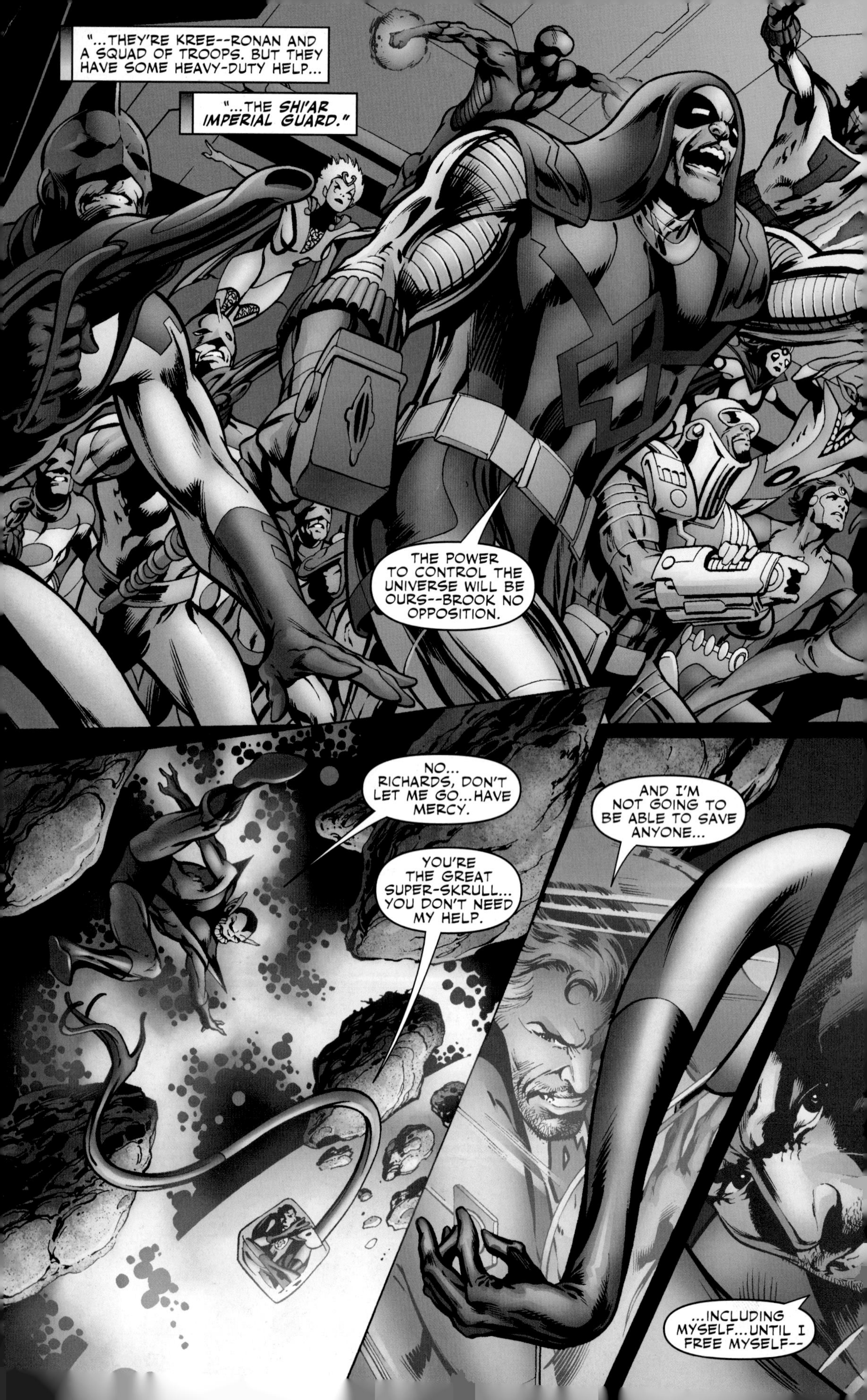
"...THEY'RE KREE--RONAN AND A SQUAD OF TROOPS. BUT THEY HAVE SOME HEAVY-DUTY HELP...
"...THE SHI'AR IMPERIAL GUARD."
THE POWER TO CONTROL THE UNIVERSE WILL BE OURS--BROOK NO OPPOSITION.
NO... RICHARDS, DON'T LET ME GO...HAVE MERCY.
YOU'RE THE GREAT SUPER-SKRULL... YOU DON'T NEED MY HELP.
AND I'M NOT GOING TO BE ABLE TO SAVE ANYONE...
...INCLUDING MYSELF...UNTIL I FREE MYSELF--

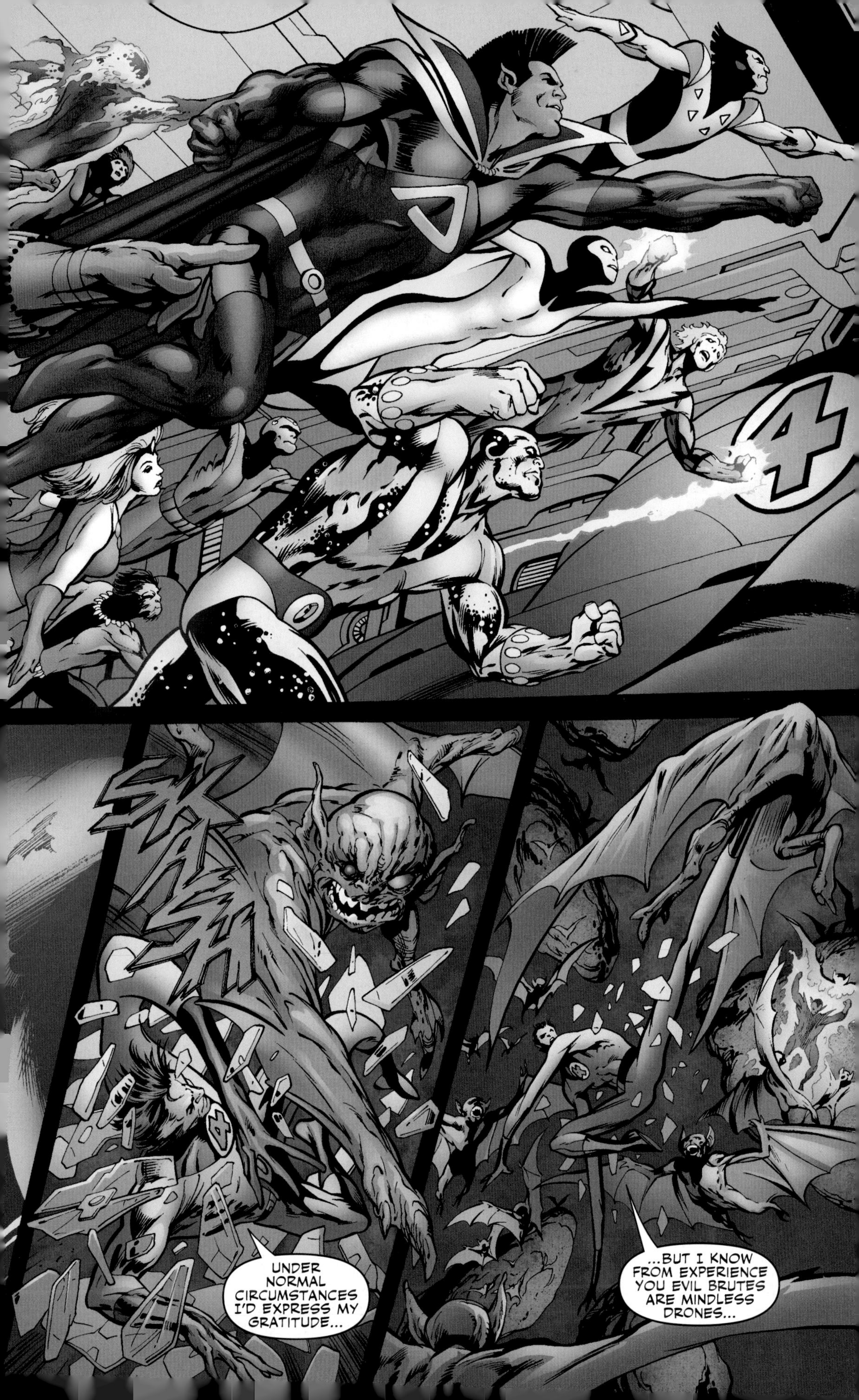
SHAM
UNDER NORMAL CIRCUMSTANCES I'D EXPRESS MY GRATITUDE...
...BUT I KNOW FROM EXPERIENCE YOU EVIL BRUTES ARE MINDLESS DRONES...

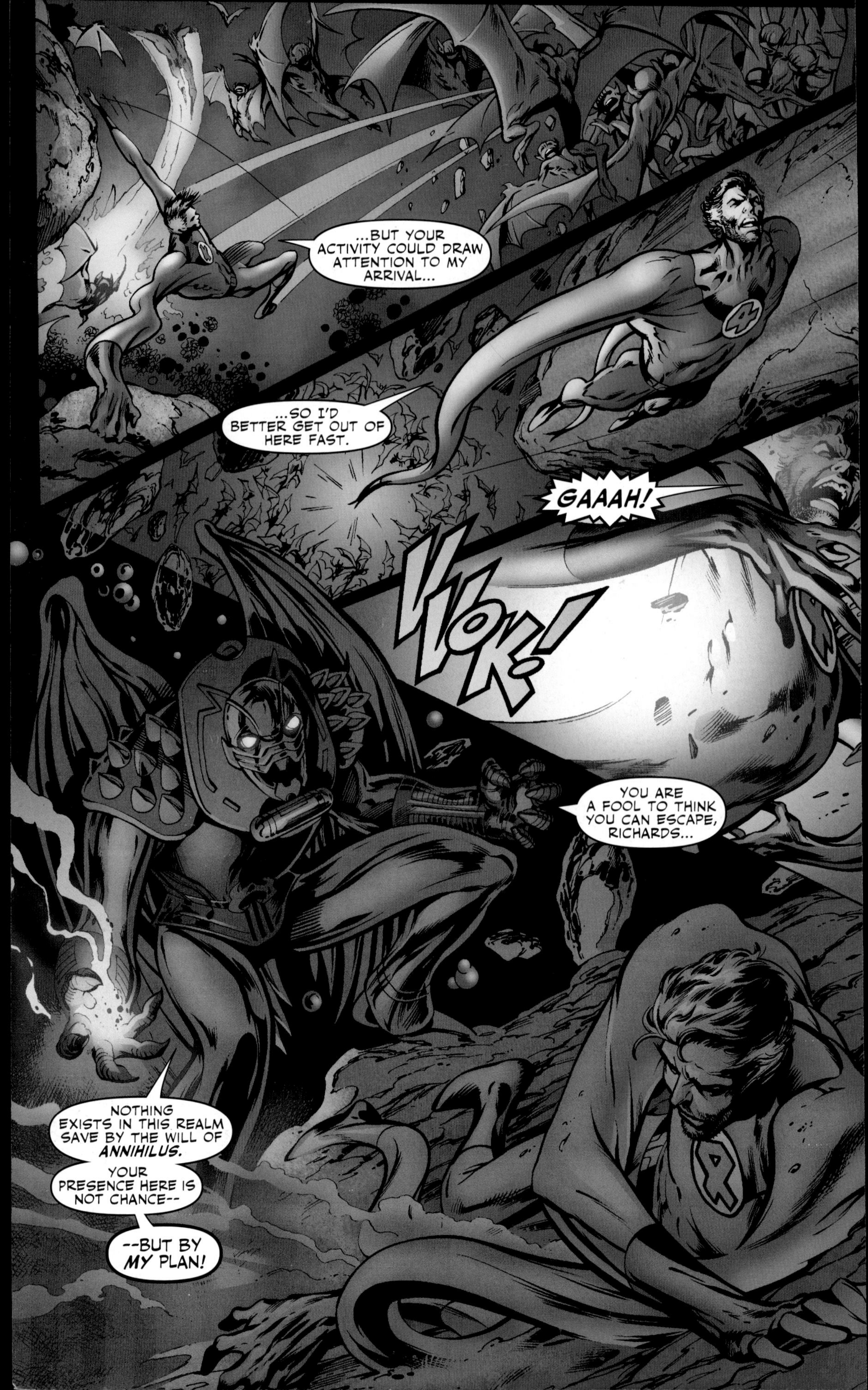
...BUT YOUR ACTIVITY COULD DRAW ATTENTION TO MY ARRIVAL...
...SO I'D BETTER GET OUT OF HERE FAST.
GAAAH!
VOK!
YOU ARE A FOOL TO THINK YOU CAN ESCAPE, RICHARDS...
NOTHING EXISTS IN THIS REALM SAVE BY THE WILL OF ANNIHILUS.
YOUR PRESENCE HERE IS NOT CHANCE--
--BUT BY MY PLAN!

THE END THE END THE END THE END THE END

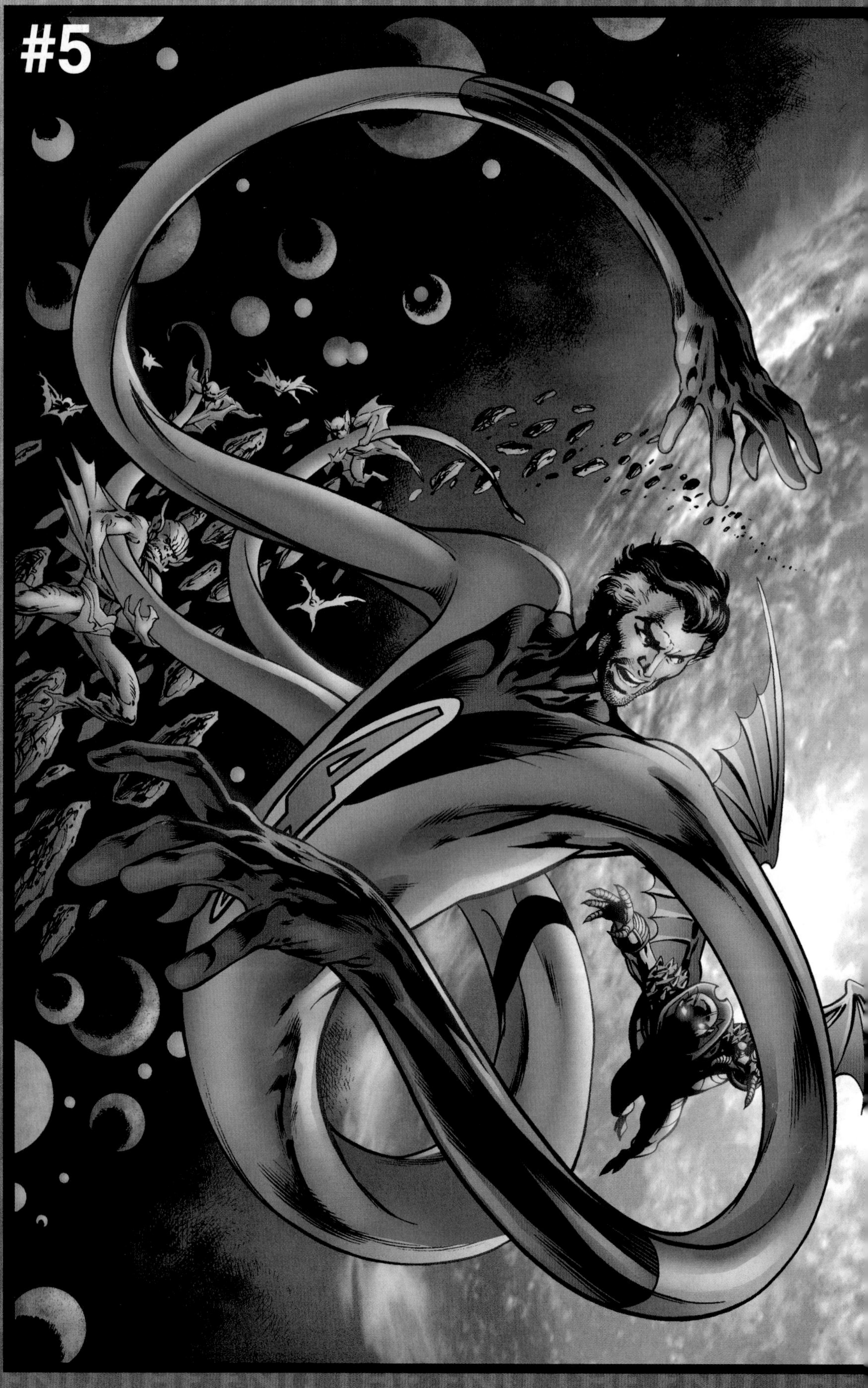
#5

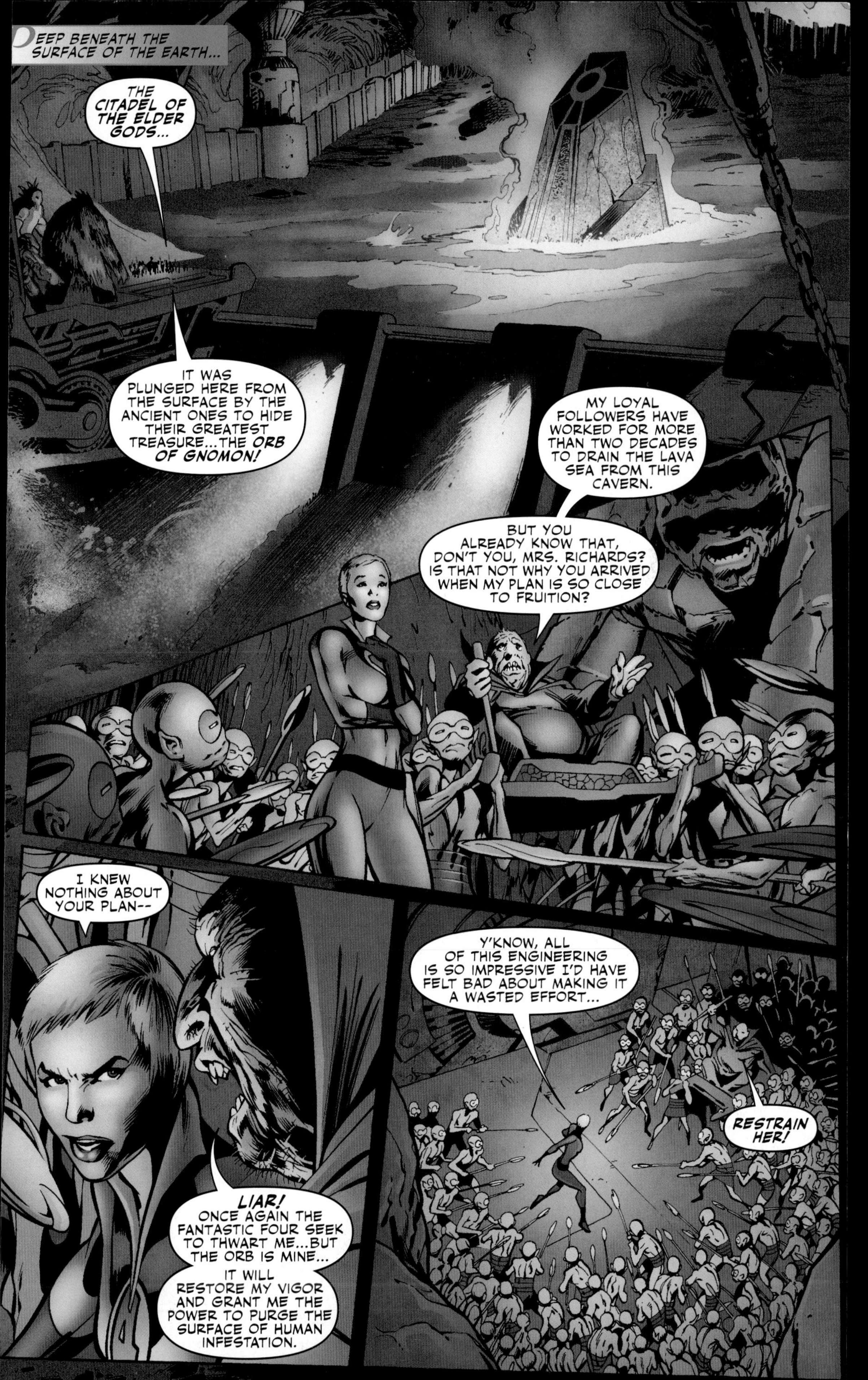
DEEP BENEATH THE SURFACE OF THE EARTH...
THE CITADEL OF THE ELDER GODS...
IT WAS PLUNGED HERE FROM THE SURFACE BY THE ANCIENT ONES TO HIDE THEIR GREATEST TREASURE...THE ORB OF GNOMON!
MY LOYAL FOLLOWERS HAVE WORKED FOR MORE THAN TWO DECADES TO DRAIN THE LAVA SEA FROM THIS CAVERN.
BUT YOU ALREADY KNOW THAT, DON'T YOU, MRS. RICHARDS? IS THAT NOT WHY YOU ARRIVED WHEN MY PLAN IS SO CLOSE TO FRUITION?
I KNEW NOTHING ABOUT YOUR PLAN--
LIAR! ONCE AGAIN THE FANTASTIC FOUR SEEK TO THWART ME...BUT THE ORB IS MINE...
IT WILL RESTORE MY VIGOR AND GRANT ME THE POWER TO PURGE THE SURFACE OF HUMAN INFESTATION.
Y'KNOW, ALL OF THIS ENGINEERING IS SO IMPRESSIVE I'D HAVE FELT BAD ABOUT MAKING IT A WASTED EFFORT...
RESTRAIN HER!

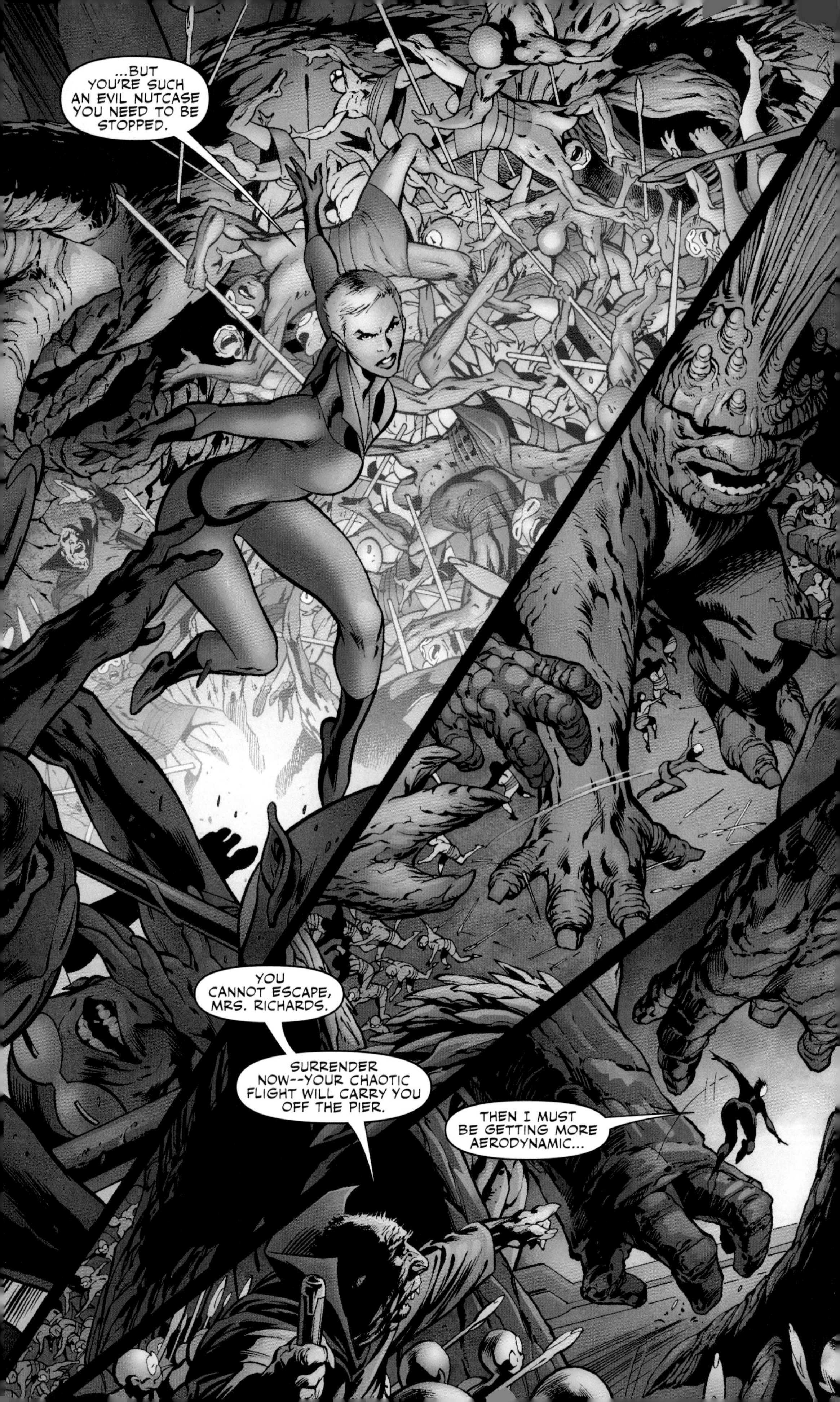
...BUT YOU'RE SUCH AN EVIL NUTCASE YOU NEED TO BE STOPPED.
YOU CANNOT ESCAPE, MRS. RICHARDS.
SURRENDER NOW--YOUR CHAOTIC FLIGHT WILL CARRY YOU OFF THE PIER.
THEN I MUST BE GETTING MORE AERODYNAMIC...

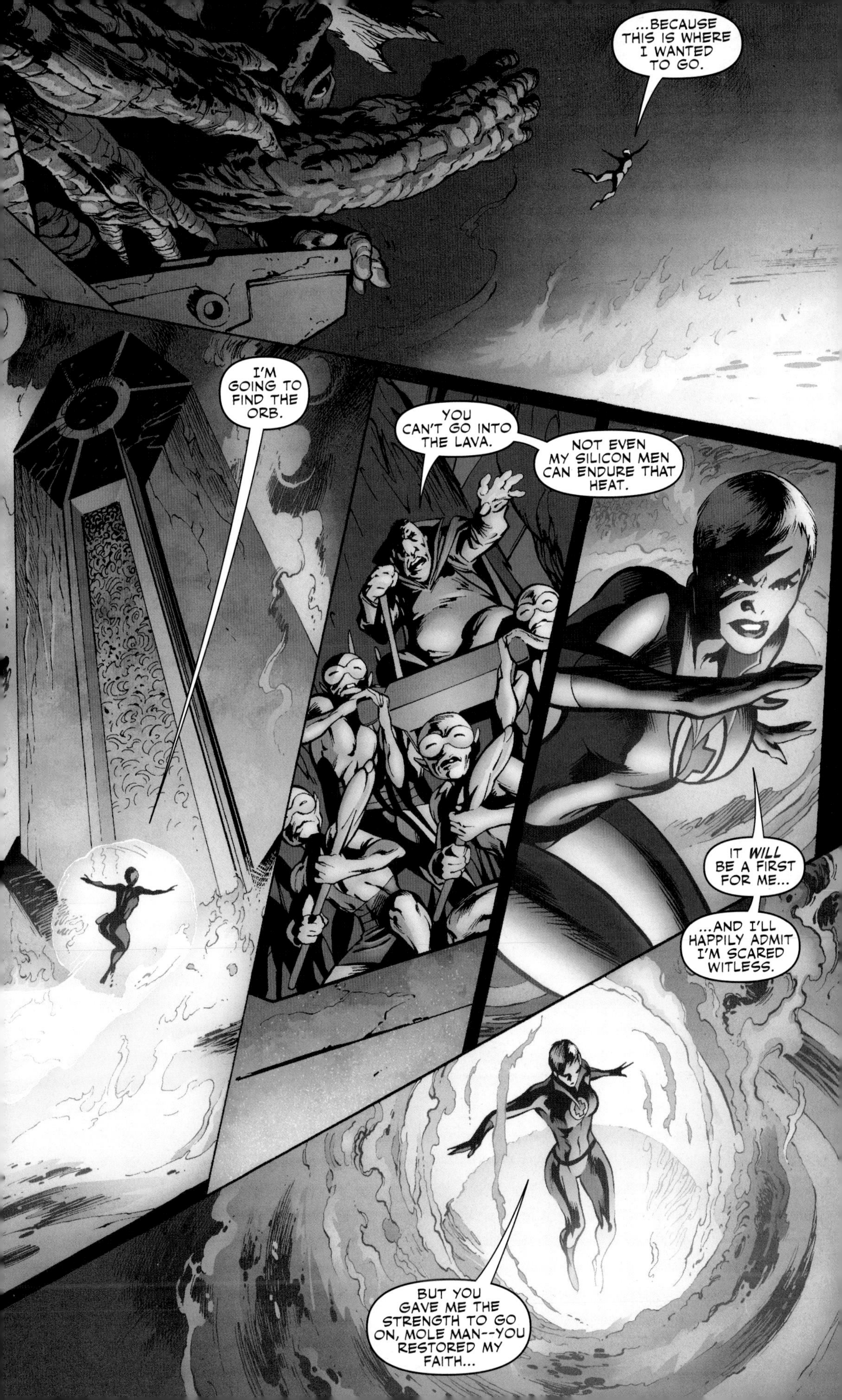
...BECAUSE THIS IS WHERE I WANTED TO GO.
I'M GOING TO FIND THE ORB.
YOU CAN'T GO INTO THE LAVA.
NOT EVEN MY SILICON MEN CAN ENDURE THAT HEAT.
IT WILL BE A FIRST FOR ME...
...AND I'LL HAPPILY ADMIT I'M SCARED WITLESS.
BUT YOU GAVE ME THE STRENGTH TO GO ON, MOLE MAN--YOU RESTORED MY FAITH...

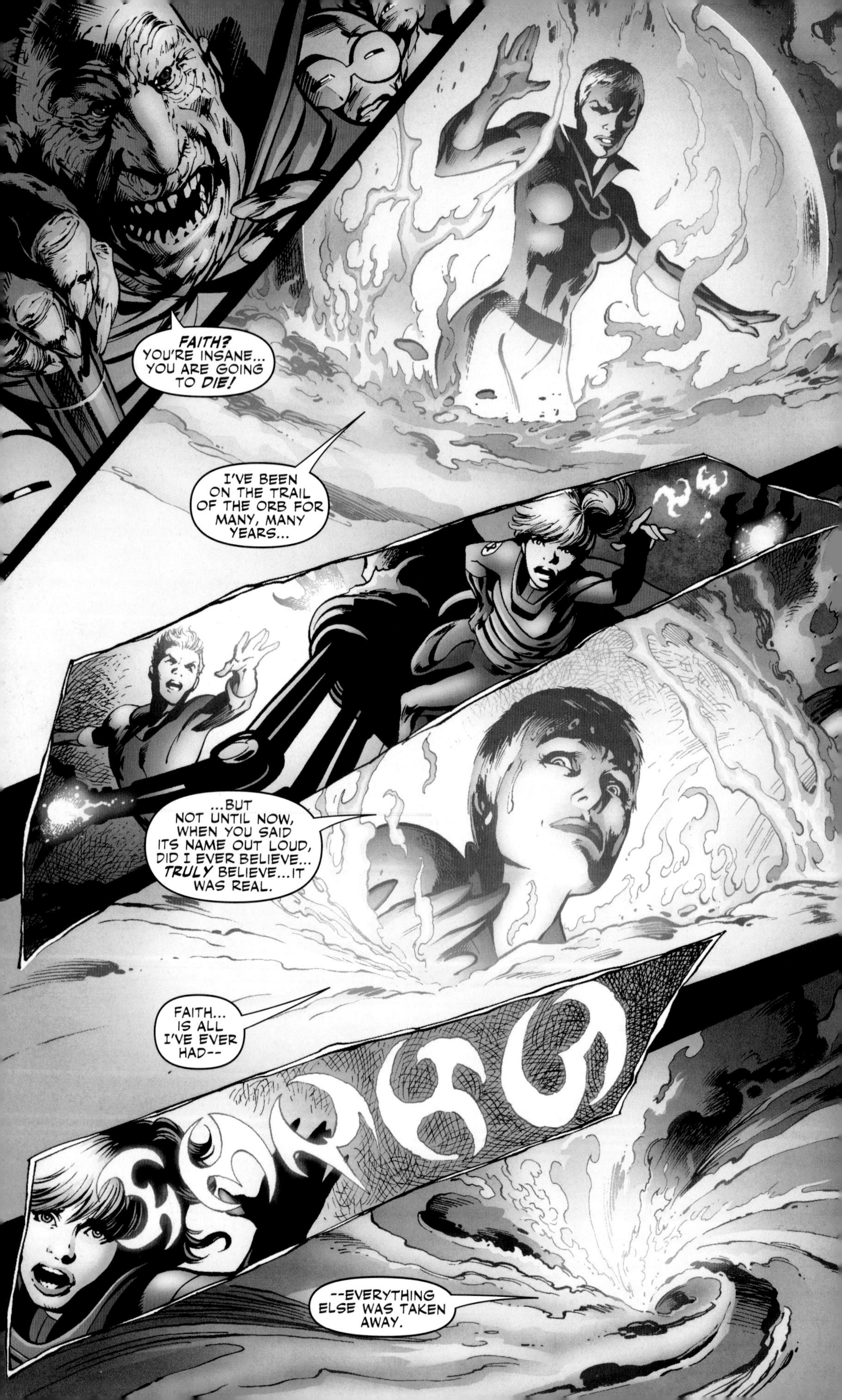
FAITH? YOU'RE INSANE... YOU ARE GOING TO DIE!
I'VE BEEN ON THE TRAIL OF THE ORB FOR MANY, MANY YEARS...
...BUT NOT UNTIL NOW, WHEN YOU SAID ITS NAME OUT LOUD, DID I EVER BELIEVE... TRULY BELIEVE...IT WAS REAL.
FAITH... IS ALL I'VE EVER HAD--
--EVERYTHING ELSE WAS TAKEN AWAY.

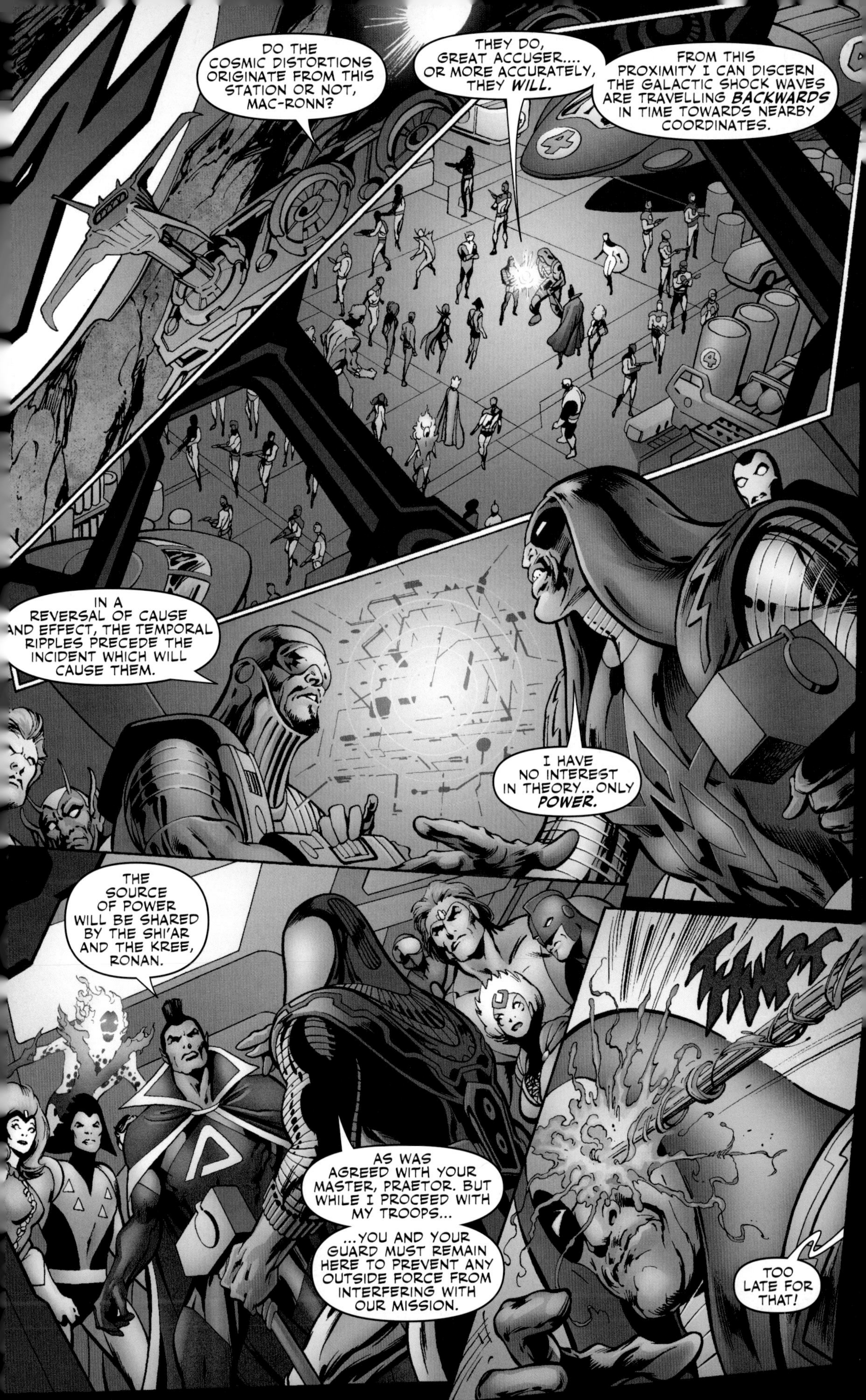
DO THE COSMIC DISTORTIONS ORIGINATE FROM THIS STATION OR NOT, MAC-RONN?
THEY DO, GREAT ACCUSER.... OR MORE ACCURATELY, THEY WILL.
FROM THIS PROXIMITY I CAN DISCERN THE GALACTIC SHOCK WAVES ARE TRAVELLING BACKWARDS IN TIME TOWARDS NEARBY COORDINATES.
IN A REVERSAL OF CAUSE AND EFFECT, THE TEMPORAL RIPPLES PRECEDE THE INCIDENT WHICH WILL CAUSE THEM.
I HAVE NO INTEREST IN THEORY...ONLY POWER.
THE SOURCE OF POWER WILL BE SHARED BY THE SHI'AR AND THE KREE, RONAN.
AS WAS AGREED WITH YOUR MASTER, PRAETOR. BUT WHILE I PROCEED WITH MY TROOPS...
...YOU AND YOUR GUARD MUST REMAIN HERE TO PREVENT ANY OUTSIDE FORCE FROM INTERFERING WITH OUR MISSION.
TOO LATE FOR THAT!

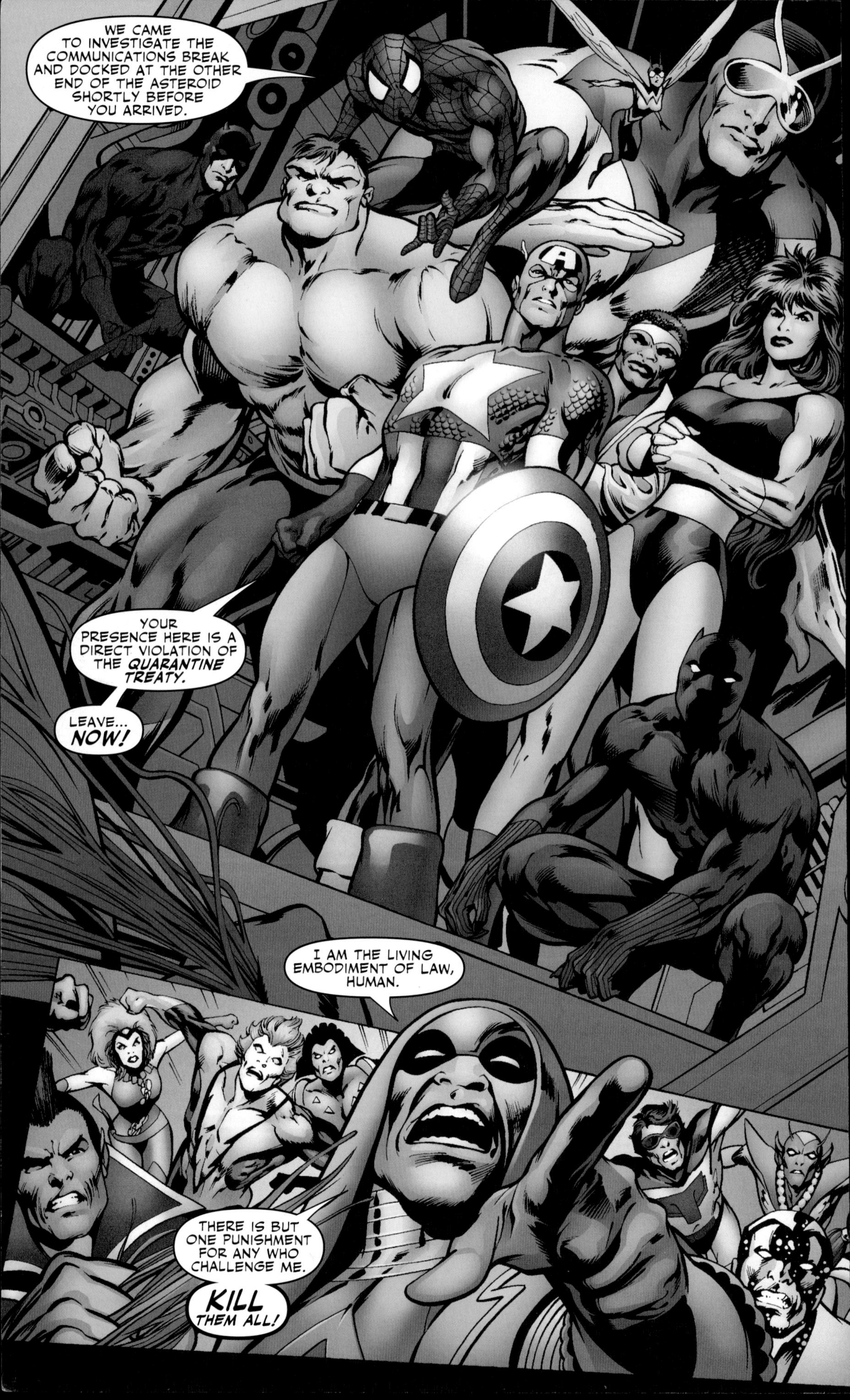

WE CAME TO INVESTIGATE THE COMMUNICATIONS BREAK AND DOCKED AT THE OTHER END OF THE ASTEROID SHORTLY BEFORE YOU ARRIVED.
YOUR PRESENCE HERE IS A DIRECT VIOLATION OF THE *QUARANTINE TREATY.*
LEAVE... ***NOW!***
I AM THE LIVING EMBODIMENT OF LAW, HUMAN.
THERE IS BUT ONE PUNISHMENT FOR ANY WHO CHALLENGE ME.
KILL THEM ALL!

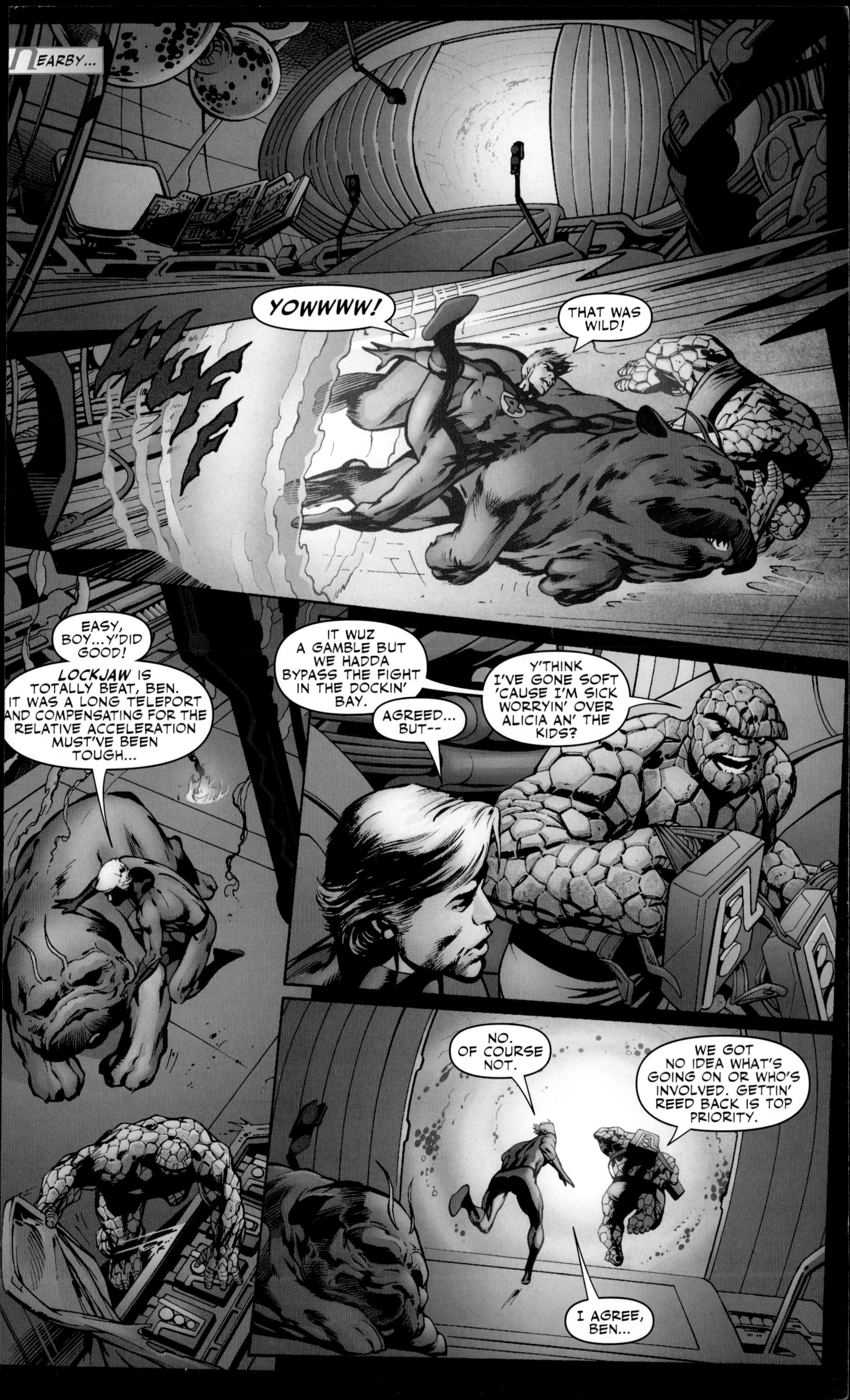
NEARBY...
YOWWWW!
THAT WAS WILD!
EASY, BOY...Y'DID GOOD!
LOCKJAW IS TOTALLY BEAT, BEN. IT WAS A LONG TELEPORT AND COMPENSATING FOR THE RELATIVE ACCELERATION MUST'VE BEEN TOUGH...
IT WUZ A GAMBLE BUT WE HADDA BYPASS THE FIGHT IN THE DOCKIN' BAY.
AGREED... BUT--
Y'THINK I'VE GONE SOFT 'CAUSE I'M SICK WORRYIN' OVER ALICIA AN' THE KIDS?
NO. OF COURSE NOT.
WE GOT NO IDEA WHAT'S GOING ON OR WHO'S INVOLVED. GETTIN' REED BACK IS TOP PRIORITY.
I AGREE, BEN...

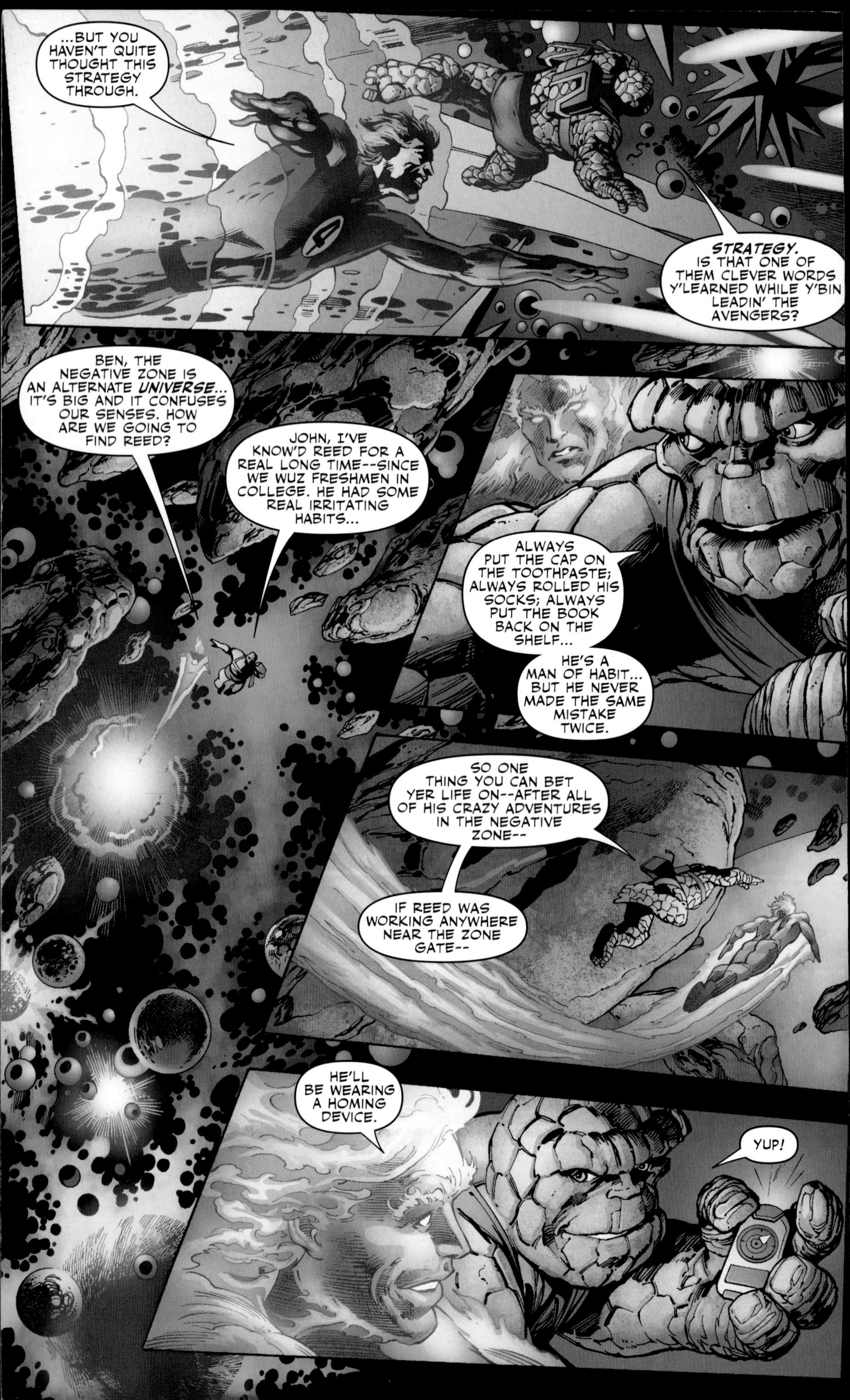
...BUT YOU HAVEN'T QUITE THOUGHT THIS STRATEGY THROUGH.
STRATEGY. IS THAT ONE OF THEM CLEVER WORDS Y'LEARNED WHILE Y'BIN LEADIN' THE AVENGERS?
BEN, THE NEGATIVE ZONE IS AN ALTERNATE UNIVERSE... IT'S BIG AND IT CONFUSES OUR SENSES. HOW ARE WE GOING TO FIND REED?
JOHN, I'VE KNOW'D REED FOR A REAL LONG TIME--SINCE WE WUZ FRESHMEN IN COLLEGE. HE HAD SOME REAL IRRITATING HABITS...
ALWAYS PUT THE CAP ON THE TOOTHPASTE; ALWAYS ROLLED HIS SOCKS; ALWAYS PUT THE BOOK BACK ON THE SHELF...
HE'S A MAN OF HABIT... BUT HE NEVER MADE THE SAME MISTAKE TWICE.
SO ONE THING YOU CAN BET YER LIFE ON--AFTER ALL OF HIS CRAZY ADVENTURES IN THE NEGATIVE ZONE--
IF REED WAS WORKING ANYWHERE NEAR THE ZONE GATE--
HE'LL BE WEARING A HOMING DEVICE.
YUP!

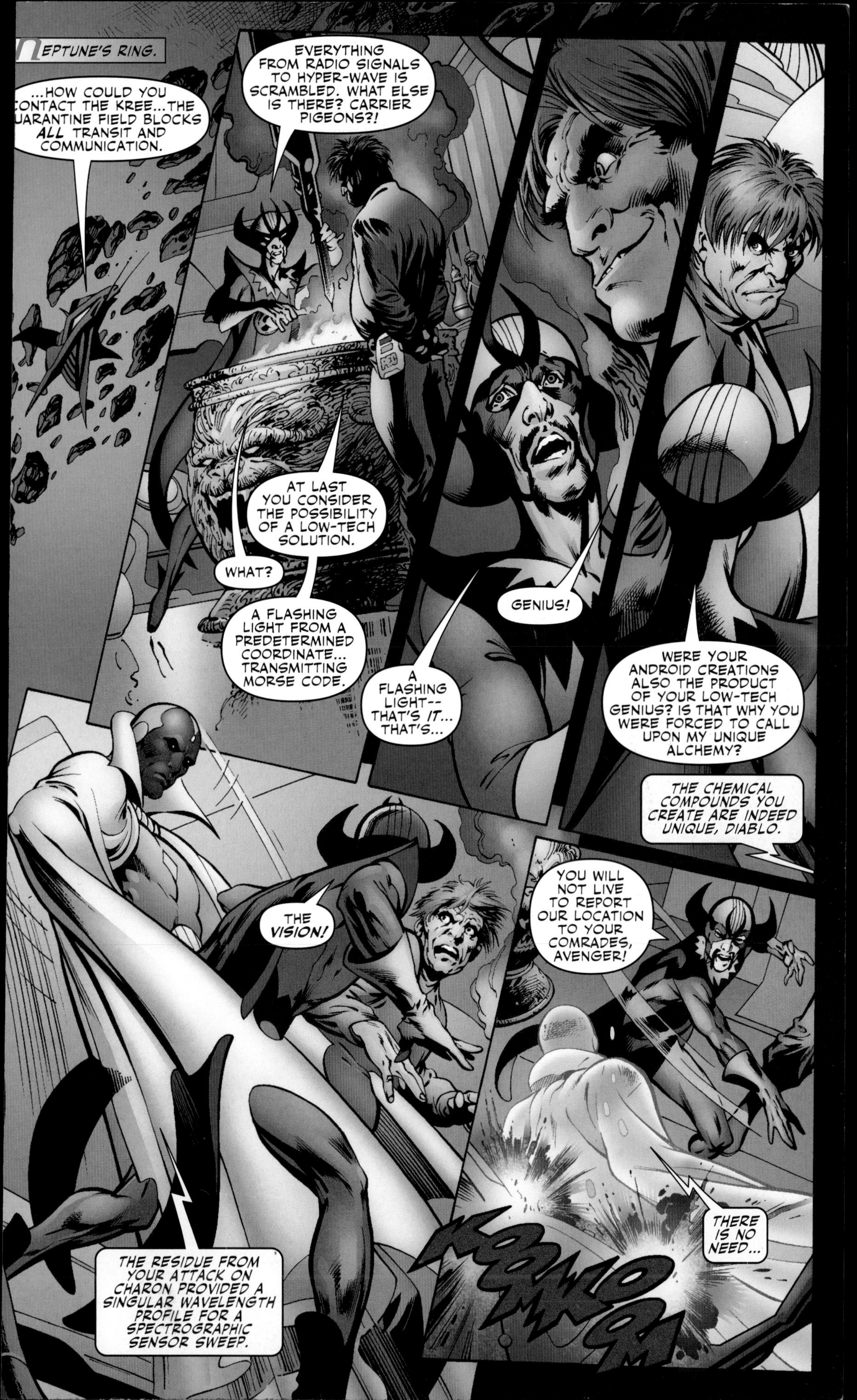
NEPTUNE'S RING.
...HOW COULD YOU CONTACT THE KREE...THE QUARANTINE FIELD BLOCKS ALL TRANSIT AND COMMUNICATION.
EVERYTHING FROM RADIO SIGNALS TO HYPER-WAVE IS SCRAMBLED. WHAT ELSE IS THERE? CARRIER PIGEONS?!
AT LAST YOU CONSIDER THE POSSIBILITY OF A LOW-TECH SOLUTION.
WHAT?
A FLASHING LIGHT FROM A PREDETERMINED COORDINATE... TRANSMITTING MORSE CODE.
A FLASHING LIGHT-- THAT'S IT... THAT'S...
GENIUS!
WERE YOUR ANDROID CREATIONS ALSO THE PRODUCT OF YOUR LOW-TECH GENIUS? IS THAT WHY YOU WERE FORCED TO CALL UPON MY UNIQUE ALCHEMY?
THE CHEMICAL COMPOUNDS YOU CREATE ARE INDEED UNIQUE, DIABLO.
THE VISION!
YOU WILL NOT LIVE TO REPORT OUR LOCATION TO YOUR COMRADES, AVENGER!
THE RESIDUE FROM YOUR ATTACK ON CHARON PROVIDED A SINGULAR WAVELENGTH PROFILE FOR A SPECTROGRAPHIC SENSOR SWEEP.
KRAKOOOM
THERE IS NO NEED...

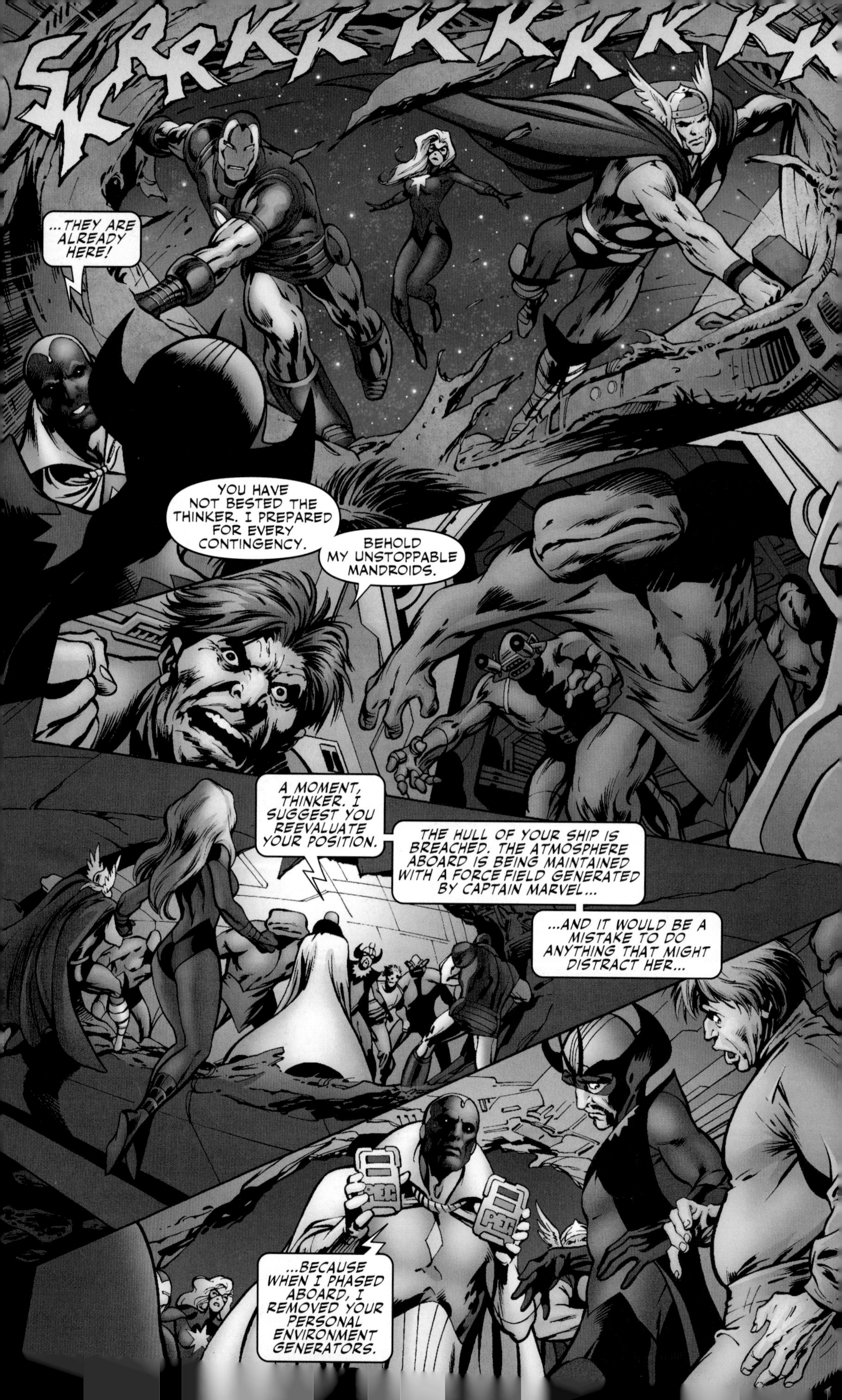

SKRRKKKKKKKK
...THEY ARE ALREADY HERE!
YOU HAVE NOT BESTED THE THINKER. I PREPARED FOR EVERY CONTINGENCY.
BEHOLD MY UNSTOPPABLE MANDROIDS.
A MOMENT, THINKER. I SUGGEST YOU REEVALUATE YOUR POSITION.
THE HULL OF YOUR SHIP IS BREACHED. THE ATMOSPHERE ABOARD IS BEING MAINTAINED WITH A FORCE FIELD GENERATED BY CAPTAIN MARVEL...
...AND IT WOULD BE A MISTAKE TO DO ANYTHING THAT MIGHT DISTRACT HER...
...BECAUSE WHEN I PHASED ABOARD, I REMOVED YOUR PERSONAL ENVIRONMENT GENERATORS.
PEG
PEG

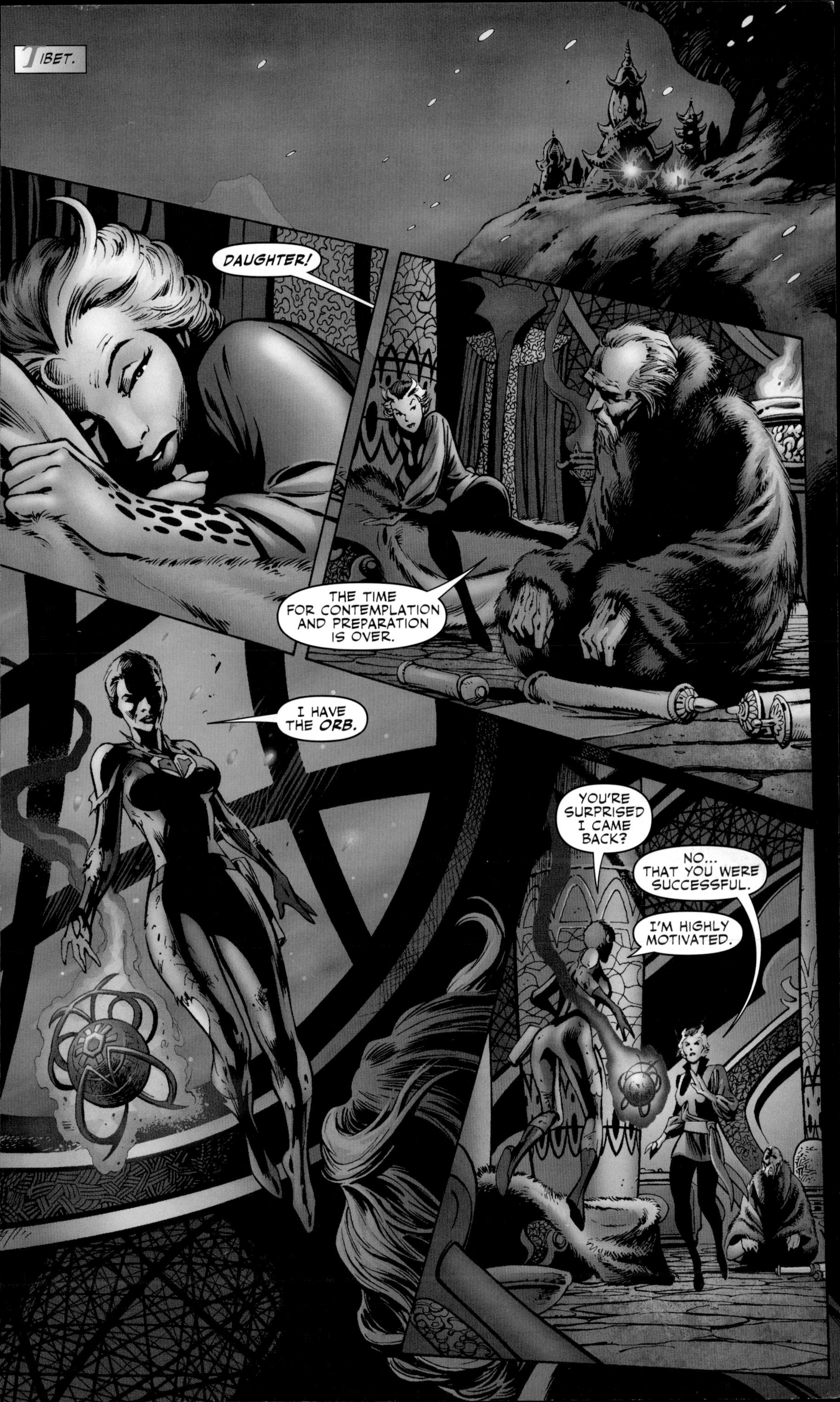

TIBET.
DAUGHTER!
THE TIME FOR CONTEMPLATION AND PREPARATION IS OVER.
I HAVE THE ORB.
YOU'RE SURPRISED I CAME BACK?
NO... THAT YOU WERE SUCCESSFUL.
I'M HIGHLY MOTIVATED.

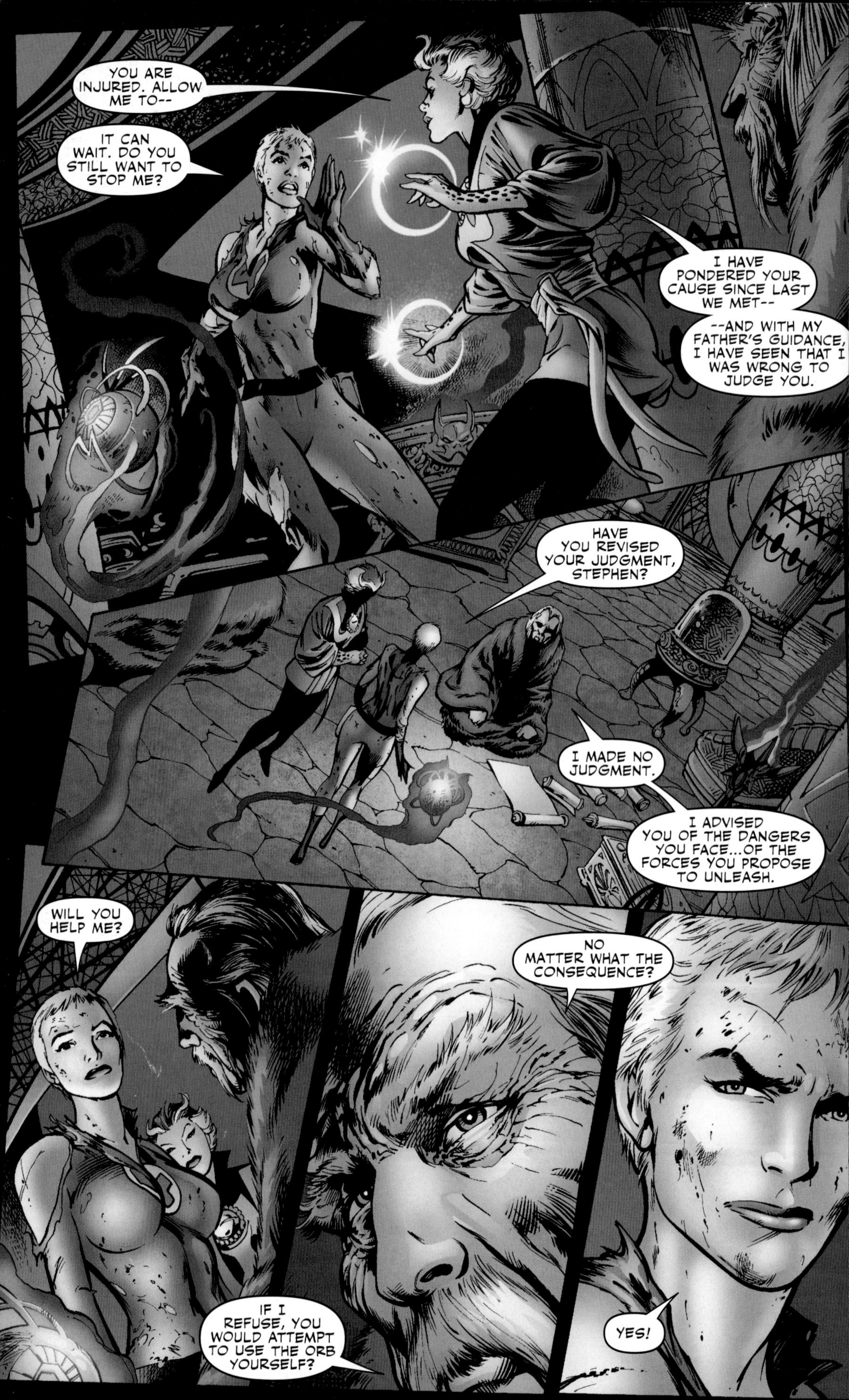
YOU ARE INJURED. ALLOW ME TO--
IT CAN WAIT. DO YOU STILL WANT TO STOP ME?
I HAVE PONDERED YOUR CAUSE SINCE LAST WE MET--
--AND WITH MY FATHER'S GUIDANCE, I HAVE SEEN THAT I WAS WRONG TO JUDGE YOU.
HAVE YOU REVISED YOUR JUDGMENT, STEPHEN?
I MADE NO JUDGMENT.
I ADVISED YOU OF THE DANGERS YOU FACE...OF THE FORCES YOU PROPOSE TO UNLEASH.
WILL YOU HELP ME?
IF I REFUSE, YOU WOULD ATTEMPT TO USE THE ORB YOURSELF?
NO MATTER WHAT THE CONSEQUENCE?
YES!

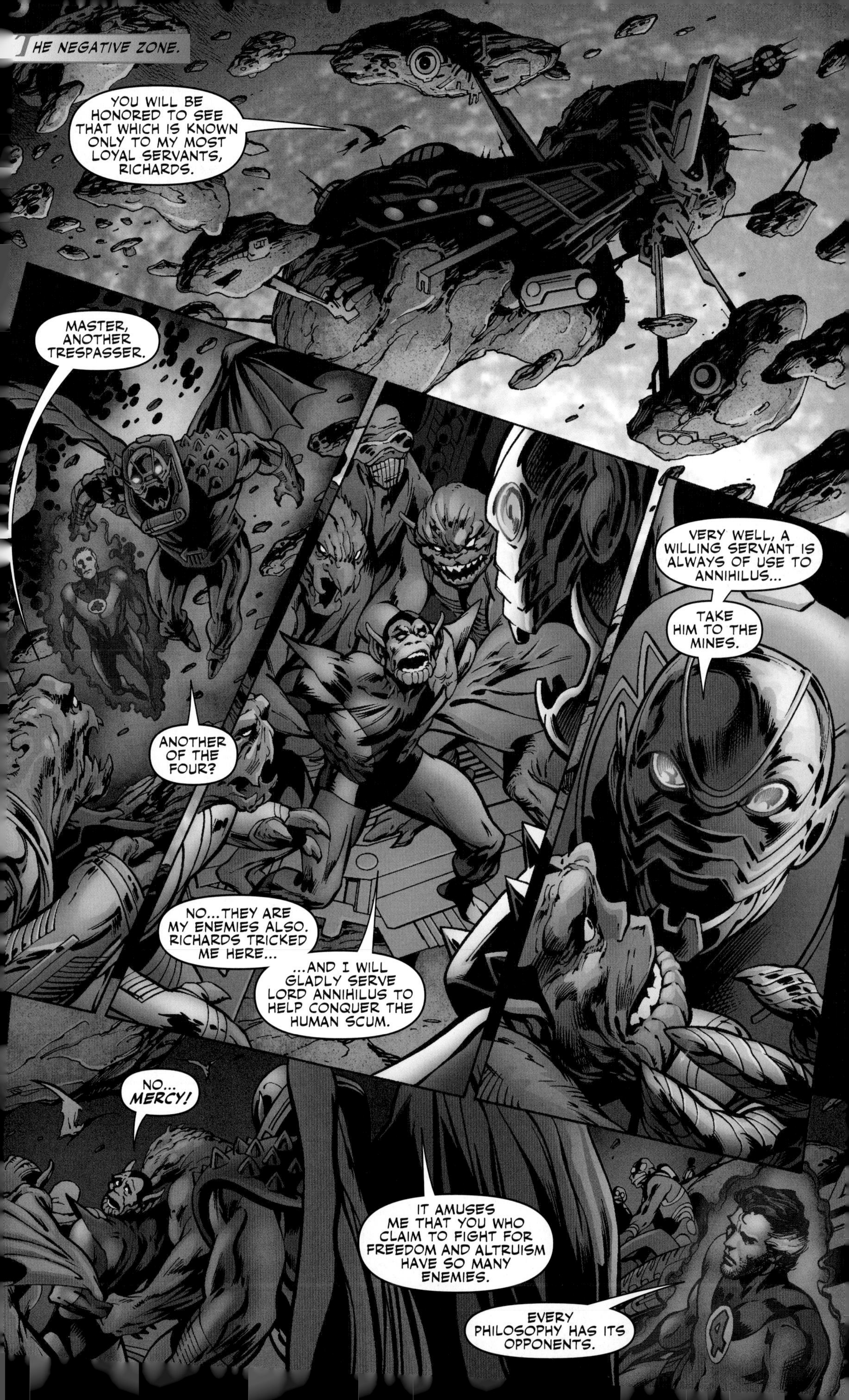
THE NEGATIVE ZONE.
YOU WILL BE HONORED TO SEE THAT WHICH IS KNOWN ONLY TO MY MOST LOYAL SERVANTS, RICHARDS.
MASTER, ANOTHER TRESPASSER.
ANOTHER OF THE FOUR?
NO...THEY ARE MY ENEMIES ALSO. RICHARDS TRICKED ME HERE...
...AND I WILL GLADLY SERVE LORD ANNIHILUS TO HELP CONQUER THE HUMAN SCUM.
VERY WELL, A WILLING SERVANT IS ALWAYS OF USE TO ANNIHILUS...
TAKE HIM TO THE MINES.
NO... MERCY!
IT AMUSES ME THAT YOU WHO CLAIM TO FIGHT FOR FREEDOM AND ALTRUISM HAVE SO MANY ENEMIES.
EVERY PHILOSOPHY HAS ITS OPPONENTS.

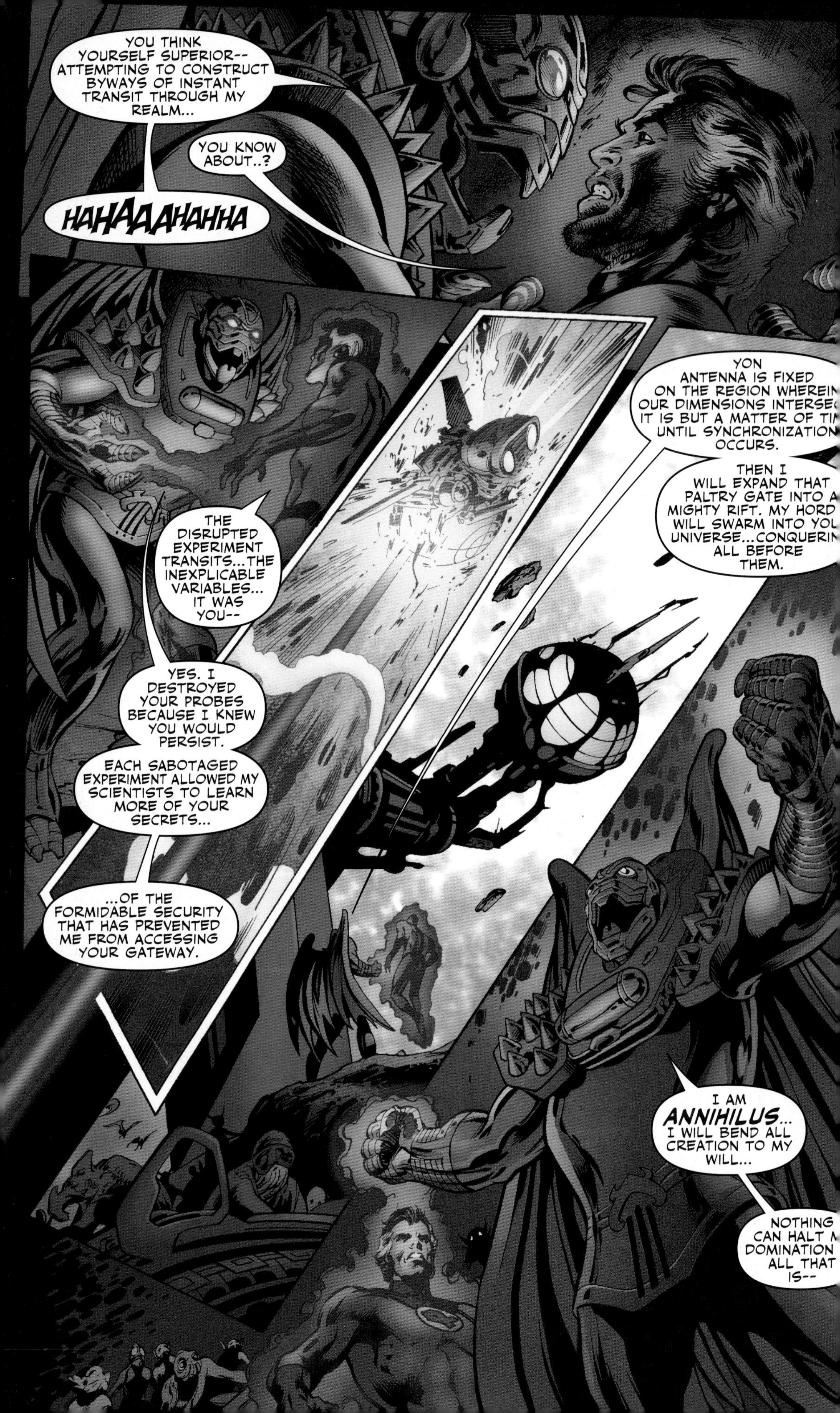
YOU THINK YOURSELF SUPERIOR-- ATTEMPTING TO CONSTRUCT BYWAYS OF INSTANT TRANSIT THROUGH MY REALM...
YOU KNOW ABOUT..?
HAHAAAAHAHHA
THE DISRUPTED EXPERIMENT TRANSITS...THE INEXPLICABLE VARIABLES... IT WAS YOU--
YES. I DESTROYED YOUR PROBES BECAUSE I KNEW YOU WOULD PERSIST.
EACH SABOTAGED EXPERIMENT ALLOWED MY SCIENTISTS TO LEARN MORE OF YOUR SECRETS...
...OF THE FORMIDABLE SECURITY THAT HAS PREVENTED ME FROM ACCESSING YOUR GATEWAY.
YON ANTENNA IS FIXED ON THE REGION WHEREIN OUR DIMENSIONS INTERSE IT IS BUT A MATTER OF TI UNTIL SYNCHRONIZATION OCCURS.
THEN I WILL EXPAND THAT PALTRY GATE INTO A MIGHTY RIFT. MY HORD WILL SWARM INTO YOU UNIVERSE...CONQUERIN ALL BEFORE THEM.
I AM ANNIHILUS... I WILL BEND ALL CREATION TO MY WILL...
NOTHING CAN HALT DOMINATION ALL THAT IS--

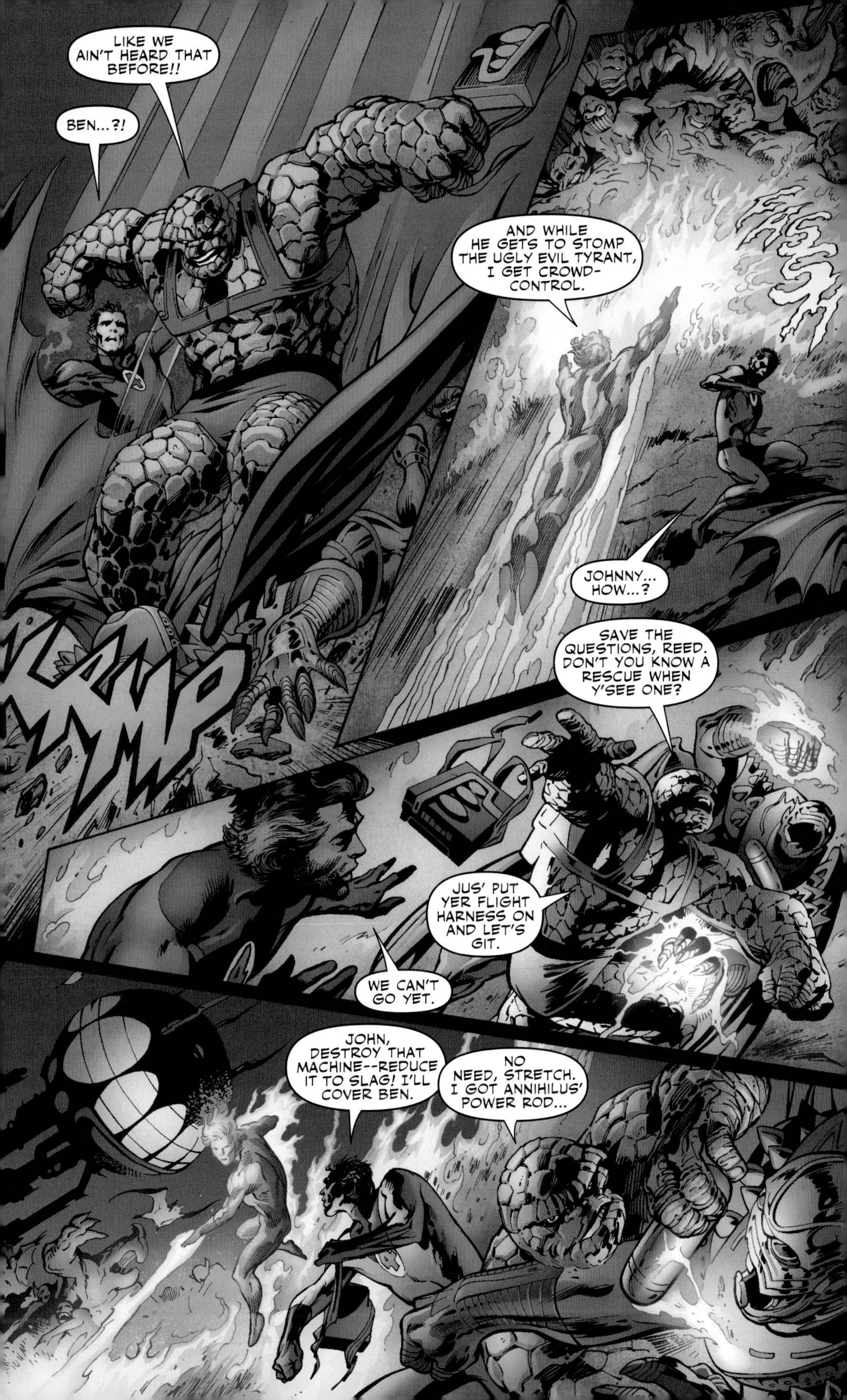
LIKE WE AIN'T HEARD THAT BEFORE!!
BEN...?!
AND WHILE HE GETS TO STOMP THE UGLY EVIL TYRANT, I GET CROWD-CONTROL.
JOHNNY... HOW...?
SAVE THE QUESTIONS, REED. DON'T YOU KNOW A RESCUE WHEN Y'SEE ONE?
JUS' PUT YER FLIGHT HARNESS ON AND LET'S GIT.
WE CAN'T GO YET.
JOHN, DESTROY THAT MACHINE--REDUCE IT TO SLAG! I'LL COVER BEN.
NO NEED, STRETCH. I GOT ANNIHILUS' POWER ROD...

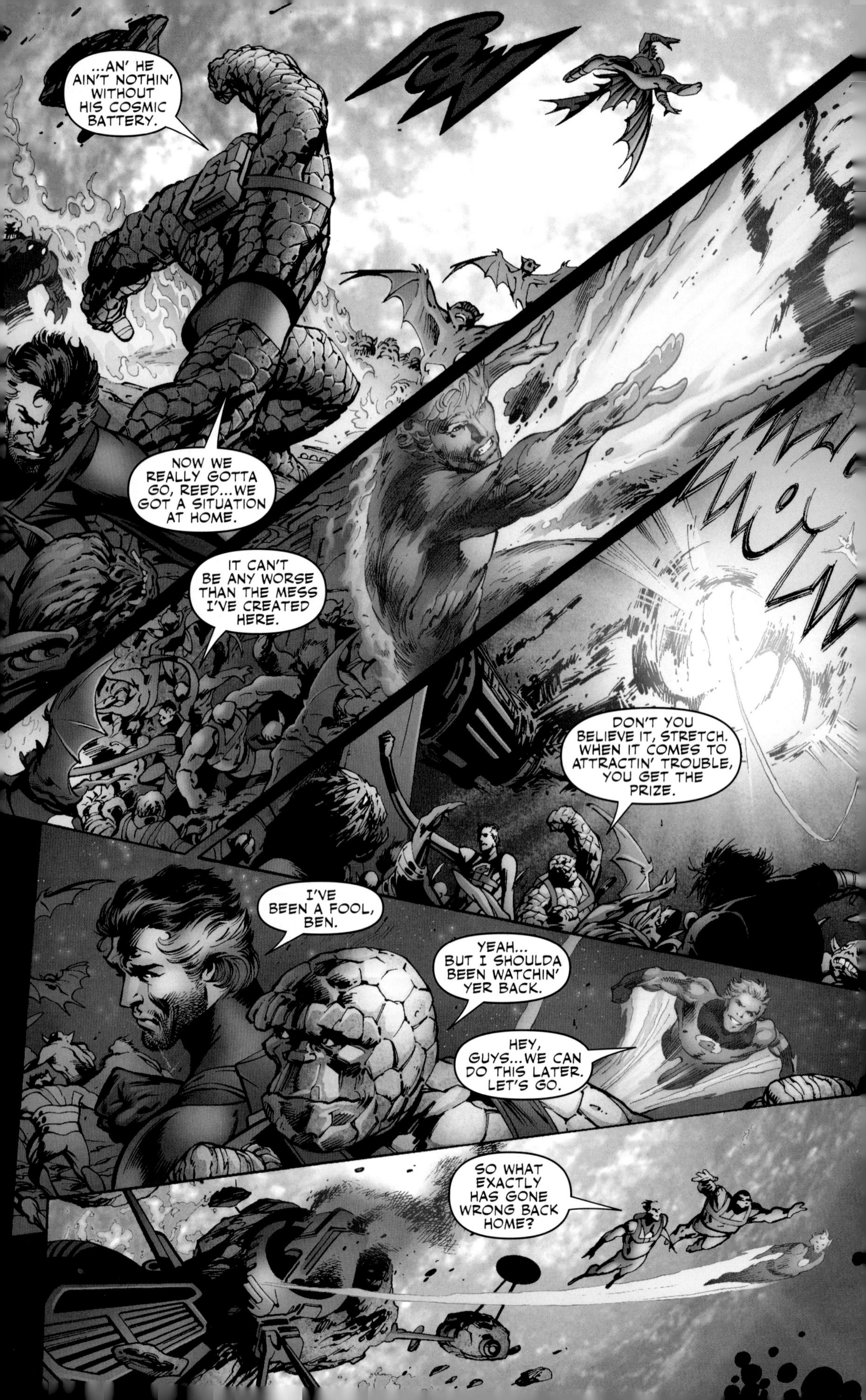
...AN' HE AIN'T NOTHIN' WITHOUT HIS COSMIC BATTERY.
NOW WE REALLY GOTTA GO, REED...WE GOT A SITUATION AT HOME.
IT CAN'T BE ANY WORSE THAN THE MESS I'VE CREATED HERE.
DON'T YOU BELIEVE IT, STRETCH. WHEN IT COMES TO ATTRACTIN' TROUBLE, YOU GET THE PRIZE.
I'VE BEEN A FOOL, BEN.
YEAH... BUT I SHOULDA BEEN WATCHIN' YER BACK.
HEY, GUYS...WE CAN DO THIS LATER. LET'S GO.
SO WHAT EXACTLY HAS GONE WRONG BACK HOME?

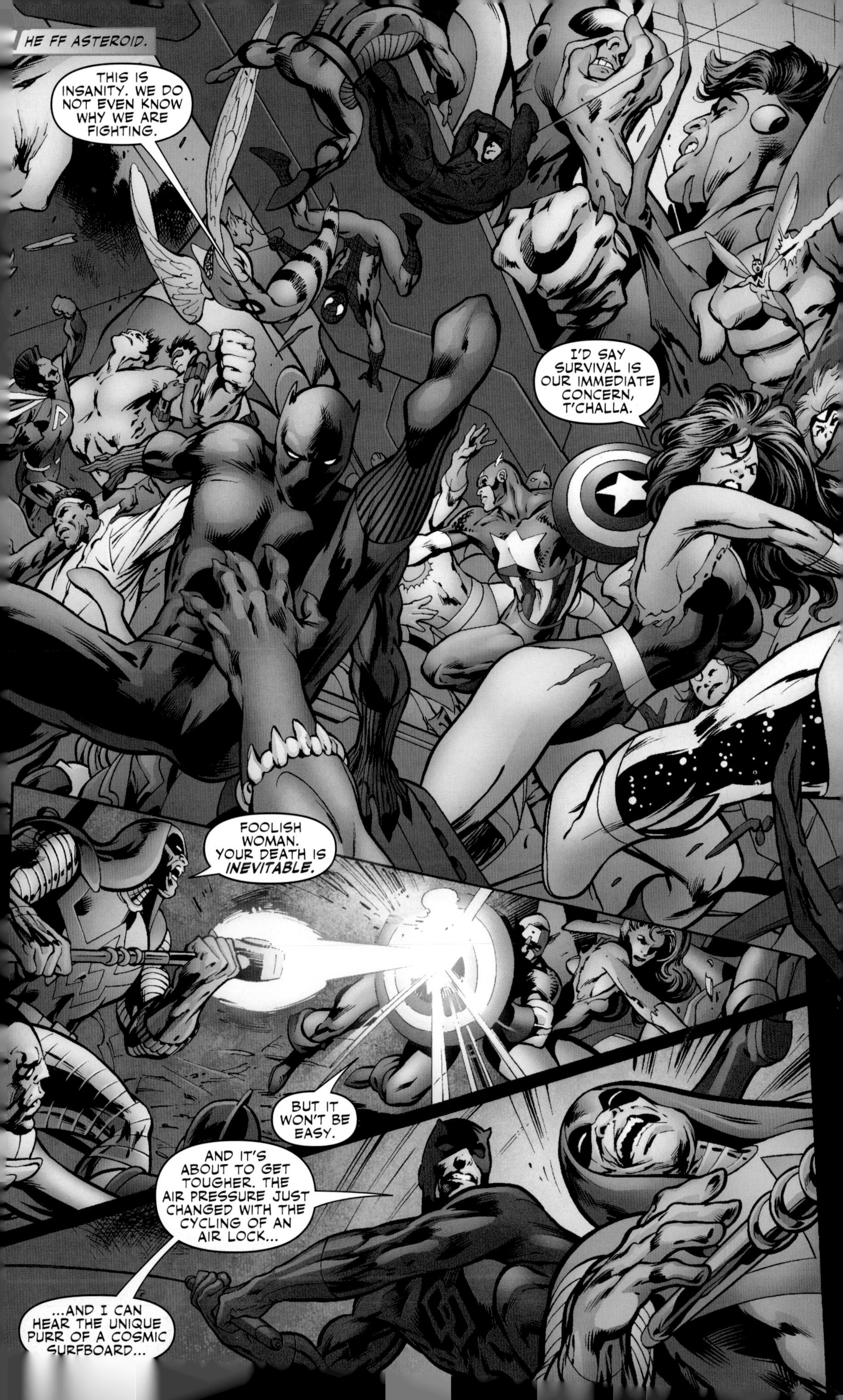
HE FF ASTEROID.
THIS IS INSANITY. WE DO NOT EVEN KNOW WHY WE ARE FIGHTING.
I'D SAY SURVIVAL IS OUR IMMEDIATE CONCERN, T'CHALLA.
FOOLISH WOMAN. YOUR DEATH IS *INEVITABLE.*
BUT IT WON'T BE EASY.
AND IT'S ABOUT TO GET TOUGHER. THE AIR PRESSURE JUST CHANGED WITH THE CYCLING OF AN AIR LOCK...
...AND I CAN HEAR THE UNIQUE PURR OF A COSMIC SURFBOARD...

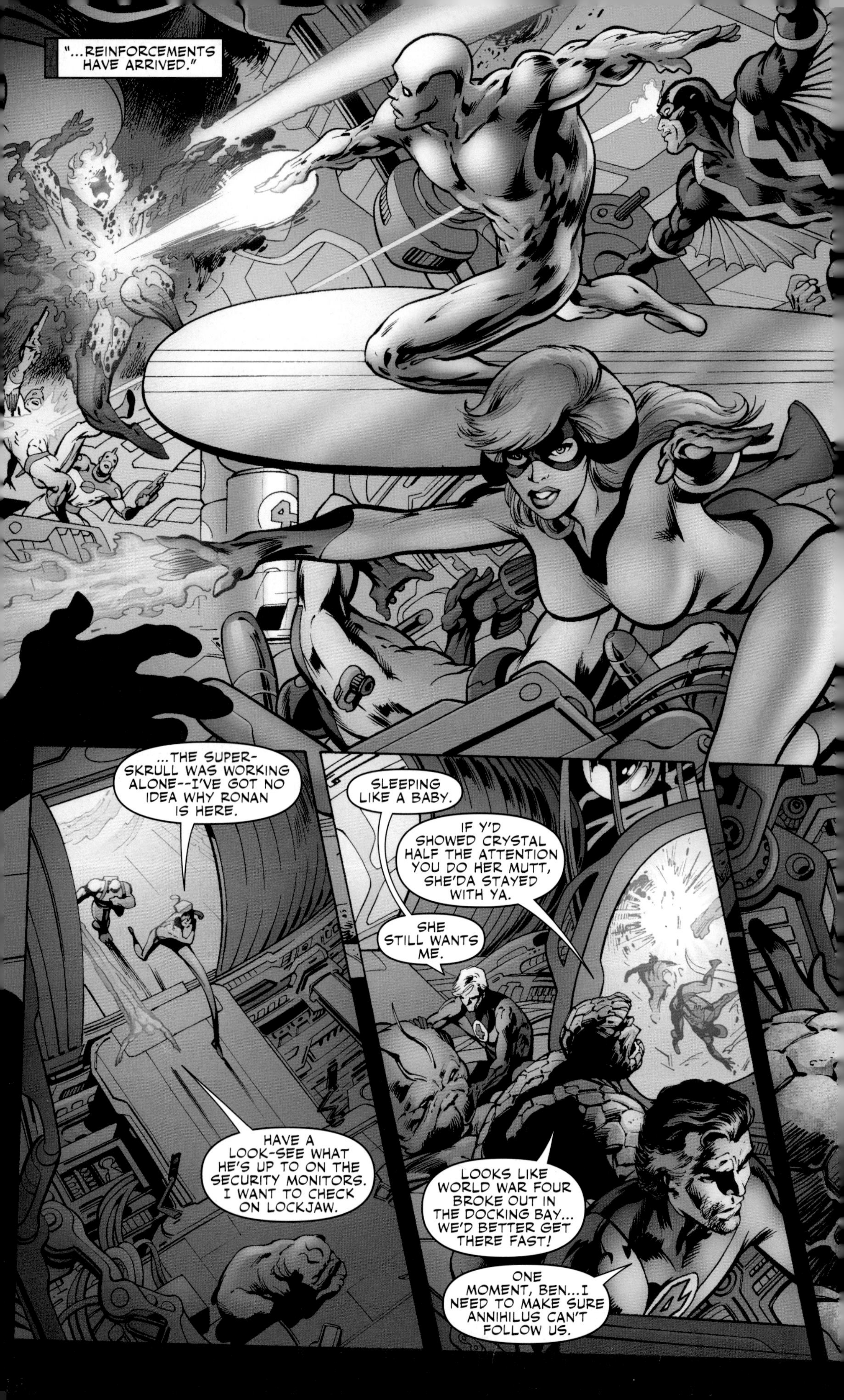
"...REINFORCEMENTS HAVE ARRIVED."
...THE SUPER-SKRULL WAS WORKING ALONE--I'VE GOT NO IDEA WHY RONAN IS HERE.
HAVE A LOOK-SEE WHAT HE'S UP TO ON THE SECURITY MONITORS. I WANT TO CHECK ON LOCKJAW.
SLEEPING LIKE A BABY.
IF Y'D SHOWED CRYSTAL HALF THE ATTENTION YOU DO HER MUTT, SHE'DA STAYED WITH YA.
SHE STILL WANTS ME.
LOOKS LIKE WORLD WAR FOUR BROKE OUT IN THE DOCKING BAY... WE'D BETTER GET THERE FAST!
ONE MOMENT, BEN...I NEED TO MAKE SURE ANNIHILUS CAN'T FOLLOW US.

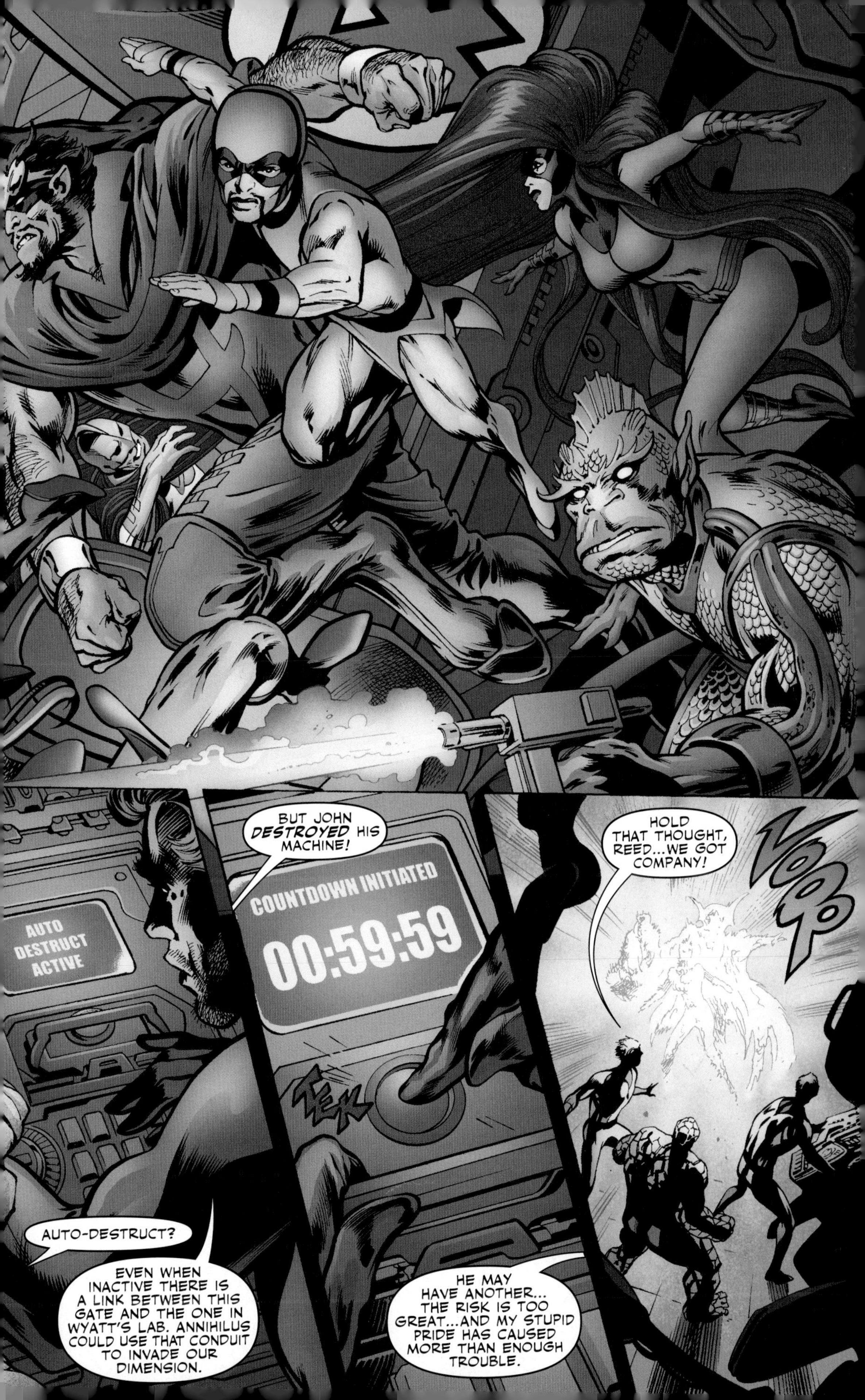
AUTO DESTRUCT ACTIVE
BUT JOHN DESTROYED HIS MACHINE!
COUNTDOWN INITIATED
00:59:59
TEK
AUTO-DESTRUCT?
EVEN WHEN INACTIVE THERE IS A LINK BETWEEN THIS GATE AND THE ONE IN WYATT'S LAB. ANNIHILUS COULD USE THAT CONDUIT TO INVADE OUR DIMENSION.
HE MAY HAVE ANOTHER... THE RISK IS TOO GREAT...AND MY STUPID PRIDE HAS CAUSED MORE THAN ENOUGH TROUBLE.
HOLD THAT THOUGHT, REED...WE GOT COMPANY!
VOOM

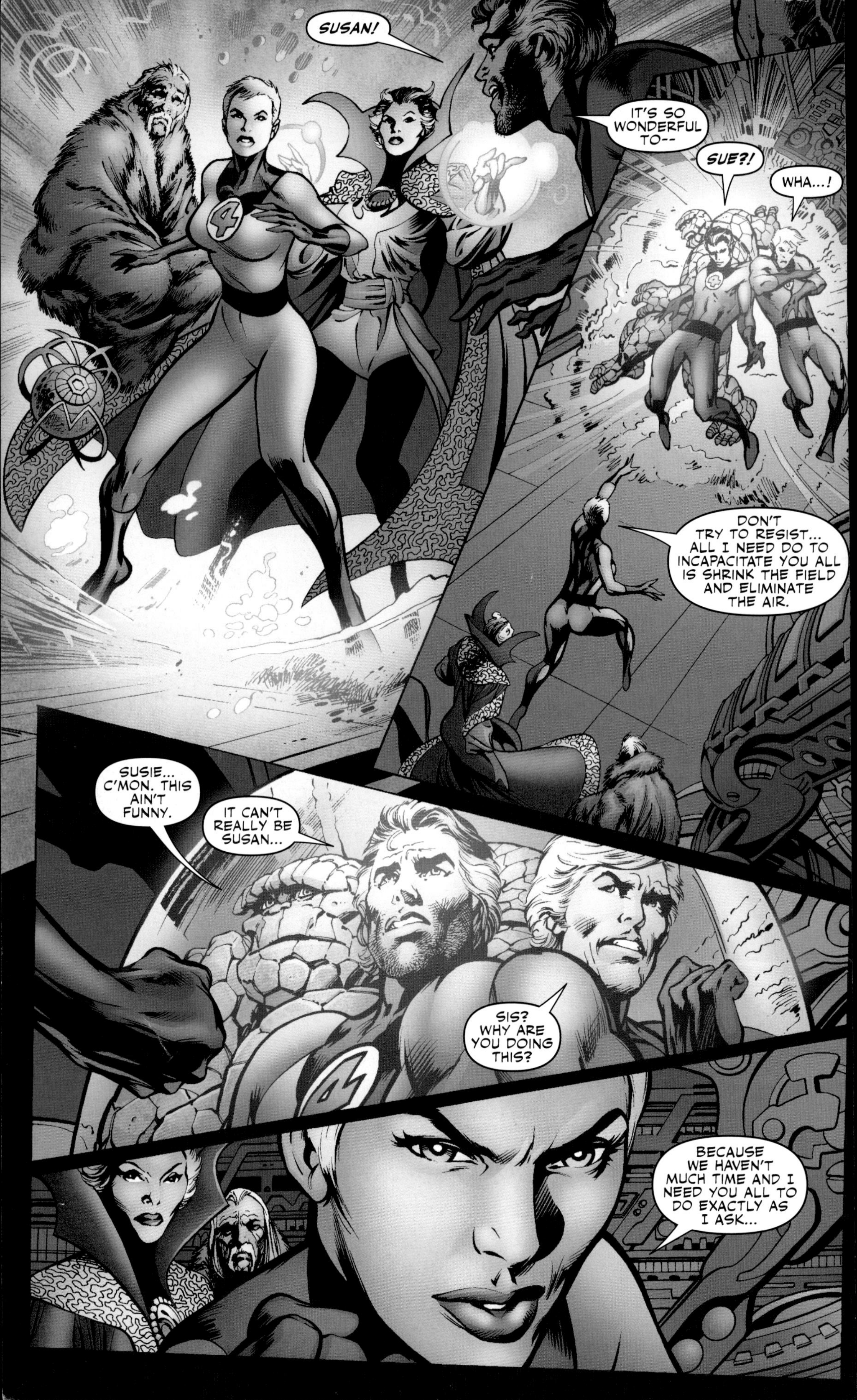
SUSAN!
IT'S SO WONDERFUL TO--
SUE?!
WHA...!
DON'T TRY TO RESIST... ALL I NEED DO TO INCAPACITATE YOU ALL IS SHRINK THE FIELD AND ELIMINATE THE AIR.
SUSIE... C'MON. THIS AIN'T FUNNY.
IT CAN'T REALLY BE SUSAN...
SIS? WHY ARE YOU DOING THIS?
BECAUSE WE HAVEN'T MUCH TIME AND I NEED YOU ALL TO DO EXACTLY AS I ASK...

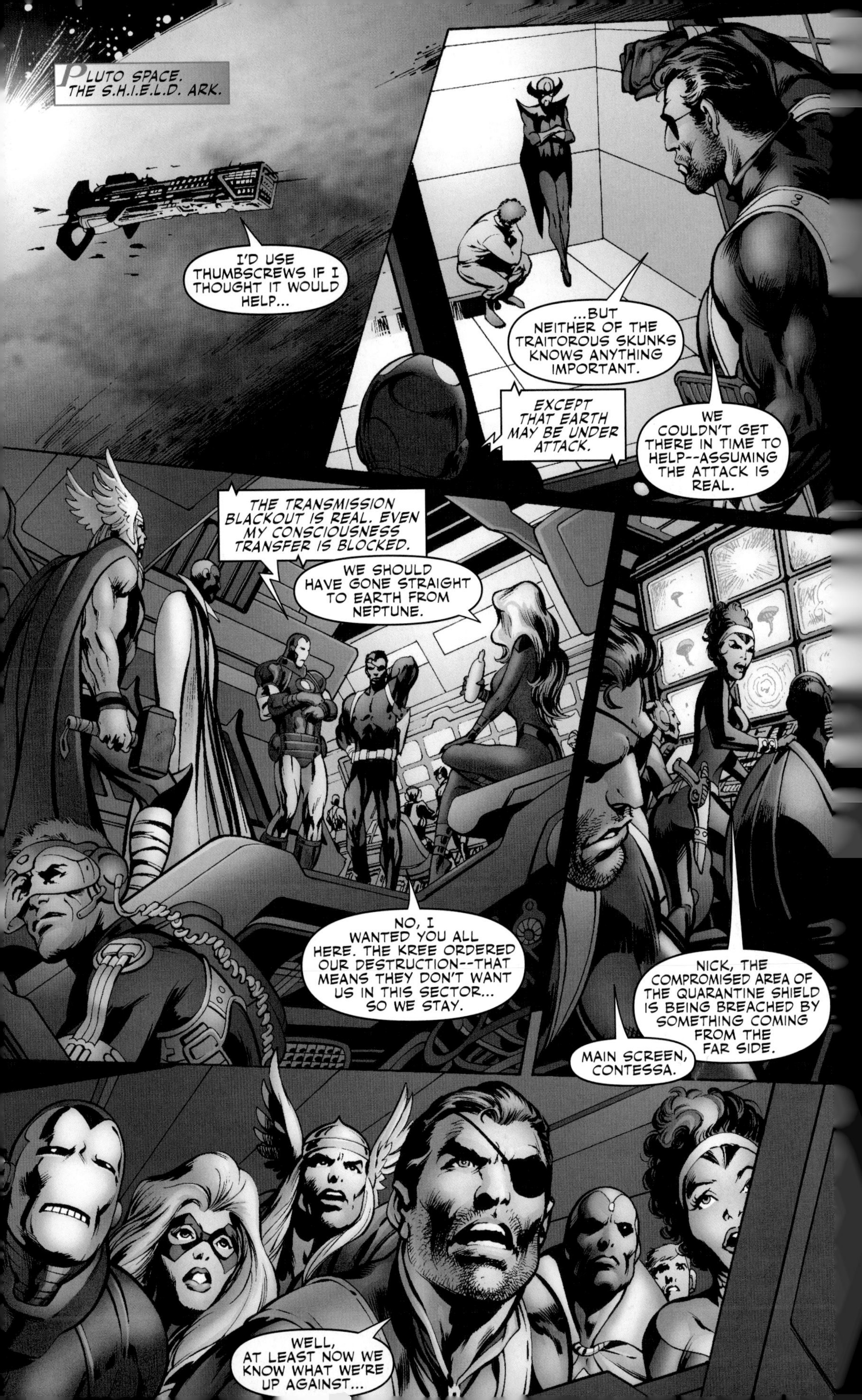
PLUTO SPACE. THE S.H.I.E.L.D. ARK.
I'D USE THUMBSCREWS IF I THOUGHT IT WOULD HELP...
...BUT NEITHER OF THE TRAITOROUS SKUNKS KNOWS ANYTHING IMPORTANT.
EXCEPT THAT EARTH MAY BE UNDER ATTACK.
WE COULDN'T GET THERE IN TIME TO HELP--ASSUMING THE ATTACK IS REAL.
THE TRANSMISSION BLACKOUT IS REAL. EVEN MY CONSCIOUSNESS TRANSFER IS BLOCKED.
WE SHOULD HAVE GONE STRAIGHT TO EARTH FROM NEPTUNE.
NO, I WANTED YOU ALL HERE. THE KREE ORDERED OUR DESTRUCTION--THAT MEANS THEY DON'T WANT US IN THIS SECTOR... SO WE STAY.
NICK, THE COMPROMISED AREA OF THE QUARANTINE SHIELD IS BEING BREACHED BY SOMETHING COMING FROM THE FAR SIDE.
MAIN SCREEN, CONTESSA.
WELL, AT LEAST NOW WE KNOW WHAT WE'RE UP AGAINST...

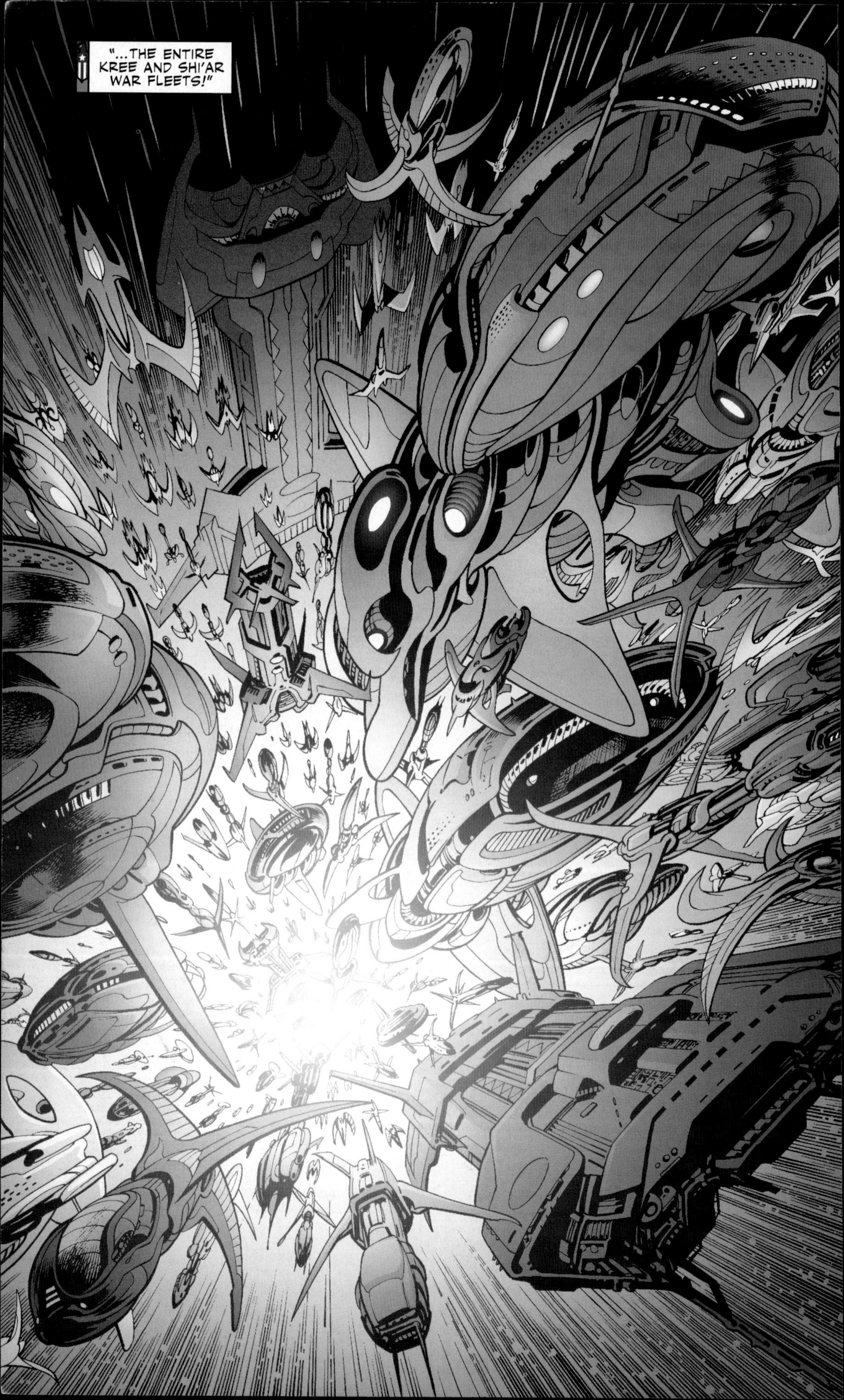
"...THE ENTIRE KREE AND SHI'AR WAR FLEETS!"

THE END THE END THE END THE END THE END THE END

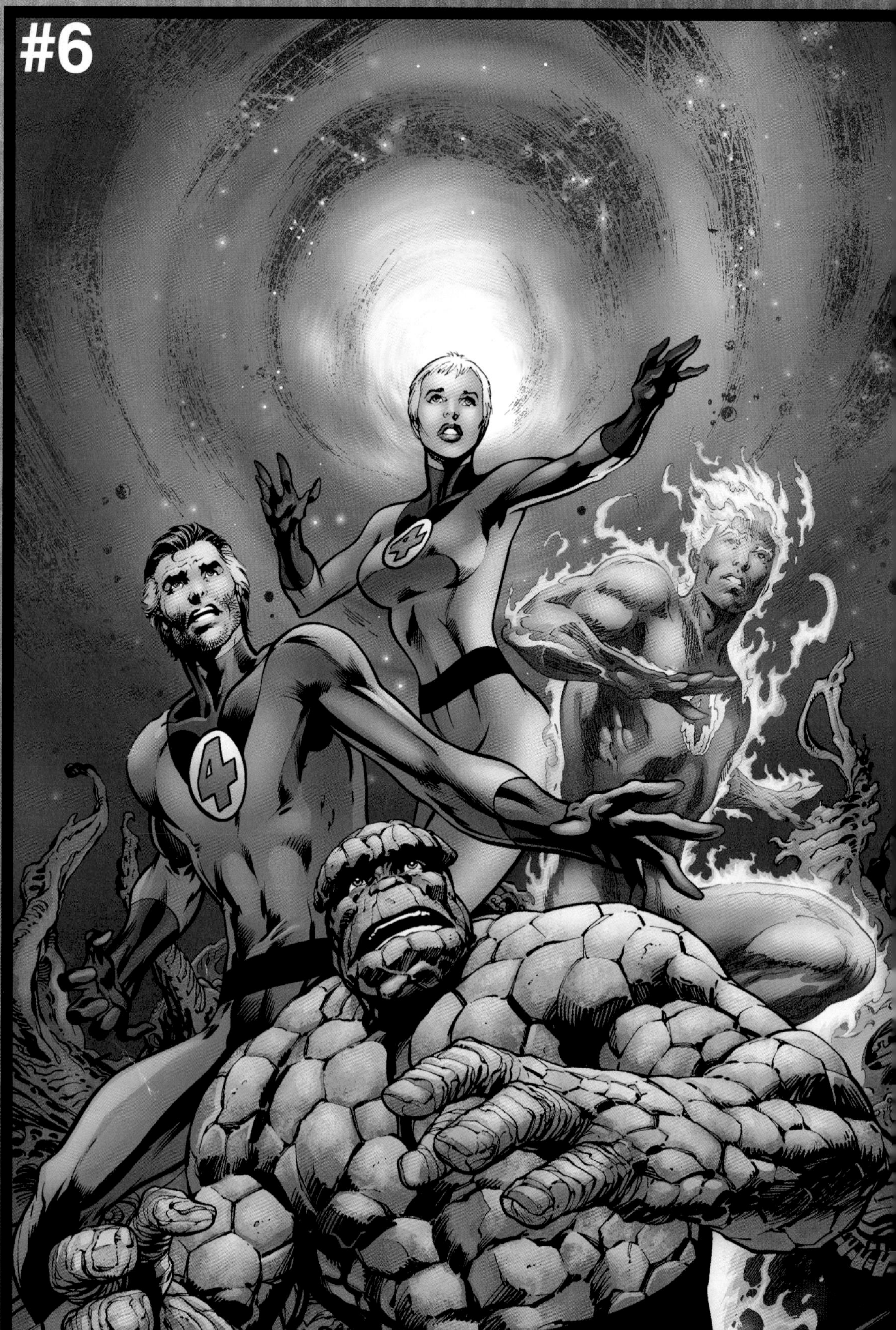
#6

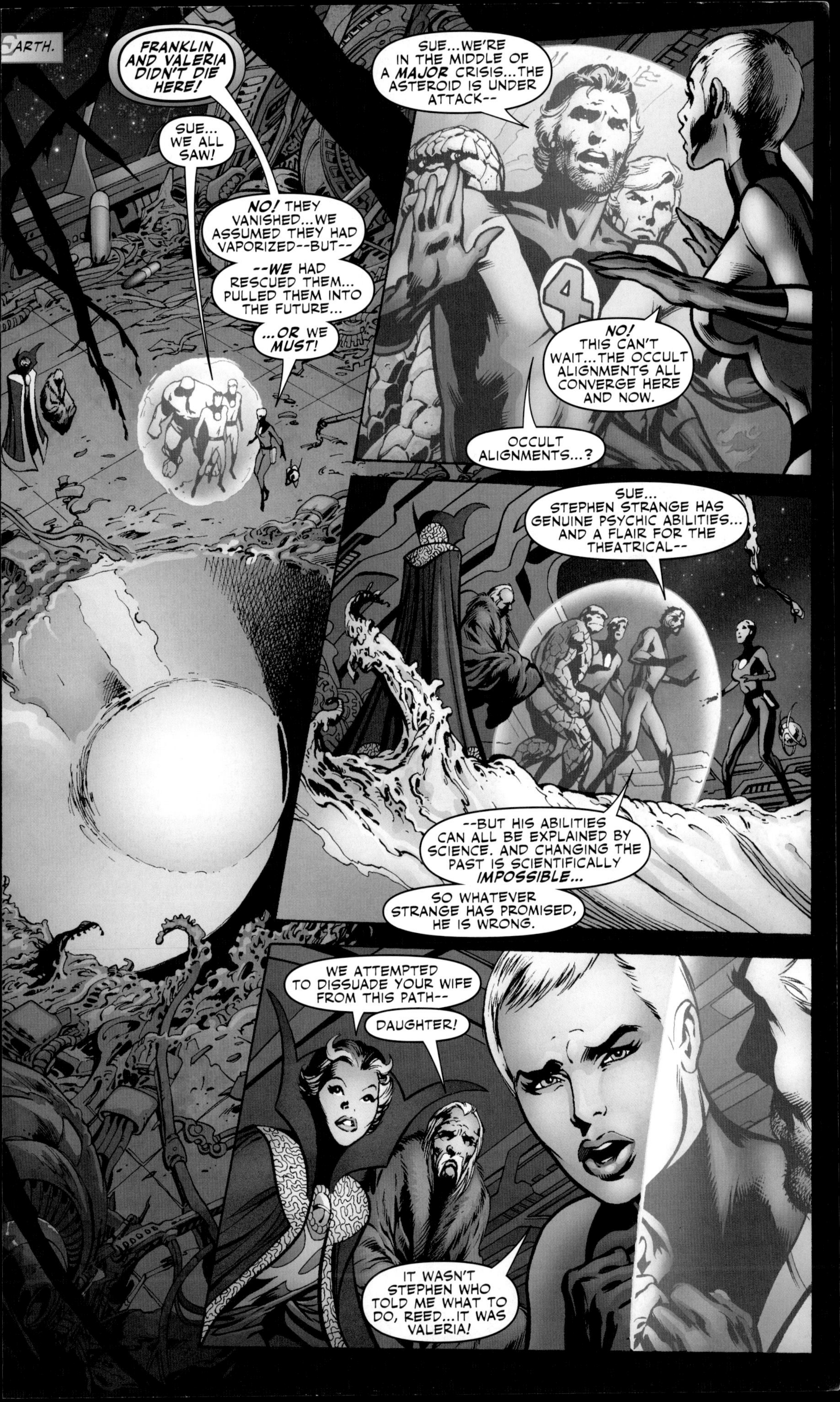
EARTH.
FRANKLIN AND VALERIA DIDN'T DIE HERE!
SUE... WE ALL SAW!
NO! THEY VANISHED...WE ASSUMED THEY HAD VAPORIZED--BUT--
--WE HAD RESCUED THEM... PULLED THEM INTO THE FUTURE...
...OR WE MUST!
SUE...WE'RE IN THE MIDDLE OF A MAJOR CRISIS...THE ASTEROID IS UNDER ATTACK--
NO! THIS CAN'T WAIT...THE OCCULT ALIGNMENTS ALL CONVERGE HERE AND NOW.
OCCULT ALIGNMENTS...?
SUE... STEPHEN STRANGE HAS GENUINE PSYCHIC ABILITIES... AND A FLAIR FOR THE THEATRICAL--
--BUT HIS ABILITIES CAN ALL BE EXPLAINED BY SCIENCE. AND CHANGING THE PAST IS SCIENTIFICALLY IMPOSSIBLE...
SO WHATEVER STRANGE HAS PROMISED, HE IS WRONG.
WE ATTEMPTED TO DISSUADE YOUR WIFE FROM THIS PATH--
DAUGHTER!
IT WASN'T STEPHEN WHO TOLD ME WHAT TO DO, REED...IT WAS VALERIA!

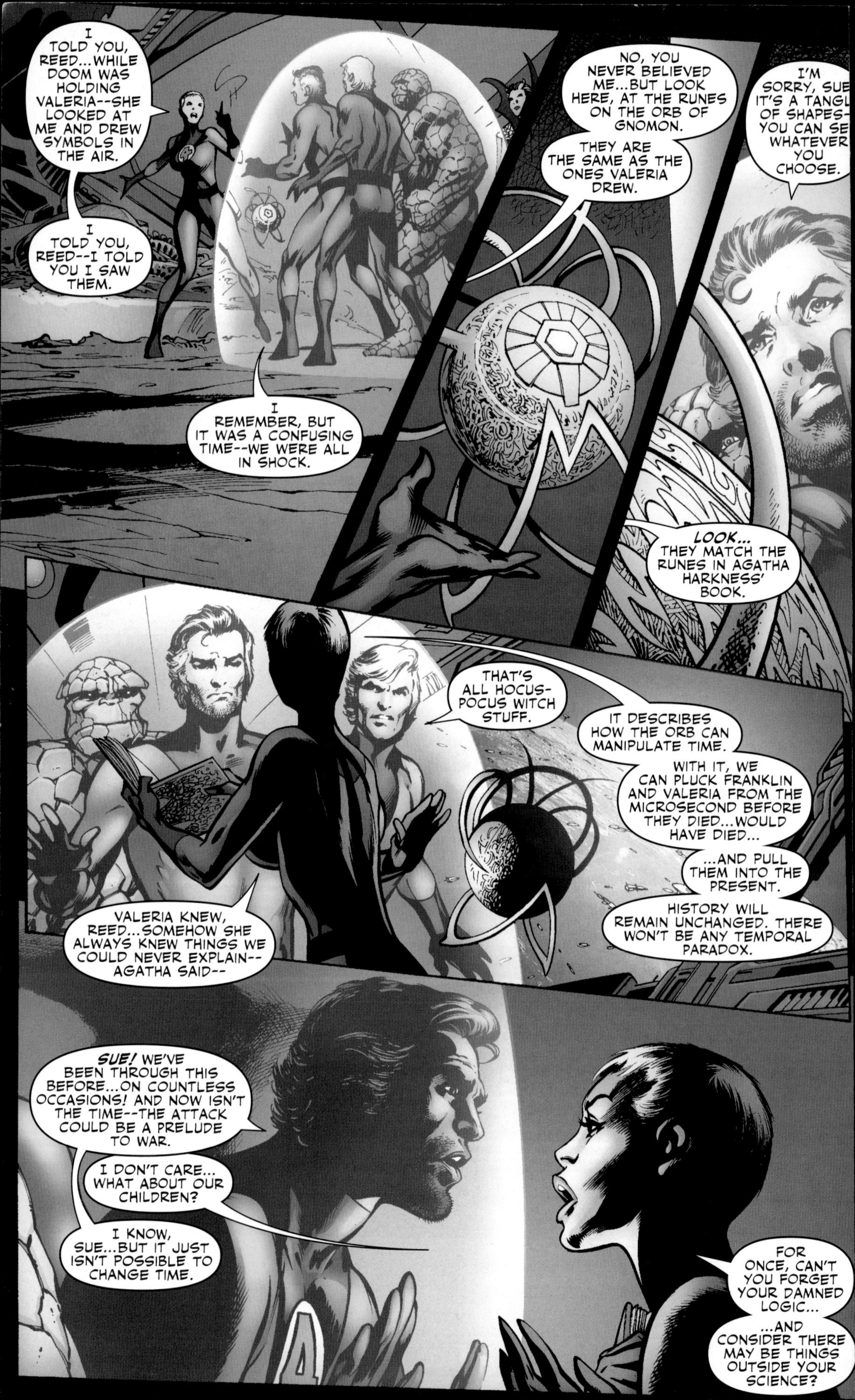

I TOLD YOU, REED...WHILE DOOM WAS HOLDING VALERIA--SHE LOOKED AT ME AND DREW SYMBOLS IN THE AIR.
I TOLD YOU, REED--I TOLD YOU I SAW THEM.
I REMEMBER, BUT IT WAS A CONFUSING TIME--WE WERE ALL IN SHOCK.
NO, YOU NEVER BELIEVED ME...BUT LOOK HERE, AT THE RUNES ON THE ORB OF GNOMON.
THEY ARE THE SAME AS THE ONES VALERIA DREW.
I'M SORRY, SUE IT'S A TANGL OF SHAPES- YOU CAN SE WHATEVER YOU CHOOSE.
LOOK... THEY MATCH THE RUNES IN AGATHA HARKNESS' BOOK.
THAT'S ALL HOCUS-POCUS WITCH STUFF.
IT DESCRIBES HOW THE ORB CAN MANIPULATE TIME.
WITH IT, WE CAN PLUCK FRANKLIN AND VALERIA FROM THE MICROSECOND BEFORE THEY DIED...WOULD HAVE DIED...
...AND PULL THEM INTO THE PRESENT.
HISTORY WILL REMAIN UNCHANGED. THERE WON'T BE ANY TEMPORAL PARADOX.
VALERIA KNEW, REED...SOMEHOW SHE ALWAYS KNEW THINGS WE COULD NEVER EXPLAIN--AGATHA SAID--
SUE! WE'VE BEEN THROUGH THIS BEFORE...ON COUNTLESS OCCASIONS! AND NOW ISN'T THE TIME--THE ATTACK COULD BE A PRELUDE TO WAR.
I DON'T CARE... WHAT ABOUT OUR CHILDREN?
I KNOW, SUE...BUT IT JUST ISN'T POSSIBLE TO CHANGE TIME.
FOR ONCE, CAN'T YOU FORGET YOUR DAMNED LOGIC...
...AND CONSIDER THERE MAY BE THINGS OUTSIDE YOUR SCIENCE?

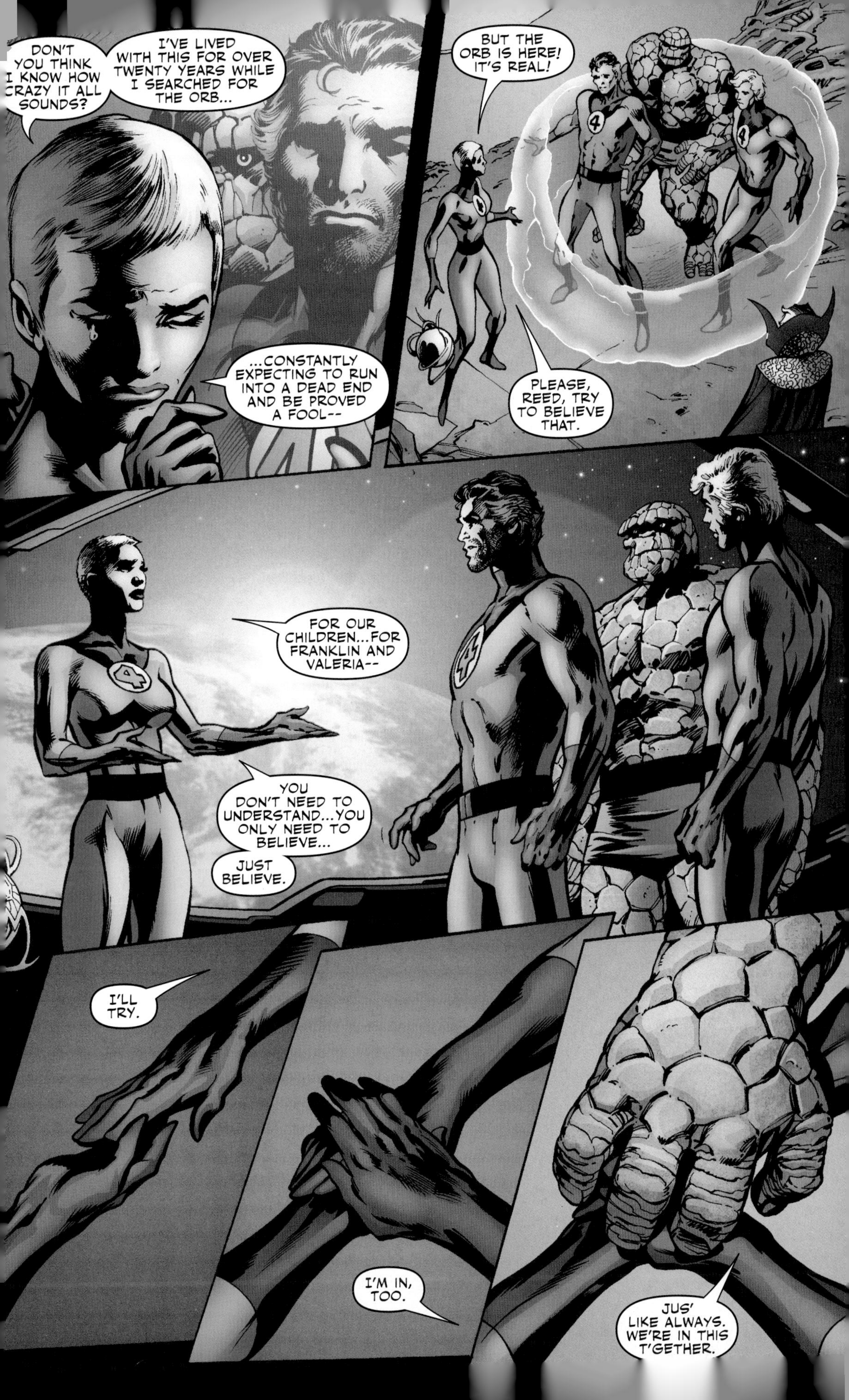
DON'T YOU THINK I KNOW HOW CRAZY IT ALL SOUNDS?
I'VE LIVED WITH THIS FOR OVER TWENTY YEARS WHILE I SEARCHED FOR THE ORB...
...CONSTANTLY EXPECTING TO RUN INTO A DEAD END AND BE PROVED A FOOL--
BUT THE ORB IS HERE! IT'S REAL!
PLEASE, REED, TRY TO BELIEVE THAT.
FOR OUR CHILDREN...FOR FRANKLIN AND VALERIA--
YOU DON'T NEED TO UNDERSTAND...YOU ONLY NEED TO BELIEVE...
JUST BELIEVE.
I'LL TRY.
I'M IN, TOO.
JUS' LIKE ALWAYS. WE'RE IN THIS T'GETHER.

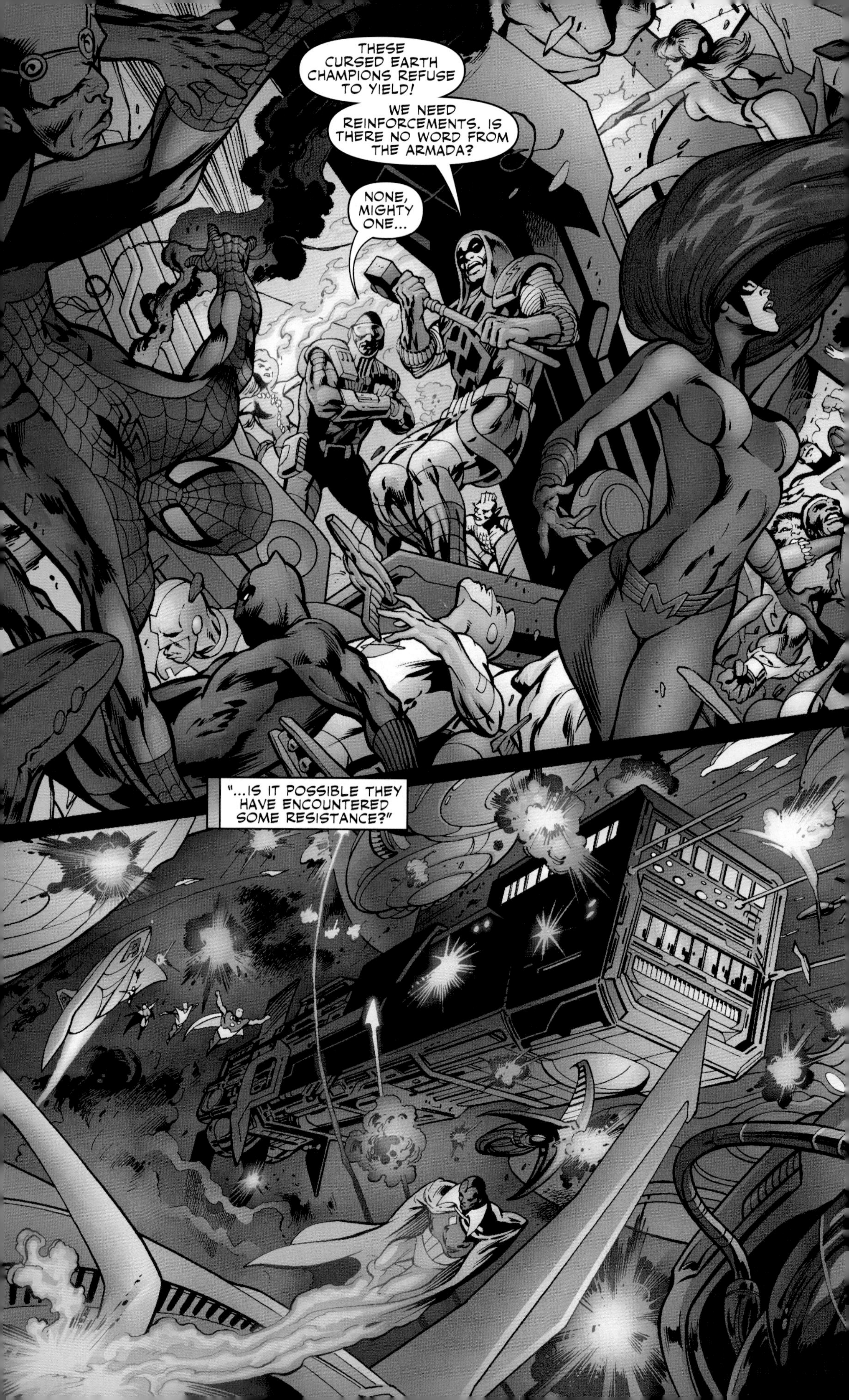
THESE CURSED EARTH CHAMPIONS REFUSE TO YIELD!
WE NEED REINFORCEMENTS. IS THERE NO WORD FROM THE ARMADA?
NONE, MIGHTY ONE...
"...IS IT POSSIBLE THEY HAVE ENCOUNTERED SOME RESISTANCE?"

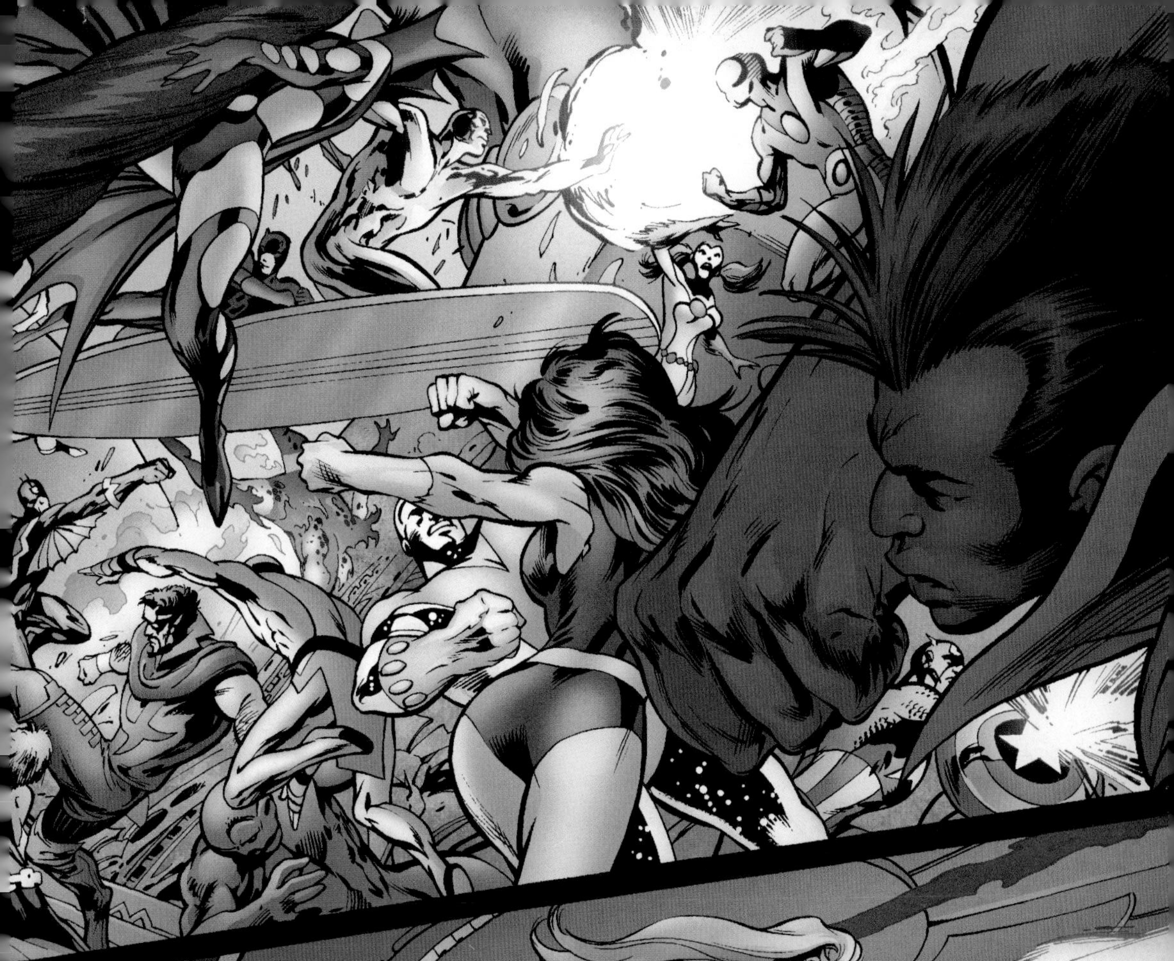

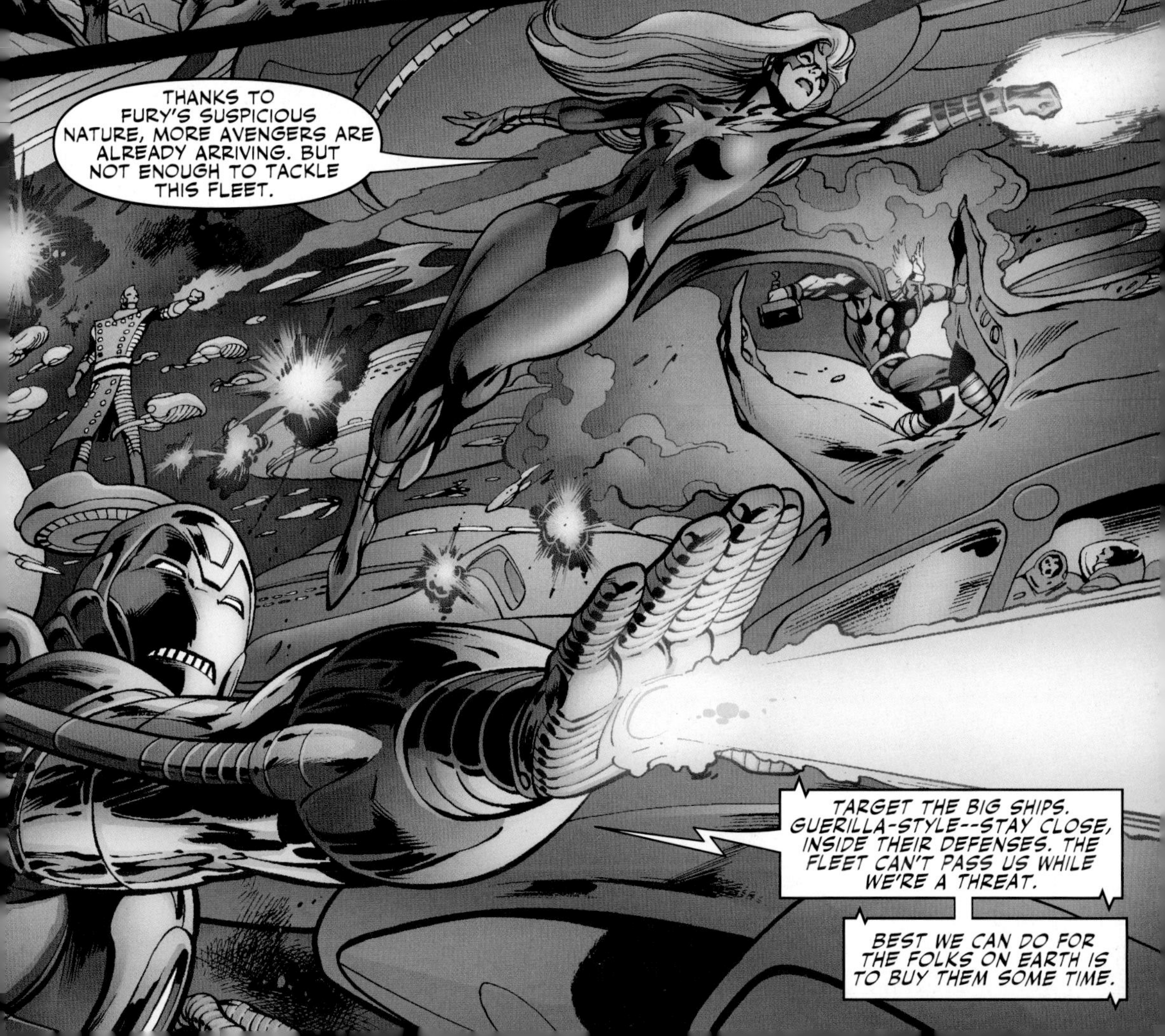
THANKS TO FURY'S SUSPICIOUS NATURE, MORE AVENGERS ARE ALREADY ARRIVING. BUT NOT ENOUGH TO TACKLE THIS FLEET.
TARGET THE BIG SHIPS. GUERILLA-STYLE--STAY CLOSE, INSIDE THEIR DEFENSES. THE FLEET CAN'T PASS US WHILE WE'RE A THREAT.
BEST WE CAN DO FOR THE FOLKS ON EARTH IS TO BUY THEM SOME TIME.

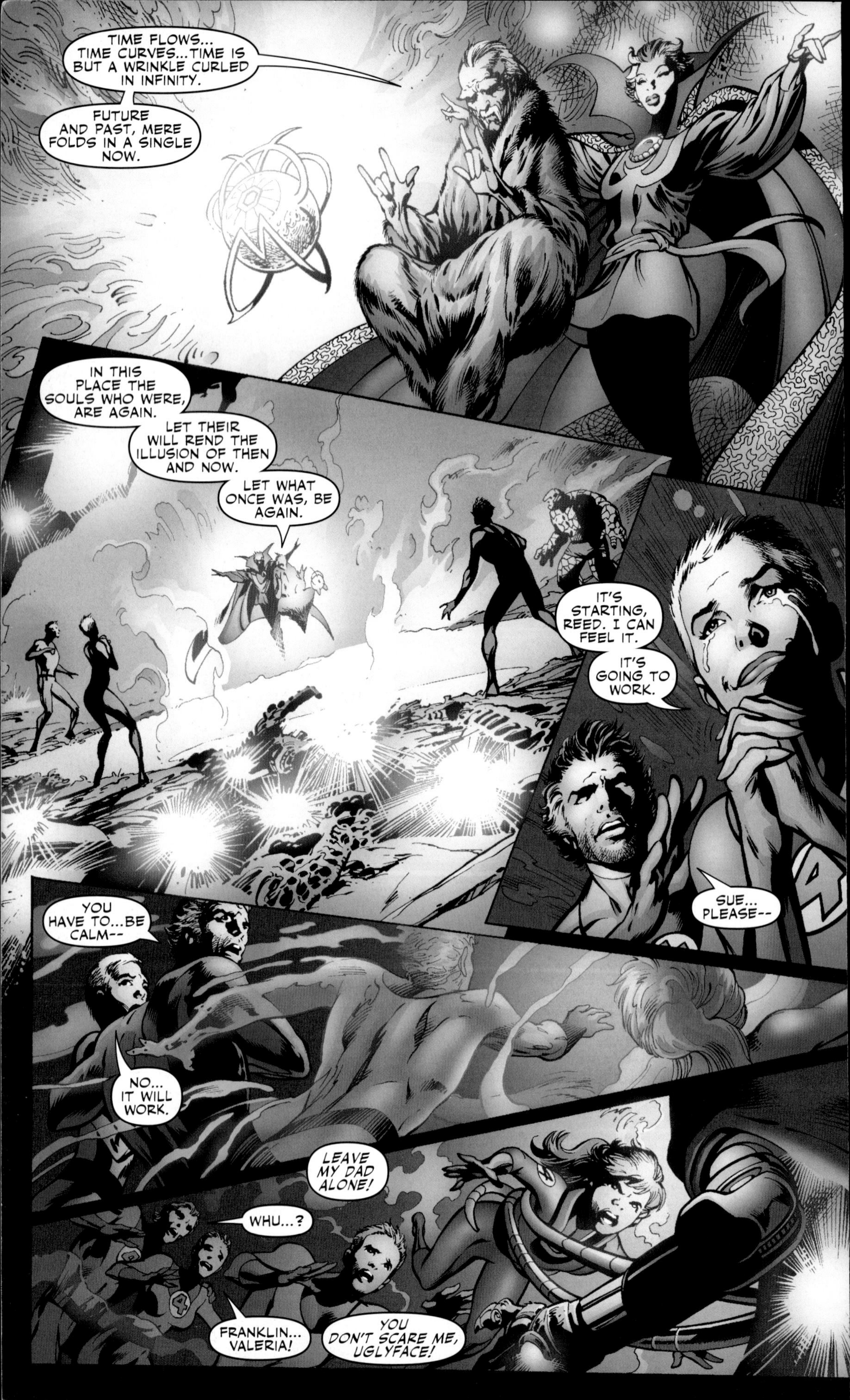
TIME FLOWS... TIME CURVES...TIME IS BUT A WRINKLE CURLED IN INFINITY.
FUTURE AND PAST, MERE FOLDS IN A SINGLE NOW.
IN THIS PLACE THE SOULS WHO WERE, ARE AGAIN.
LET THEIR WILL REND THE ILLUSION OF THEN AND NOW.
LET WHAT ONCE WAS, BE AGAIN.
IT'S STARTING, REED. I CAN FEEL IT.
IT'S GOING TO WORK.
SUE... PLEASE--
YOU HAVE TO...BE CALM--
NO... IT WILL WORK.
LEAVE MY DAD ALONE!
WHU...?
FRANKLIN... VALERIA!
YOU DON'T SCARE ME, UGLYFACE!

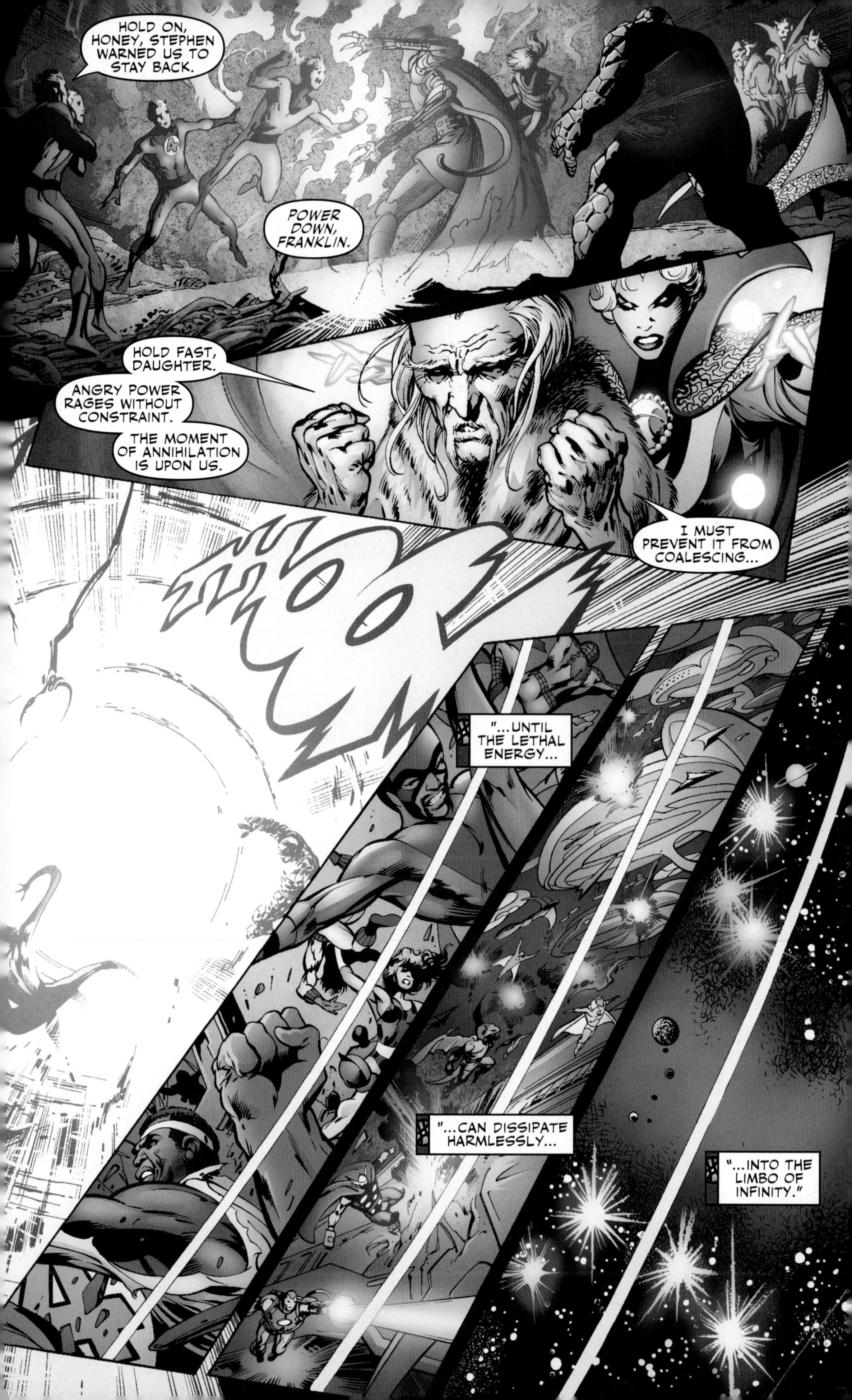
HOLD ON, HONEY, STEPHEN WARNED US TO STAY BACK.
POWER DOWN, FRANKLIN.
HOLD FAST, DAUGHTER.
ANGRY POWER RAGES WITHOUT CONSTRAINT.
THE MOMENT OF ANNIHILATION IS UPON US.
I MUST PREVENT IT FROM COALESCING...
FWOOM
"...UNTIL THE LETHAL ENERGY...
"...CAN DISSIPATE HARMLESSLY...
"...INTO THE LIMBO OF INFINITY."

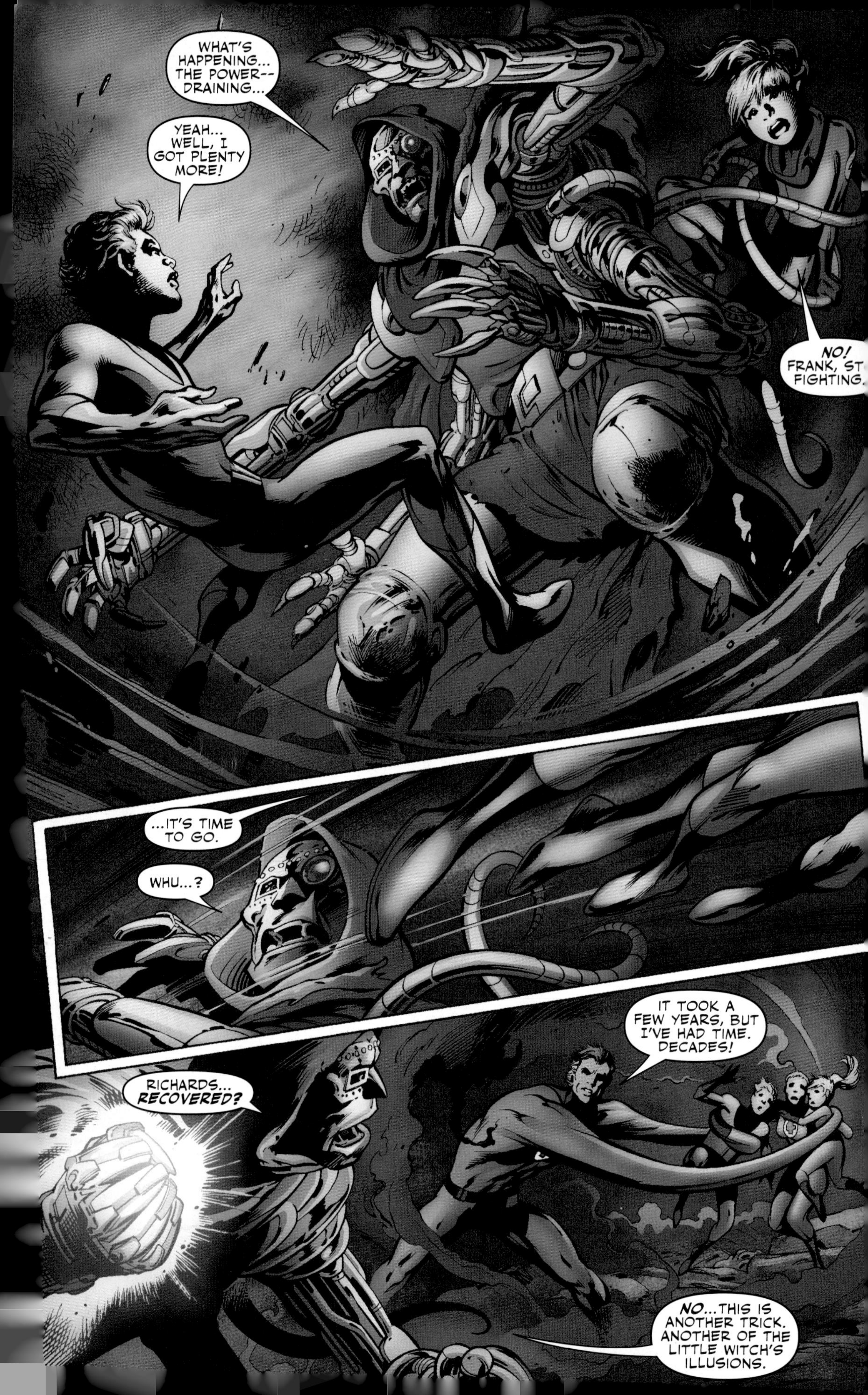
WHAT'S HAPPENING... THE POWER-- DRAINING...
YEAH... WELL, I GOT PLENTY MORE!
NO! FRANK, ST FIGHTING.
...IT'S TIME TO GO.
WHU...?
RICHARDS... RECOVERED?
IT TOOK A FEW YEARS, BUT I'VE HAD TIME. DECADES!
NO...THIS IS ANOTHER TRICK. ANOTHER OF THE LITTLE WITCH'S ILLUSIONS.

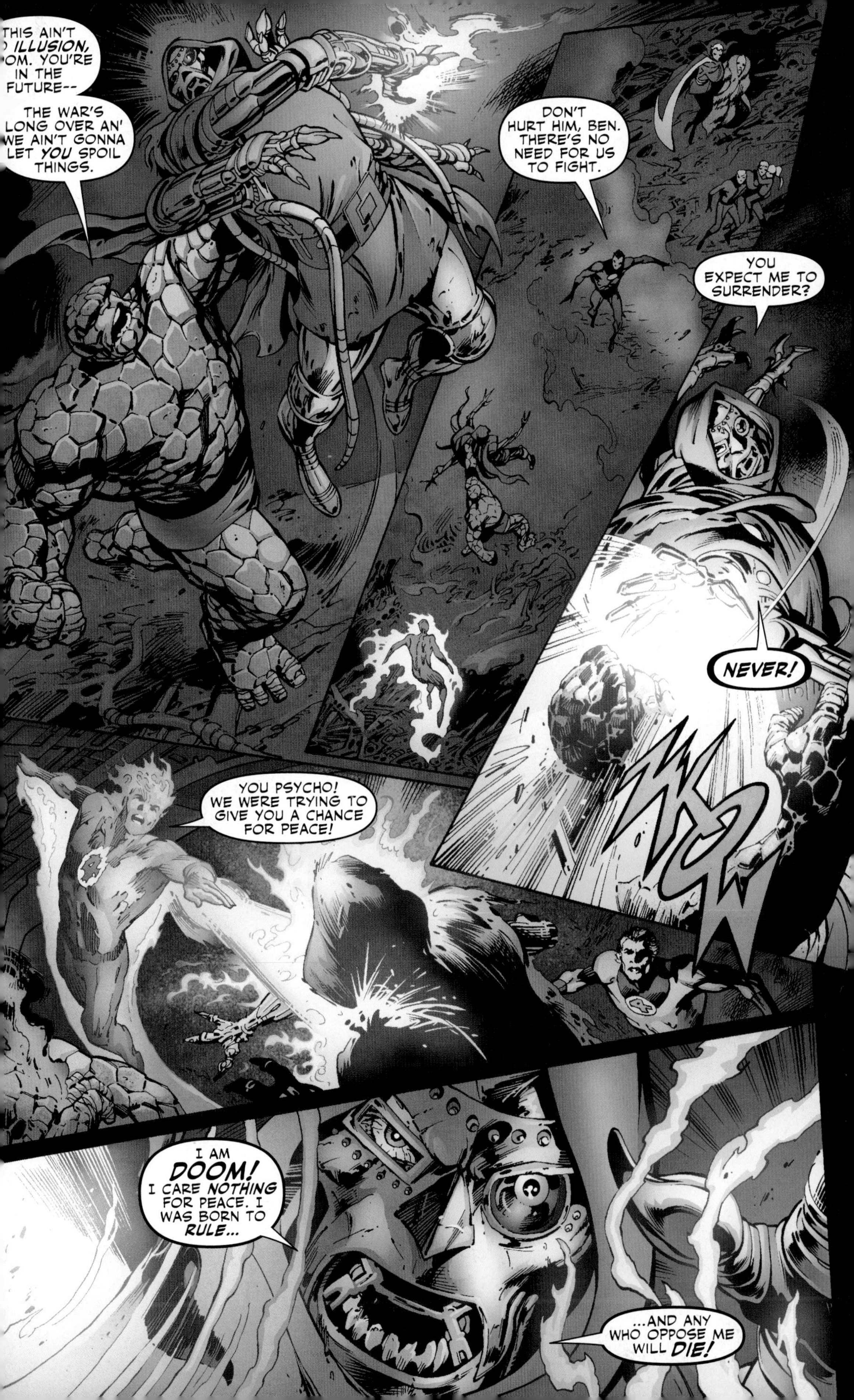
THIS AIN'T ... ILLUSION, ...OM. YOU'RE IN THE FUTURE--
THE WAR'S LONG OVER AN' WE AIN'T GONNA LET YOU SPOIL THINGS.
DON'T HURT HIM, BEN. THERE'S NO NEED FOR US TO FIGHT.
YOU EXPECT ME TO SURRENDER?
NEVER!
YOU PSYCHO! WE WERE TRYING TO GIVE YOU A CHANCE FOR PEACE!
I AM DOOM! I CARE NOTHING FOR PEACE. I WAS BORN TO RULE...
...AND ANY WHO OPPOSE ME WILL DIE!

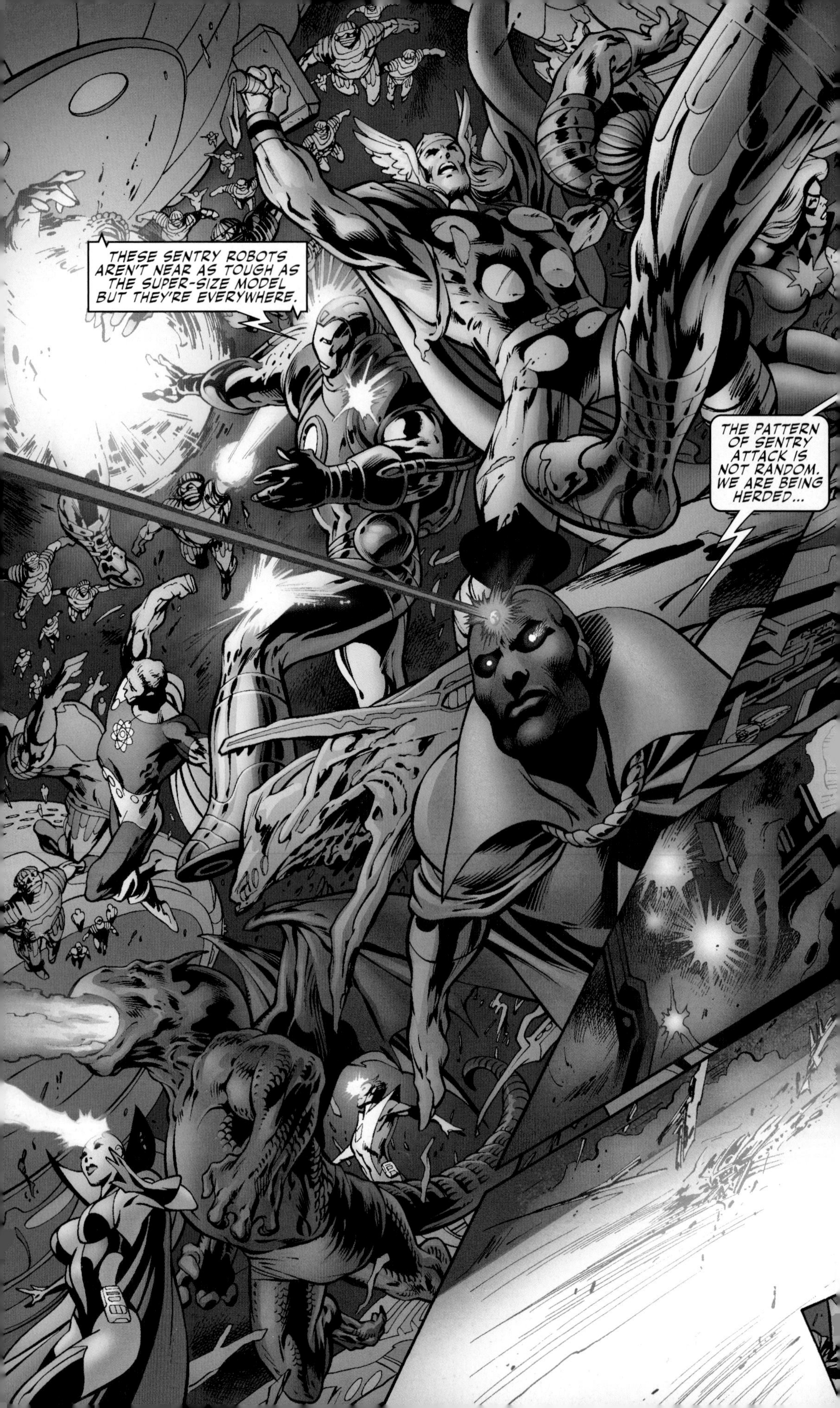
THESE SENTRY ROBOTS AREN'T NEAR AS TOUGH AS THE SUPER-SIZE MODEL BUT THEY'RE EVERYWHERE.
THE PATTERN OF SENTRY ATTACK IS NOT RANDOM. WE ARE BEING HERDED...

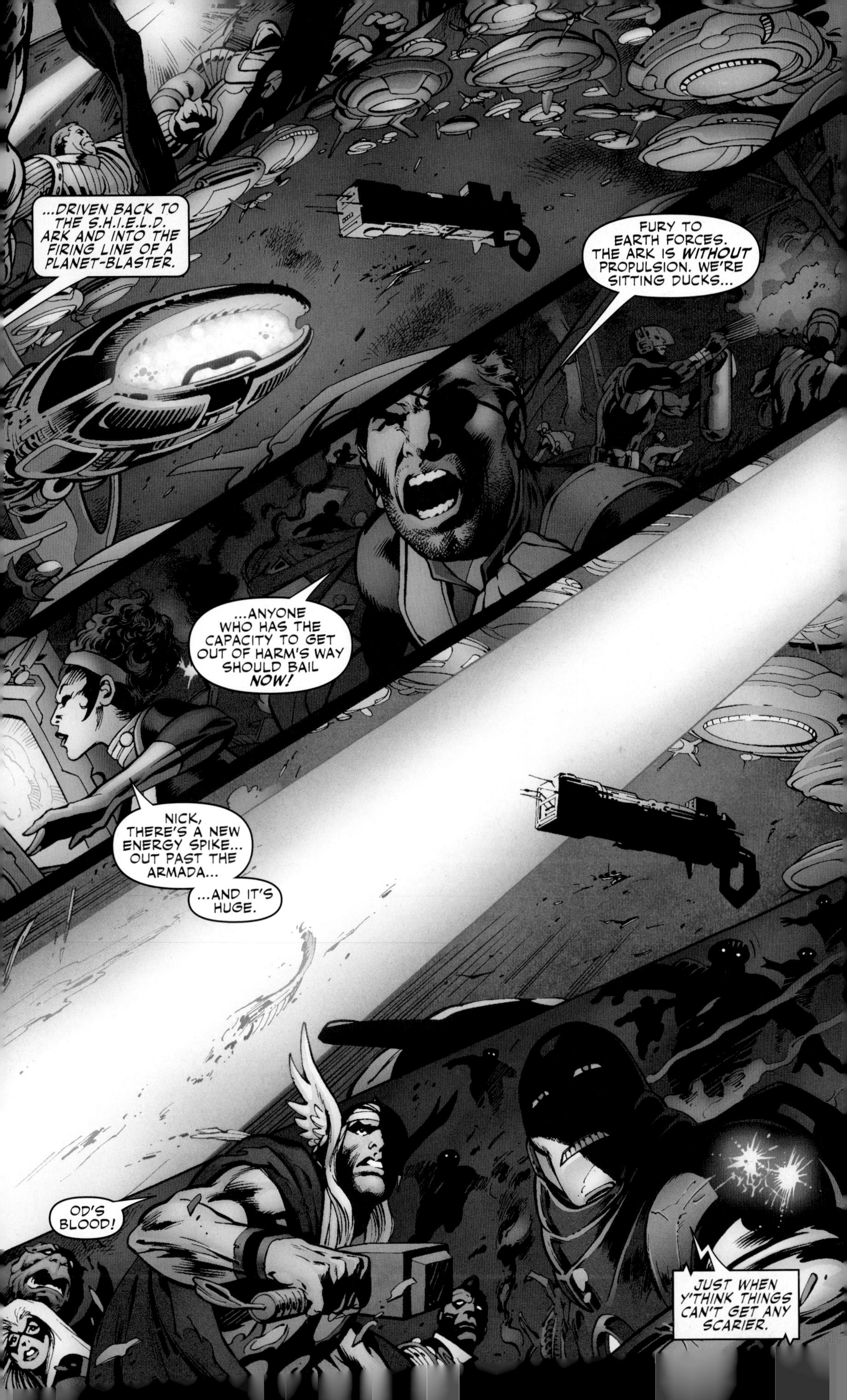
...DRIVEN BACK TO THE S.H.I.E.L.D. ARK AND INTO THE FIRING LINE OF A PLANET-BLASTER.
FURY TO EARTH FORCES. THE ARK IS *WITHOUT* PROPULSION. WE'RE SITTING DUCKS...
...ANYONE WHO HAS THE CAPACITY TO GET OUT OF HARM'S WAY SHOULD BAIL *NOW!*
NICK, THERE'S A NEW ENERGY SPIKE... OUT PAST THE ARMADA...
...AND IT'S HUGE.
OD'S BLOOD!
JUST WHEN Y'THINK THINGS CAN'T GET ANY SCARIER.

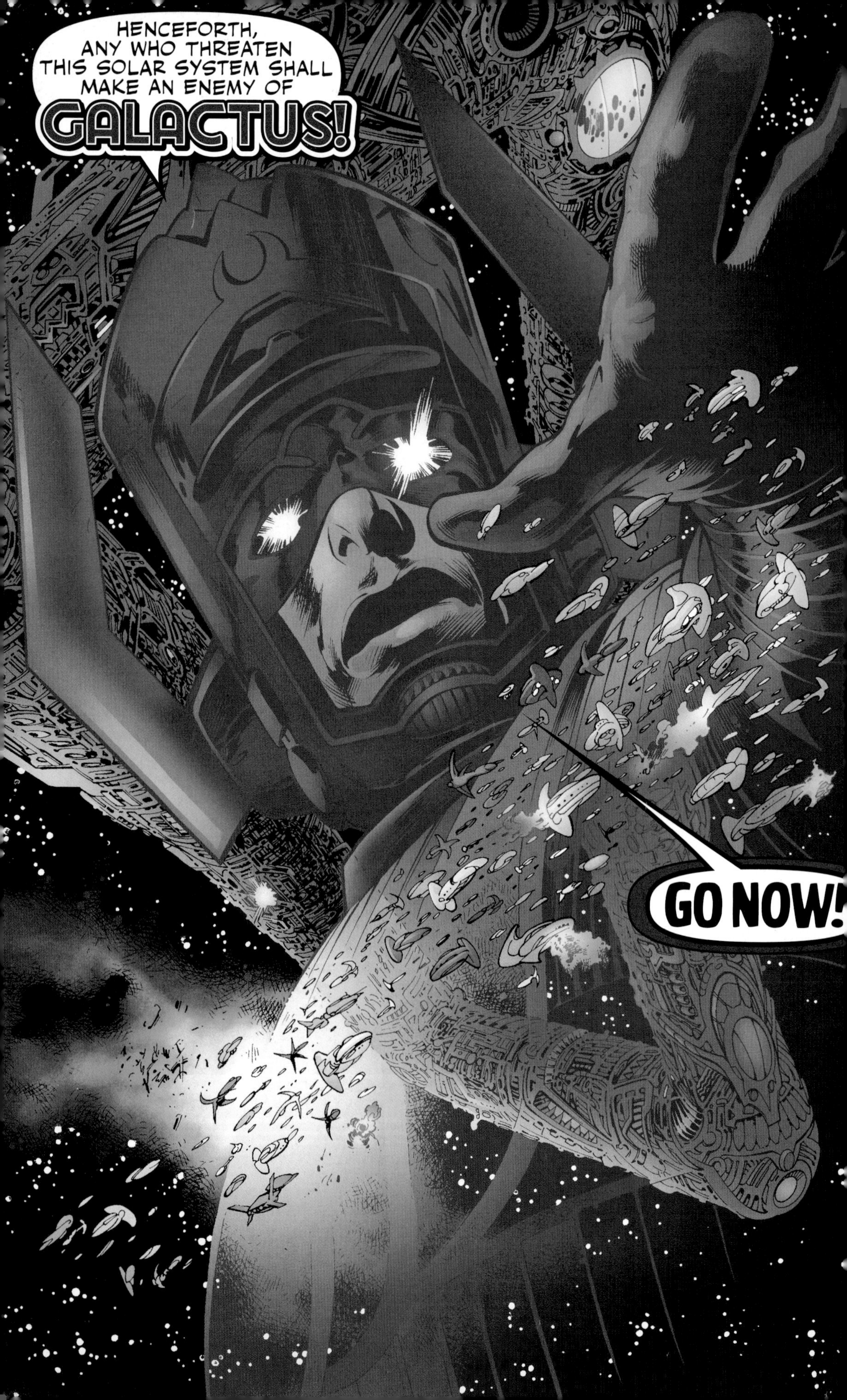
HENCEFORTH, ANY WHO THREATEN THIS SOLAR SYSTEM SHALL MAKE AN ENEMY OF GALACTUS!
GO NOW!

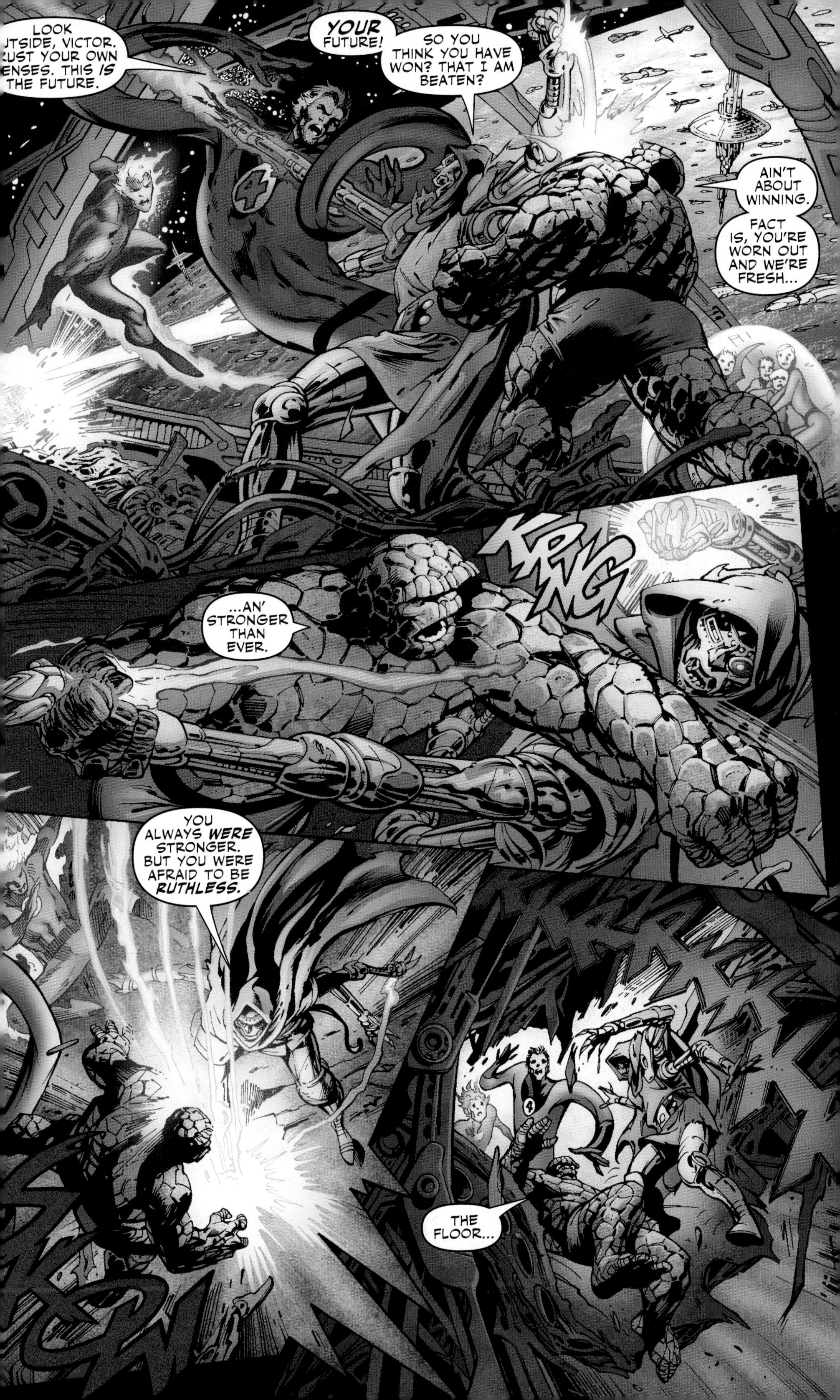

LOOK
UTSIDE, VICTOR.
RUST YOUR OWN
ENSES. THIS IS
THE FUTURE.
YOUR FUTURE!
SO YOU THINK YOU HAVE WON? THAT I AM BEATEN?
AIN'T ABOUT WINNING.
FACT IS, YOU'RE WORN OUT AND WE'RE FRESH...
KRANG
...AN' STRONGER THAN EVER.
YOU ALWAYS WERE STRONGER. BUT YOU WERE AFRAID TO BE RUTHLESS.
THE FLOOR...

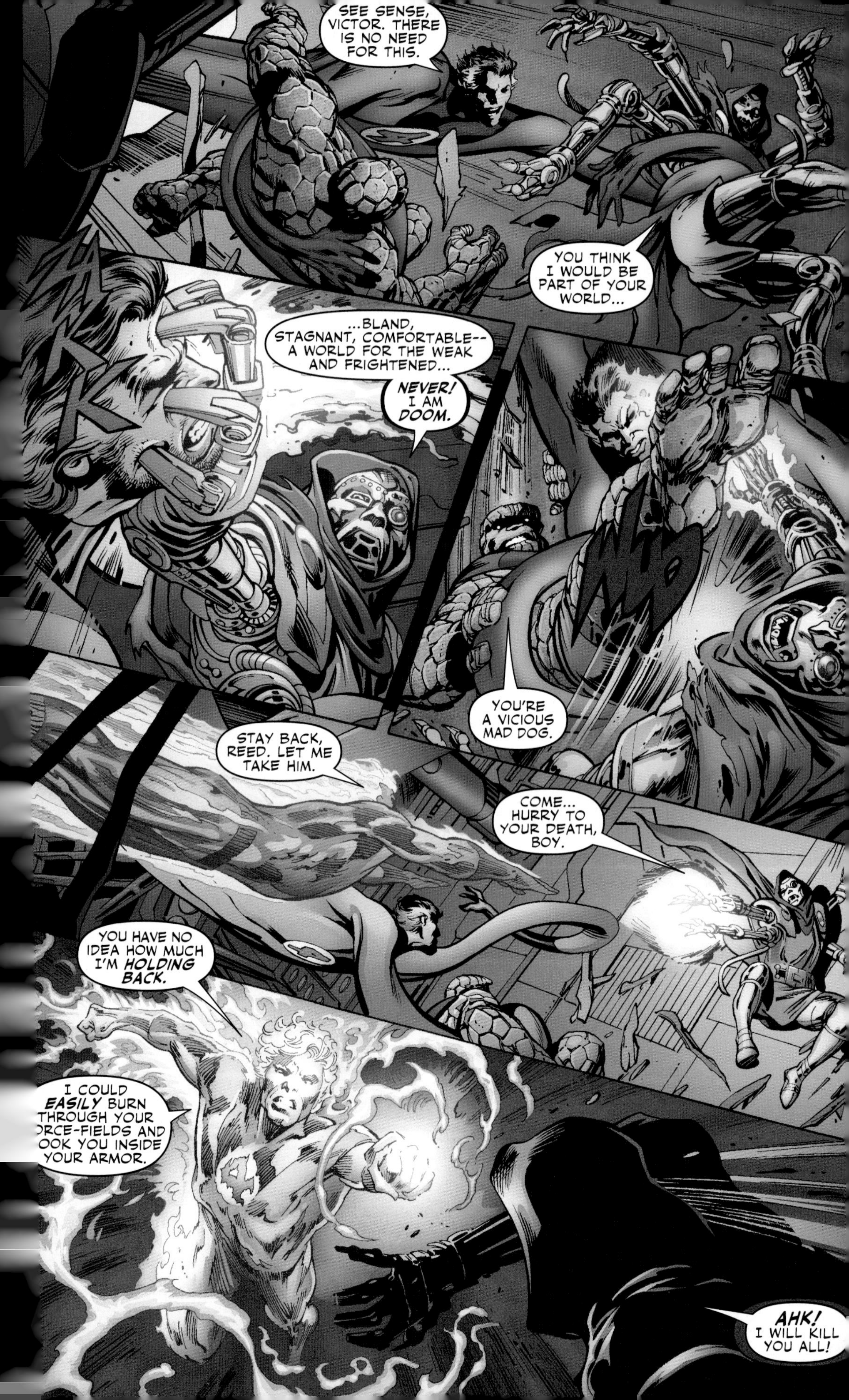
SEE SENSE, VICTOR. THERE IS NO NEED FOR THIS.
YOU THINK I WOULD BE PART OF YOUR WORLD...
...BLAND, STAGNANT, COMFORTABLE-- A WORLD FOR THE WEAK AND FRIGHTENED...
NEVER! I AM DOOM.
YOU'RE A VICIOUS MAD DOG.
STAY BACK, REED. LET ME TAKE HIM.
COME... HURRY TO YOUR DEATH, BOY.
YOU HAVE NO IDEA HOW MUCH I'M HOLDING BACK.
I COULD EASILY BURN THROUGH YOUR ORCE-FIELDS AND OOK YOU INSIDE YOUR ARMOR.
AHK! I WILL KILL YOU ALL!

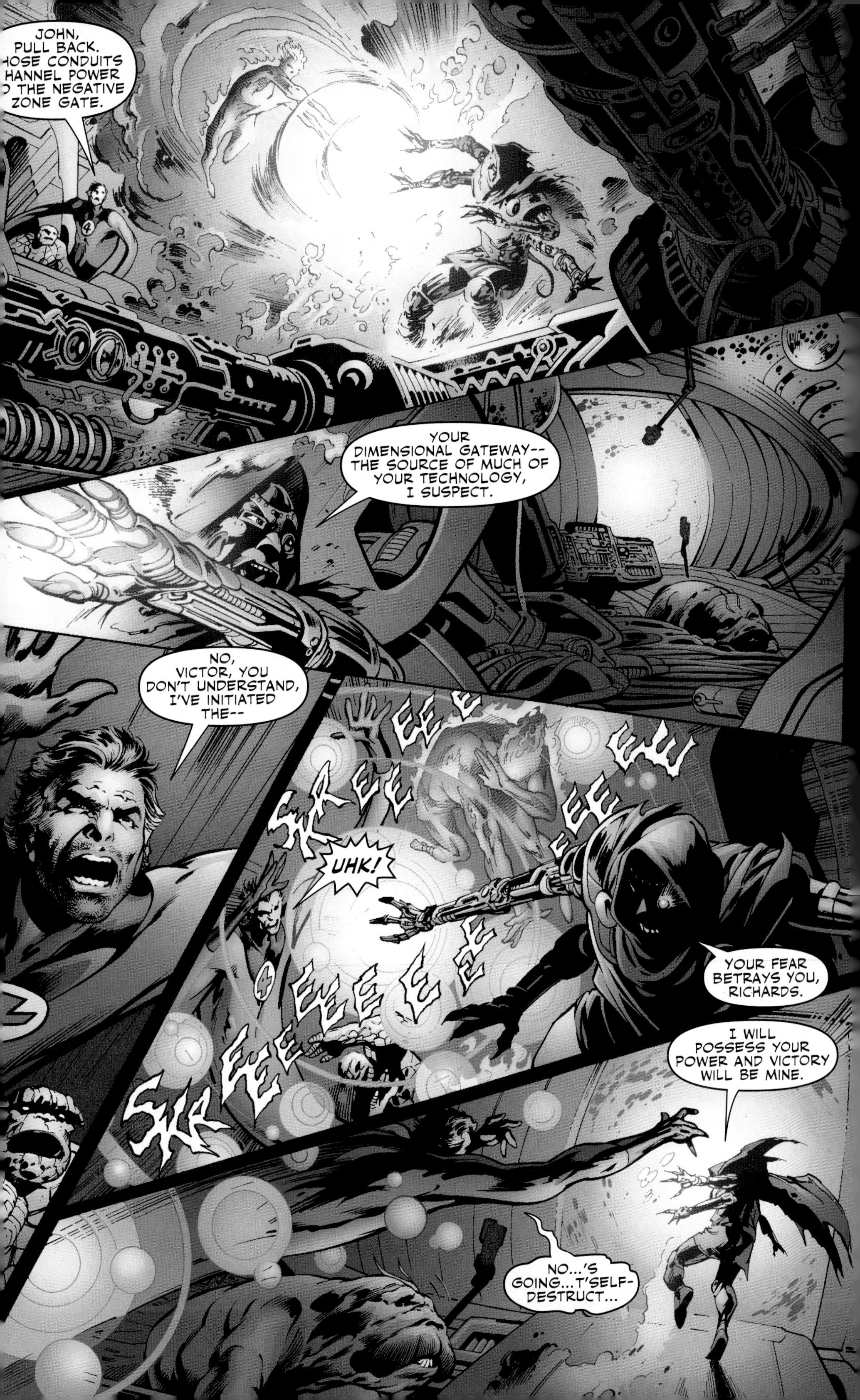
JOHN, PULL BACK. HOSE CONDUITS HANNEL POWER O THE NEGATIVE ZONE GATE.
YOUR DIMENSIONAL GATEWAY-- THE SOURCE OF MUCH OF YOUR TECHNOLOGY, I SUSPECT.
NO, VICTOR, YOU DON'T UNDERSTAND, I'VE INITIATED THE--
UHK!
YOUR FEAR BETRAYS YOU, RICHARDS.
I WILL POSSESS YOUR POWER AND VICTORY WILL BE MINE.
NO...'S GOING...T'SELF-DESTRUCT...

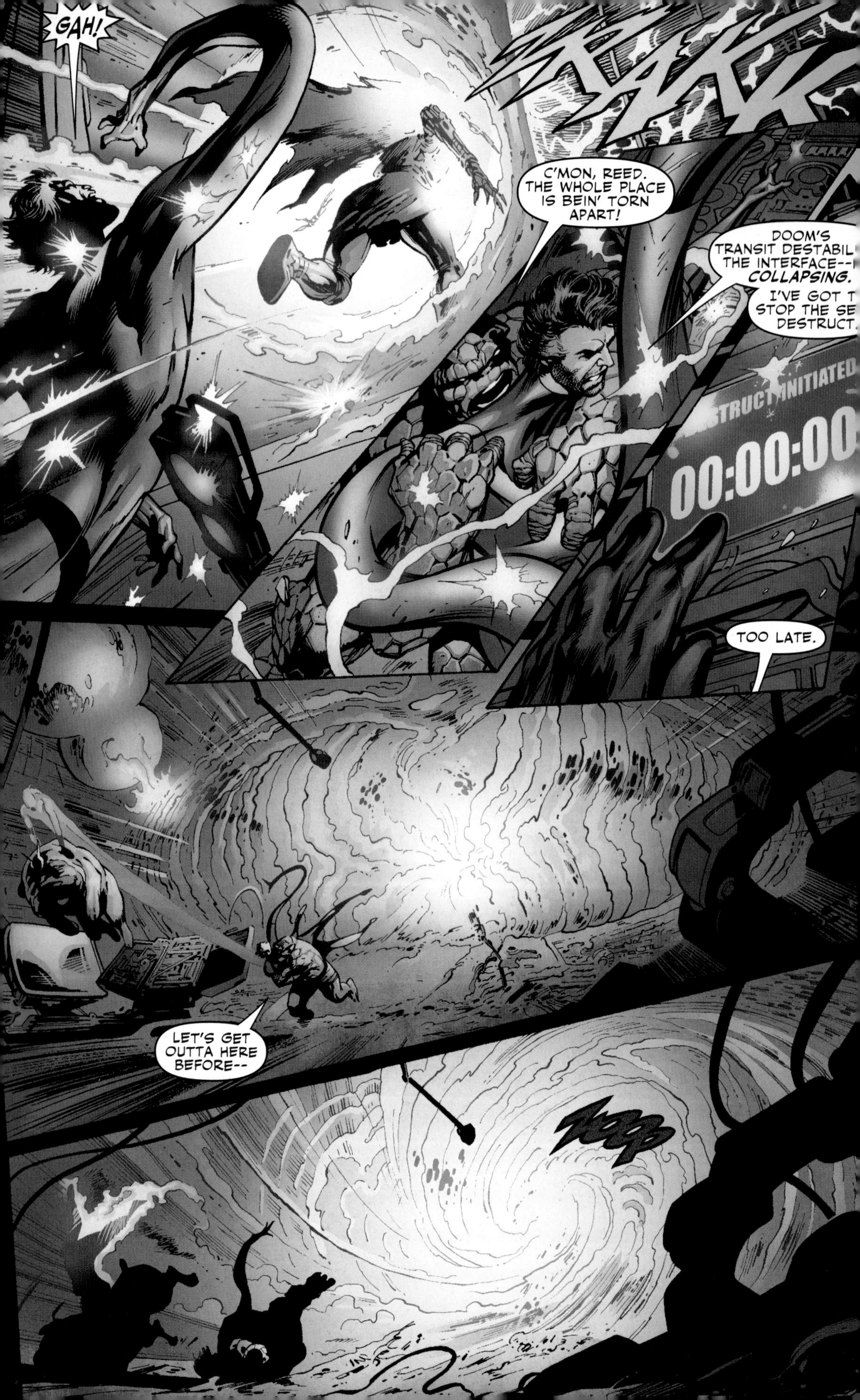
GAH!
C'MON, REED. THE WHOLE PLACE IS BEIN' TORN APART!
DOOM'S TRANSIT DESTABIL THE INTERFACE-- COLLAPSING.
I'VE GOT T STOP THE SE DESTRUCT.
STRUCT INITIATED
00:00:00
TOO LATE.
LET'S GET OUTTA HERE BEFORE--

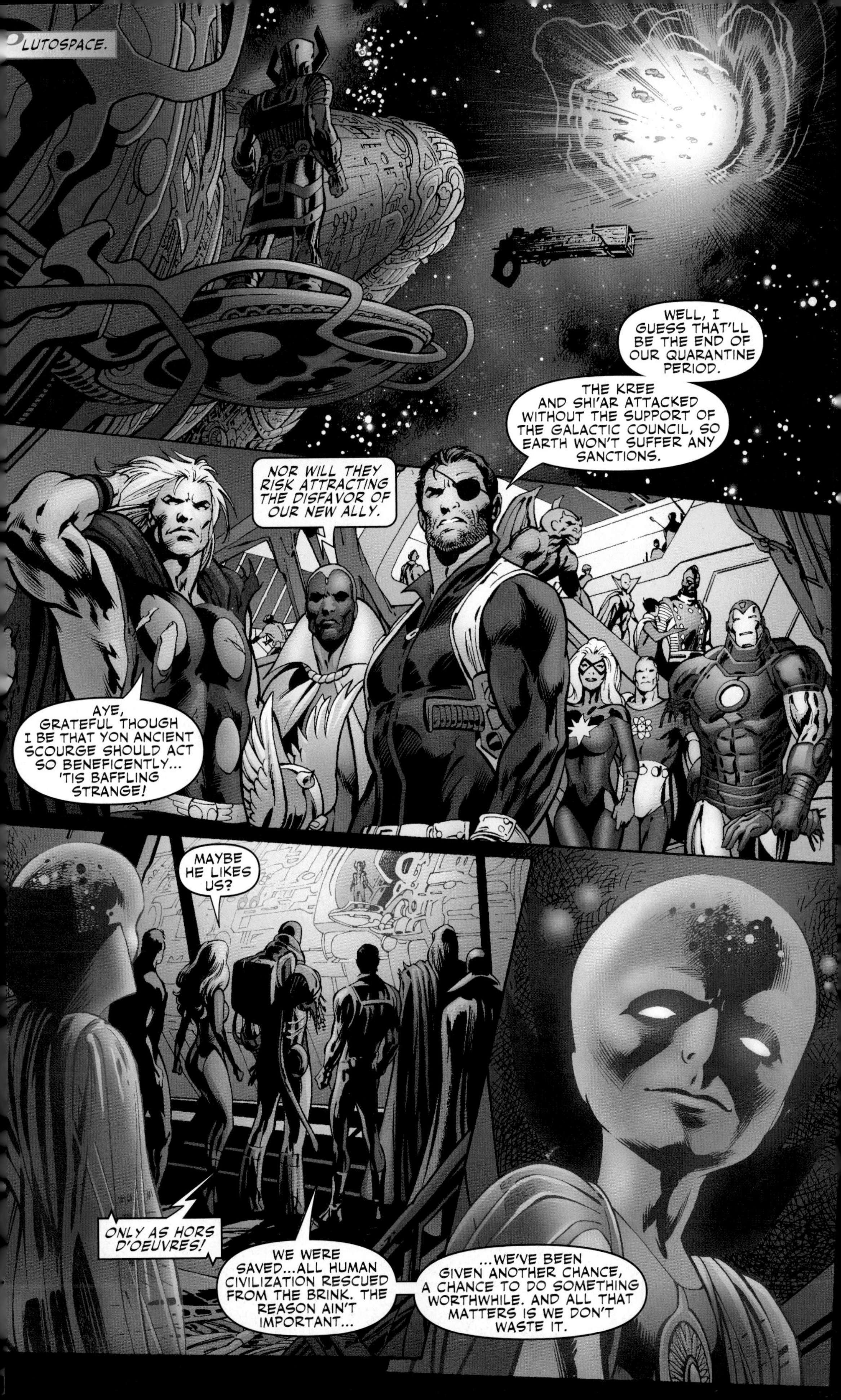

PLUTOSPACE.
WELL, I GUESS THAT'LL BE THE END OF OUR QUARANTINE PERIOD.
THE KREE AND SHI'AR ATTACKED WITHOUT THE SUPPORT OF THE GALACTIC COUNCIL, SO EARTH WON'T SUFFER ANY SANCTIONS.
NOR WILL THEY RISK ATTRACTING THE DISFAVOR OF OUR NEW ALLY.
AYE, GRATEFUL THOUGH I BE THAT YON ANCIENT SCOURGE SHOULD ACT SO BENEFICENTLY... 'TIS BAFFLING STRANGE!
MAYBE HE LIKES US?
ONLY AS HORS D'OEUVRES!
WE WERE SAVED...ALL HUMAN CIVILIZATION RESCUED FROM THE BRINK. THE REASON AIN'T IMPORTANT...
...WE'VE BEEN GIVEN ANOTHER CHANCE, A CHANCE TO DO SOMETHING WORTHWHILE. AND ALL THAT MATTERS IS WE DON'T WASTE IT.

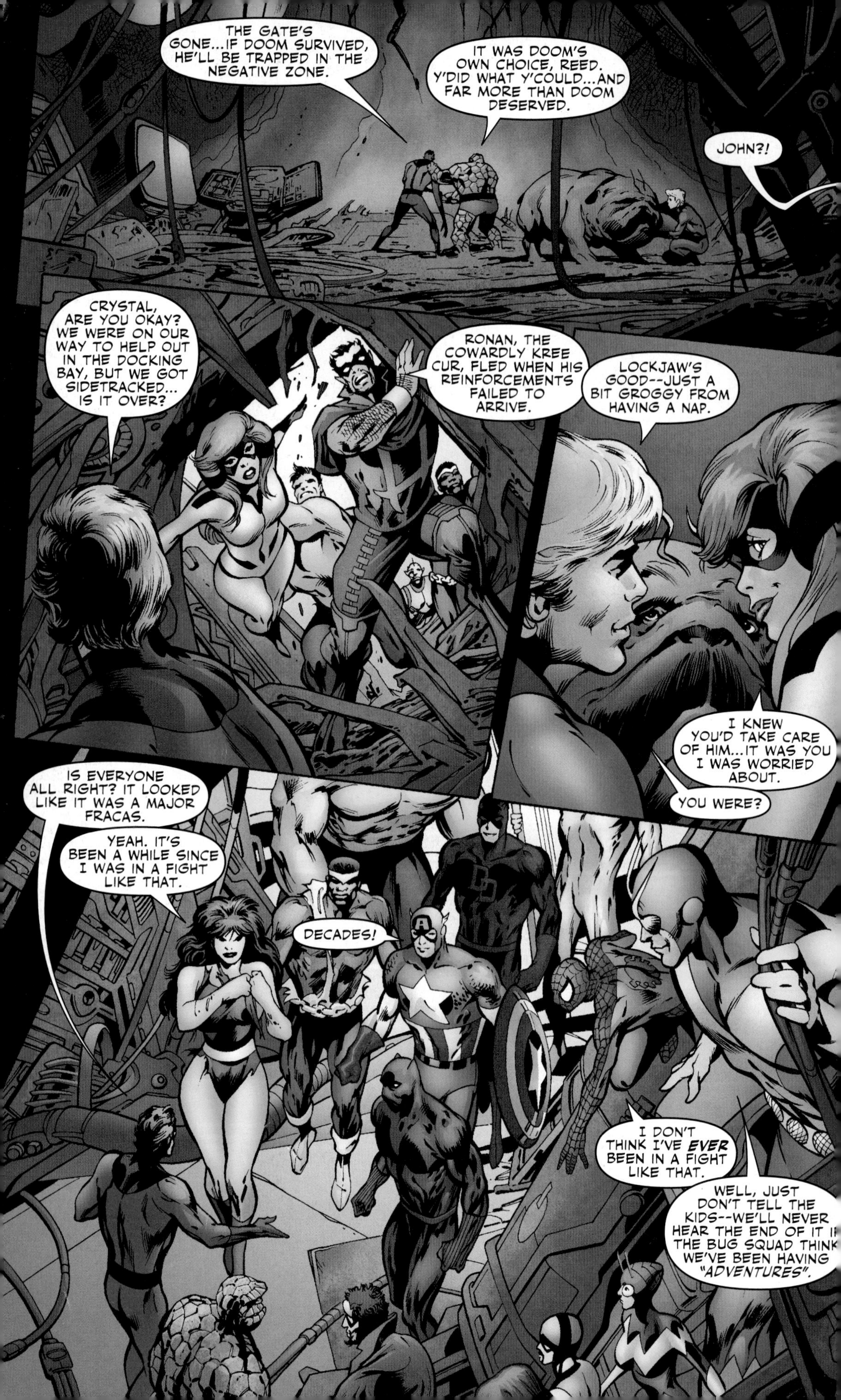
THE GATE'S GONE...IF DOOM SURVIVED, HE'LL BE TRAPPED IN THE NEGATIVE ZONE.
IT WAS DOOM'S OWN CHOICE, REED. Y'DID WHAT Y'COULD...AND FAR MORE THAN DOOM DESERVED.
JOHN?!
CRYSTAL, ARE YOU OKAY? WE WERE ON OUR WAY TO HELP OUT IN THE DOCKING BAY, BUT WE GOT SIDETRACKED... IS IT OVER?
RONAN, THE COWARDLY KREE CUR, FLED WHEN HIS REINFORCEMENTS FAILED TO ARRIVE.
LOCKJAW'S GOOD--JUST A BIT GROGGY FROM HAVING A NAP.
I KNEW YOU'D TAKE CARE OF HIM...IT WAS YOU I WAS WORRIED ABOUT.
YOU WERE?
IS EVERYONE ALL RIGHT? IT LOOKED LIKE IT WAS A MAJOR FRACAS.
YEAH. IT'S BEEN A WHILE SINCE I WAS IN A FIGHT LIKE THAT.
DECADES!
I DON'T THINK I'VE *EVER* BEEN IN A FIGHT LIKE THAT.
WELL, JUST DON'T TELL THE KIDS--WE'LL NEVER HEAR THE END OF IT IF THE BUG SQUAD THINK WE'VE BEEN HAVING *"ADVENTURES"*.

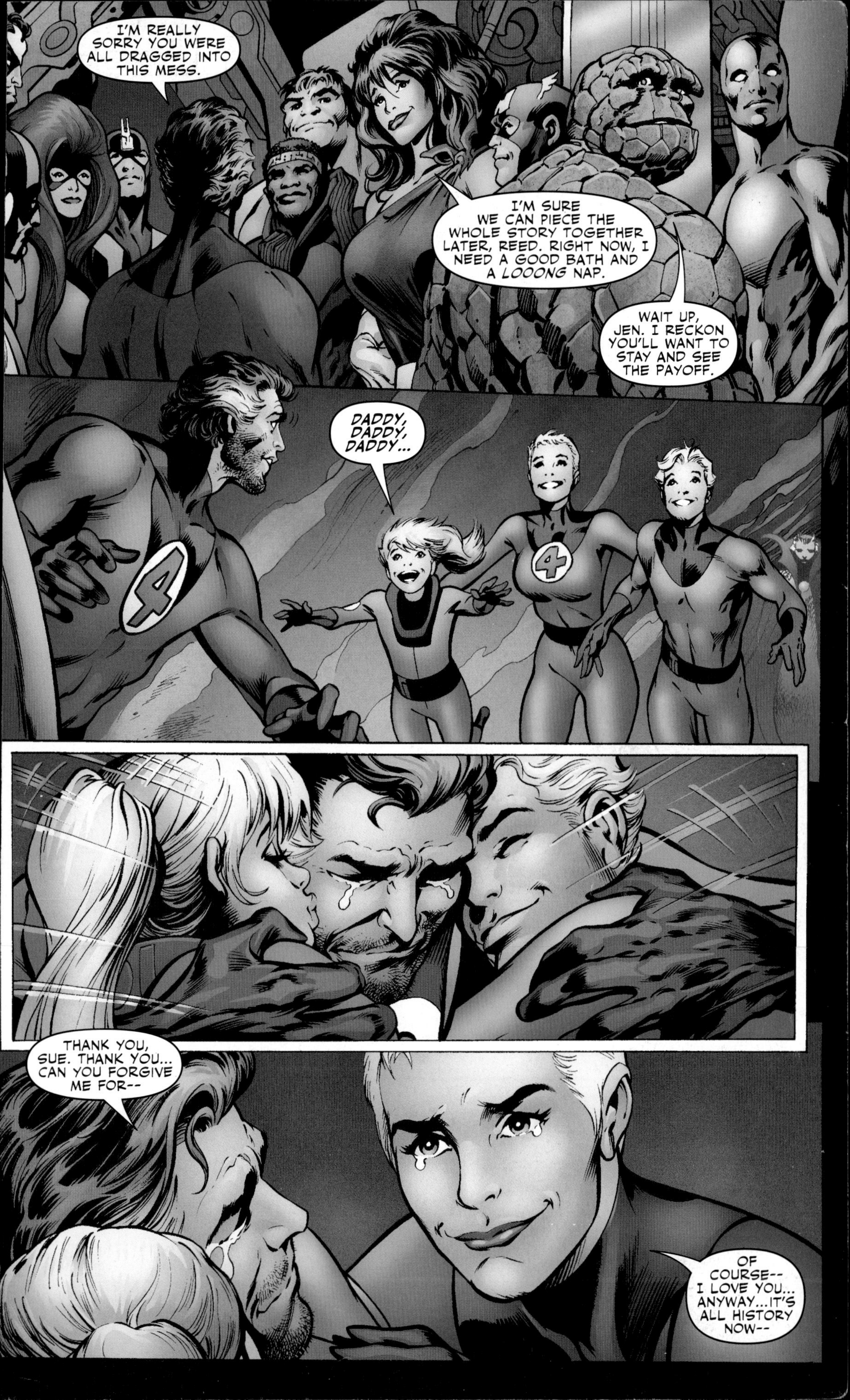
I'M REALLY SORRY YOU WERE ALL DRAGGED INTO THIS MESS.
I'M SURE WE CAN PIECE THE WHOLE STORY TOGETHER LATER, REED. RIGHT NOW, I NEED A GOOD BATH AND A *LOOONG* NAP.
WAIT UP, JEN. I RECKON YOU'LL WANT TO STAY AND SEE THE PAYOFF.
DADDY, DADDY, DADDY...
THANK YOU, SUE. THANK YOU... CAN YOU FORGIVE ME FOR--
OF COURSE-- I LOVE YOU... ANYWAY...IT'S ALL HISTORY NOW--

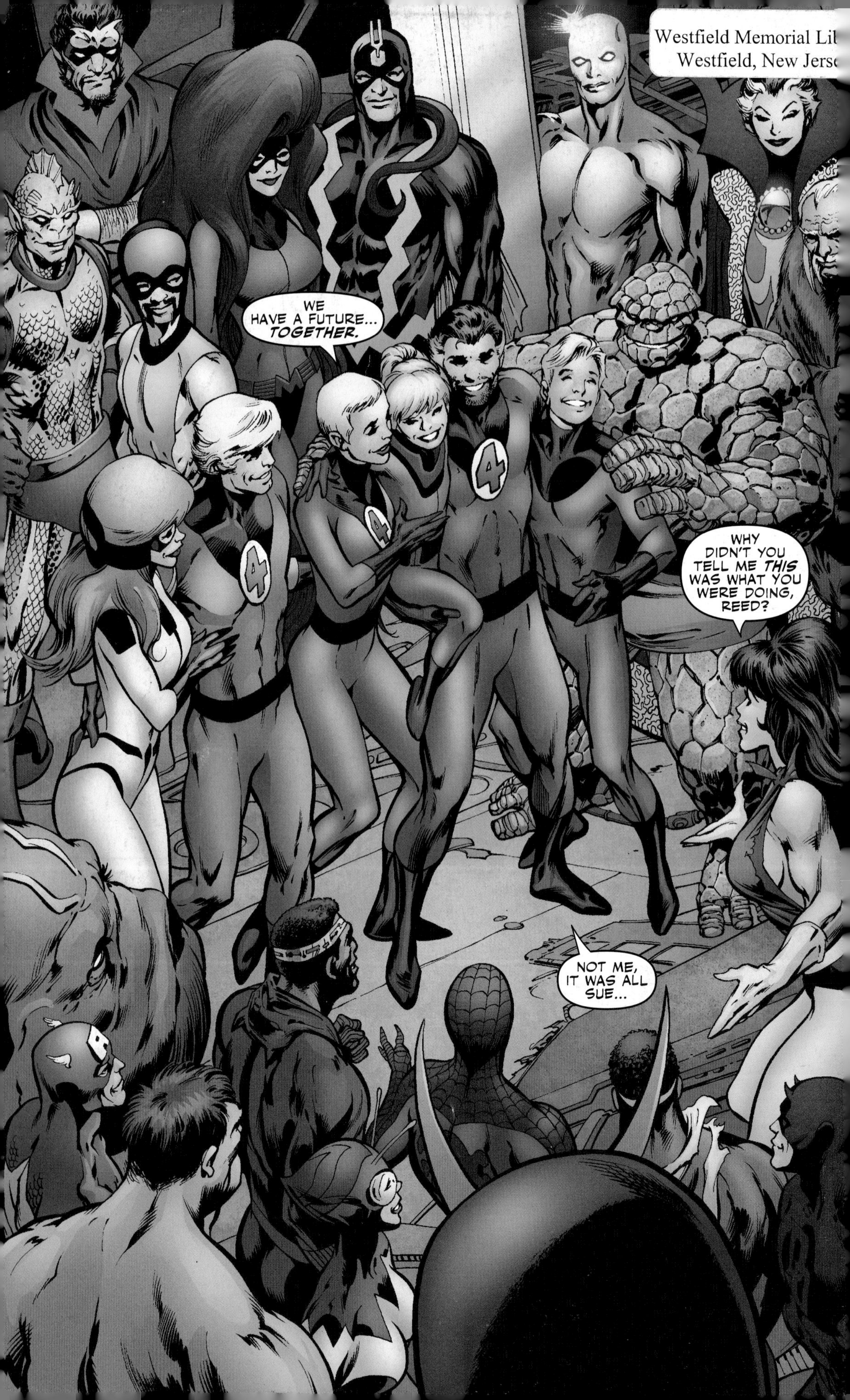
WE HAVE A FUTURE... *TOGETHER.*
WHY DIDN'T YOU TELL ME *THIS* WAS WHAT YOU WERE DOING, REED?
NOT ME, IT WAS ALL SUE...

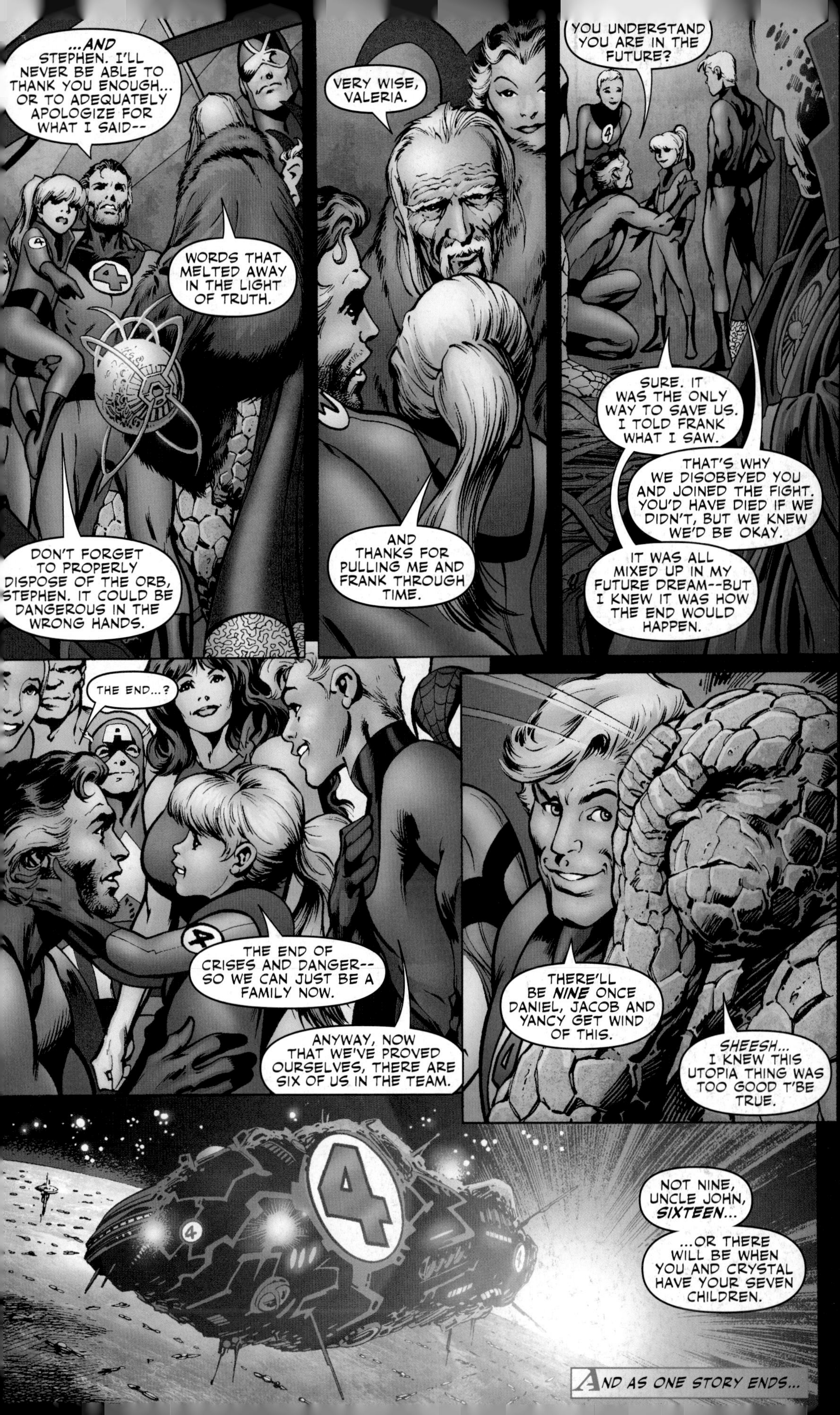
...AND STEPHEN. I'LL NEVER BE ABLE TO THANK YOU ENOUGH... OR TO ADEQUATELY APOLOGIZE FOR WHAT I SAID--
WORDS THAT MELTED AWAY IN THE LIGHT OF TRUTH.
DON'T FORGET TO PROPERLY DISPOSE OF THE ORB, STEPHEN. IT COULD BE DANGEROUS IN THE WRONG HANDS.
VERY WISE, VALERIA.
AND THANKS FOR PULLING ME AND FRANK THROUGH TIME.
YOU UNDERSTAND YOU ARE IN THE FUTURE?
SURE. IT WAS THE ONLY WAY TO SAVE US. I TOLD FRANK WHAT I SAW.
THAT'S WHY WE DISOBEYED YOU AND JOINED THE FIGHT. YOU'D HAVE DIED IF WE DIDN'T, BUT WE KNEW WE'D BE OKAY.
IT WAS ALL MIXED UP IN MY FUTURE DREAM--BUT I KNEW IT WAS HOW THE END WOULD HAPPEN.
THE END...?
THE END OF CRISES AND DANGER--SO WE CAN JUST BE A FAMILY NOW.
ANYWAY, NOW THAT WE'VE PROVED OURSELVES, THERE ARE SIX OF US IN THE TEAM.
THERE'LL BE NINE ONCE DANIEL, JACOB AND YANCY GET WIND OF THIS.
SHEESH... I KNEW THIS UTOPIA THING WAS TOO GOOD T'BE TRUE.
NOT NINE, UNCLE JOHN, SIXTEEN...
...OR THERE WILL BE WHEN YOU AND CRYSTAL HAVE YOUR SEVEN CHILDREN.
AND AS ONE STORY ENDS...

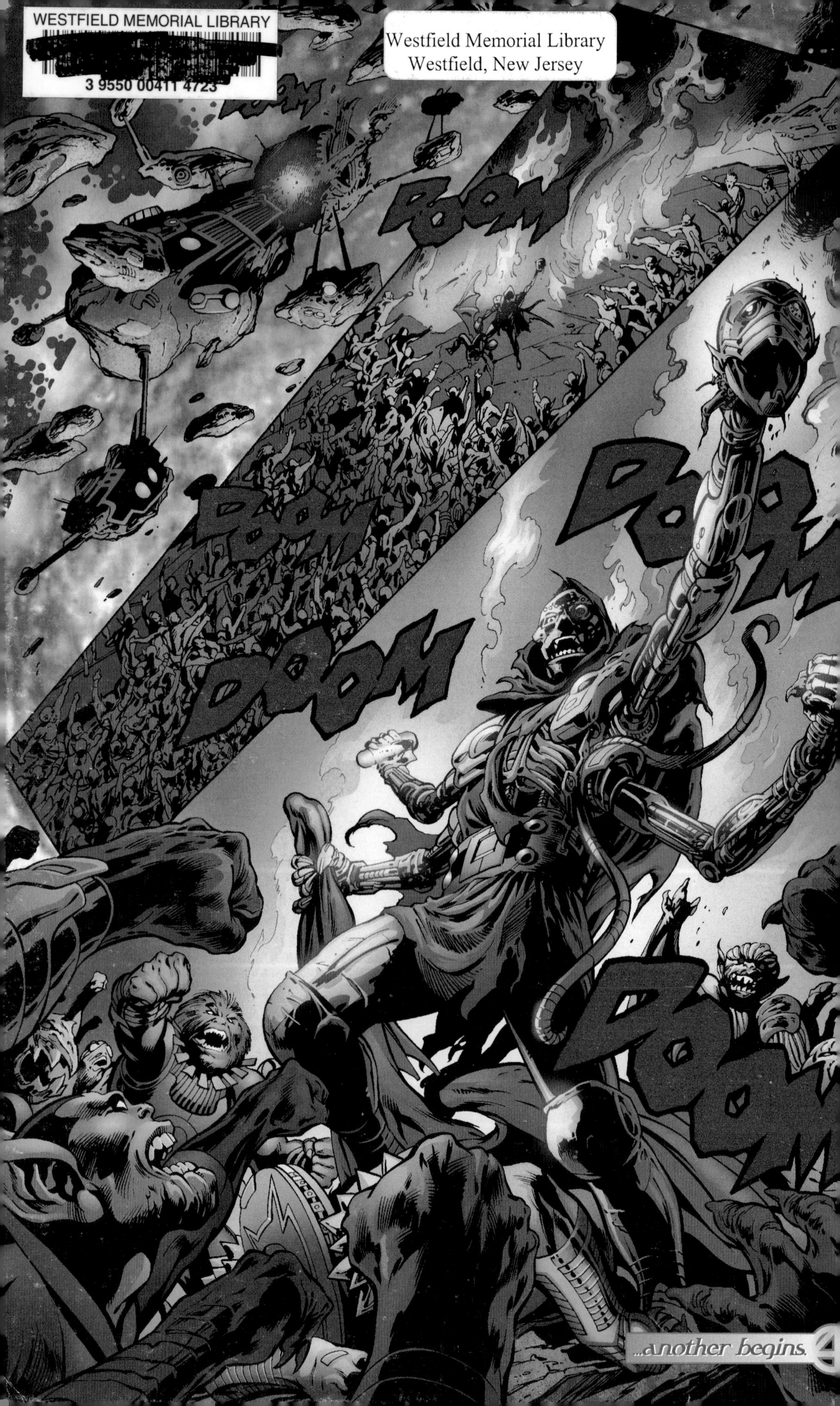
DOOM
DOOM
DOOM
...another begins.